Joseph Abruscato   Joan Wade Fossaceca   Jack Hassard   Donald Peck

HOLT SCIENCE

Holt, Rinehart and Winston, Publishers
New York · Toronto · Mexico City · London · Sydney · Tokyo

THE AUTHORS

Joseph Abruscato
Associate Dean
College of Education and Social Services
University of Vermont
Burlington, Vermont

Joan Wade Fossaceca
Teacher
Pointview Elementary School
Westerville City Schools
Westerville, Ohio

Jack Hassard
Professor
College of Education
Georgia State University
Atlanta, Georgia

Donald Peck
Supervisor of Science
Woodbridge Township School District
Woodbridge, New Jersey

Cover photos, front: Fred Bavendam/Peter Arnold, Inc.; back: Chesher/
Photo Researchers, Inc.
The diversity of marine invertebrate life is typified by the hard and soft corals of
the Bahamas shown on the front cover and the blue vase sponge on the back cover.

Photo and art credits on pages 359–360

ISBN: 0-03-003082-X
01234 069 10987

ACKNOWLEDGMENTS

Teacher Consultants

Armand Alvarez
District Science Curriculum Specialist
San Antonio Independent School District
San Antonio, Texas

Sister de Montfort Babb, I.H.M.
Earth Science Teacher
Maria Regina High School
Uniondale, New York
Instructor
Hofstra University
Hempstead, New York

Ernest Bibby
Science Consultant
Granville County Board of Education
Oxford, North Carolina

Linda C. Cardwell
Teacher
Dickinson Elementary School
Grand Prairie, Texas

Betty Eagle
Teacher
Englewood Cliffs Upper School
Englewood Cliffs, New Jersey

James A. Harris
Principal
Rothschild Elementary School
Rothschild, Wisconsin

Rachel P. Keziah
Instructional Supervisor
New Hanover County Schools
Wilmington, North Carolina

J. Peter O'Neil
Science Teacher
Waunakee Junior High School
Waunakee, Wisconsin

Raymond E. Sanders, Jr.
Assistant Science Supervisor
Calcasieu Parish Schools
Lake Charles, Louisiana

Content Consultants

John B. Jenkins
Professor of Biology
Swarthmore College
Swarthmore, Pennsylvania

Mark M. Payne, O.S.B.
Physics Teacher
St. Benedict's Preparatory School
Newark, New Jersey

Robert W. Ridky, Ph.D.
Professor of Geology
University of Maryland
College Park, Maryland

Safety Consultant

Franklin D. Kizer
Executive Secretary
Council of State Science Supervisors, Inc.
Lancaster, Virginia

Readability Consultant

Jane Kita Cooke
Assistant Professor of Education
College of New Rochelle
New Rochelle, New York

Curriculum Consultant

Lowell J. Bethel
Associate Professor, Science Education
Director, Office of Student Field Experiences
The University of Texas at Austin
Austin, Texas

Special Education Consultant

Joan Baltman
Special Education Program Coordinator
P.S. 188 Elementary School
Bronx, New York

CONTENTS

Introduction: SKILLS OF SCIENCE   viii

UNIT 1 OCEAN FRONTIERS   8

Chapter 1   THE OCEAN   10
1–1. The Ocean Bottom   10
1–2. Salts and Sediments   15
1–3. Changes in the Ocean Floor   20
Chapter Review   25

Chapter 2   OCEAN MOVEMENTS   26
2–1. Currents   26
2–2. Waves   31
2–3. Tides   37
Chapter Review   42

Chapter 3   OCEAN EXPLORATION   43
3–1. Ocean Resources   43
3–2. Ocean Life   49
3–3. The Ocean in Danger   52
3–4. Exploring the Ocean Bottom   57
People in Science: Eugenie Clark   62
Chapter Review   63
Investigating   64
Careers   65

UNIT 2 SOUND   66

Chapter 4   HEARING SOUND   68
4–1. How Sounds Are Made   68
4–2. Instruments of Sound   73
4–3. How Sound Travels   79
Chapter Review   83

Chapter 5   SOUND WAVES   84
5–1. Sound and Matter   84
5–2. Different Sounds   91
5–3. Sound Waves Reflect   97
5–4. Sound Messages   102
People in Science: Cyril Harris   108

Chapter Review   109
Investigating   110
Careers   111

UNIT 3 SENSING AND MOVING — 112

Chapter 6   YOUR SENSES   114
6–1. Sense Organs   114
6–2. Taste   119
6–3. Hearing   123
6–4. Sight   128
6–5. Touch   133
Chapter Review   138

Chapter 7   BONES AND MUSCLES   139
7–1. Bones   139
7–2. How Bones Join   145
People in Science: Augustus A. White, III   149
7–3. Muscles   150
7–4. Kinds of Muscles   155
Chapter Review   159
Investigating   160
Careers   161

UNIT 4 ELECTRICITY AND MAGNETISM — 162

Chapter 8   ELECTRICITY   164
8–1. Static Electricity   164
8–2. Current Electricity   169
8–3. One Kind of Circuit   173
8–4. Another Kind of Circuit   177
People in Science: Charles Proteus Steinmetz   181
Chapter Review   182

Chapter 9   MAGNETISM   183
9–1. Magnets   183
9–2. A Special Kind of Magnet   188
9–3. Moving Magnets   193
Chapter Review   197

Chapter 10   USING ELECTRICITY   198
10–1. Measuring Electricity   198
10–2. Producing Electricity   203
10–3. Electricity and Environment   207
10–4. Electricity in the Computer Age   211
Chapter Review   217
Investigating   218
Careers   219

UNIT 5 LIVING ORGANISMS   220

**Chapter 11   CELLS AND SIMPLE
                ORGANISMS**   222
11–1. Classifying Living Things   222
11–2. Building Blocks of Life   226
11–3. The Simplest Organisms   230
11–4. Algae and Fungi   235
Chapter Review   238

Chapter 12   PLANTS   239
12–1. Classifying Plants   239
12–2. Roots, Stems, and Leaves   243
12–3. Groups of Plants   247
People in Science: Barbara McClintock   252
Chapter Review   253

**Chapter 13   ANIMALS WITHOUT
                BACKBONES**   254
13–1. Simple Animals   254
13–2. Animals with Shells and Spines   259
13–3. Arthropods   264
Chapter Review   271

**Chapter 14   ANIMALS WITH
                BACKBONES**   272
14–1. Fish and Amphibians   272
14–2. Reptiles and Birds   278
14–3. Mammals   284
Chapter Review   289
Investigating   290
Careers   291

UNIT 6 EXPLORING THE UNIVERSE — 292

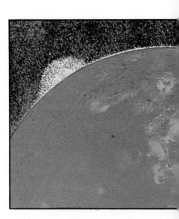

Chapter 15	**THE EARTH, MOON, AND SUN**	**294**
15–1.	Day, Night, and the Seasons	294
15–2.	The Moon	299
15–3.	The Sun	305
	Chapter Review	309
Chapter 16	**THE SOLAR SYSTEM**	**310**
16–1.	The Inner Planets	310
16–2.	The Outer Planets	317
16–3.	Asteroids, Meteors, and Comets	322
16–4.	Travel in the Solar System	325
	Chapter Review	329
Chapter 17	**THE STARS AND BEYOND**	**330**
17–1.	The Stars	330
17–2.	Constellations	337
	People in Science: Susan Jocelyn Burnell	341
17–3.	The Universe	342
	Chapter Review	347
	Investigating	348
	Careers	349
	Glossary/ Index	350

SKILLS OF SCIENCE

For Charles, the cold winter day began at 3 A.M. He turned off the alarm and slipped into warm clothes and boots. He grabbed his notebook, then headed down the road. It was still dark when he met up with the bird-counting party at the edge of town.

"Glad you could come," said Alice, the group leader. "Since this is your first bird count, just stick with me. Keep watching. Write down the name of every bird you see. If you can't identify a bird, I'll help."

Charles was one of thousands of people taking part in the Christmas Bird Count. In 1,400 different places, people spend a day each December counting the kinds of birds they see. Some of the counters are scientists. Most counters are only interested bird-watchers. The only requirement is that they be good observers. They must be able to identify different kinds or **species** of birds. Some counters go out into the field. Others stay at bird feeders. At the end of the day, the number of birds of each *species* seen in each area is added up.

Species: All of the same kind of living thing.

From a bird count, scientists can learn about the health of a bird **population**. A *population* is a group of the same kind of plants or animals living in the same place. A healthy population is one that is growing in number or staying the same. A population in trouble is one that is going down in number.

Population: A group of the same kind of plants or animals living in the same place.

SKILL BUILDING ACTIVITY

Can you identify different bird species?

A. Obtain these materials: paper, pencil.

B. Read the descriptions below. Then match each description to the correct bird.

   1. What are the correct names of birds A, B, and C?

   2. Which bird can grow to be the longest? Which bird is the smallest?

   3. Which two birds do you think are most closely related? How can you tell? (Hint: look for an important feature that they share.)

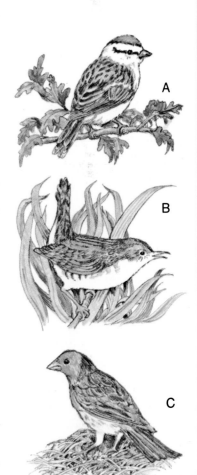

Descriptions:

Finch: Small, brown bird, from 14 to 16 centimeters long. Red forehead and underside. Sides are streaked. Short, light bill.

House wren: Small, brown bird, from 10.5 to 13.5 centimeters long. Carries tail almost straight up and down. White underside. Long, thornlike bill.

Chipping sparrow: Small, brown bird, from 12.5 to 14 centimeters long. Reddish cap. White line over eye and a black line through eye. White underside. Short, black bill.

Investigate: To study carefully.

Observe: To watch closely.

Record: To write down information.

Bird counts taken during the late 1930s brought scientists some bad news about *whooping cranes*, the birds shown in the photograph. Whooping cranes are tall, white birds that live near water. The birds were down to a population of about 20. Scientists feared that illness or a bad storm could wipe out the rest.

One flock of these birds spent the winter along the Texas coast. A second flock lived year-round in Louisiana. But no one knew where the Texas birds lived in the summer. And no one knew why the whooping crane population was so low. Wildlife scientists wanted to find out why.

In 1946 Robert Allen, the scientist shown at left, was asked to study or **investigate** the "whoopers." He began his *investigation* by watching closely or **observing** a wild flock of whoopers. He *observed* the birds that wintered at Aransas National Wildlife Refuge in Texas. From sunup to sundown Allen watched the birds. He knew when they slept and what they ate. He watched them care for their young. Like all good scientists, he carefully **recorded** his observations. *Recording* information is an important step in investigating.

Next, Allen investigated where the whoopers spend their summers. Each spring the whoopers leave Texas.

They head north to breed. They return to Texas in the fall. Allen found out where the whoopers had been spotted over the years. He was able to guess where the cranes went to, or *migrated*. Making a guess, or **hypothesis,** is part of how scientists solve a problem. Allen's *hypothesis* was that the cranes migrated to Canada. In 1952 Allen found the summer home of the whoopers: Wood Buffalo National Park. The map shows the route the cranes took to get there.

Allen learned many things at the birds' summer home. Whooping cranes lay two eggs each season. Although they are good parents, adult birds raise only one young bird a year. The whoopers also need to be alone. They must have a lot of space around them. Allen's observations led him to make these final statements or **conclusions:** The whooping cranes were dying out because they did not produce enough young cranes each year to make up for the ones that were hunted by people. Also, they were being crowded out of their living space by the growing human population.

Allen's *conclusions* helped scientists to think of *ideas* that would help the whoopers. Each idea was carefully studied and *tested*. One idea was to give the birds more food and protection from outsiders at their winter home. The idea worked. The flock of Aransas whoopers went up from 20 to 70 birds.

Hypothesis: A scientific guess.

Conclusion: A final statement based on observations.

SKILL BUILDING ACTIVITY

Keeping records of bird migrations

A. Obtain these materials: pencil, paper.

B. Study the chart below. It shows the number of whooping cranes observed during their spring and fall migrations.

WHOOPING CRANES OBSERVED

Year	Season	Number of Birds
1976	spring	14
	fall	15
1978	spring	28
	fall	29
1980	spring	31
	fall	35

1. How many cranes were observed in the fall of 1976? How many were seen in the fall of 1980? In which year were more cranes observed?
2. Draw a conclusion about what happened to the crane population between 1976 and 1980.
3. Predict what the number of birds seen in 1982 might have been.
4. What information would you need to see if your prediction is right?
5. Why do you think the number of cranes increased?

C. Draw a bar graph similar to the one shown. Draw in bars to show the number of cranes seen in the spring and fall of each year. One year has been done for you.

6. During which migration were more birds seen, spring or fall? Can you explain why?

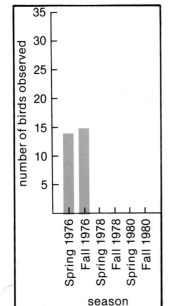

Scientists had another idea for increasing the number of whooping cranes. They took eggs from the wild flock to raise in captivity. Later, the captive birds could be released in the wild. Allen had already shown that whoopers raise only one young bird a year. Scientists predicted that taking one egg from a nest would cause no harm. This was tested and proved true. Since 1967, many eggs have been taken from whooper nests in Canada. These eggs have been flown to a research center in Maryland. There, many of the eggs have hatched. Now a captive flock of 25 birds lives there. Scientists have made a good home for the birds. They hope the birds will soon produce eggs on their own.

Scientists had still another idea. They would give whooper eggs to *sandhill cranes* to raise. Sandhill cranes are small relatives of the whoopers. Sandhill cranes live in the Rocky Mountains. Could the sandhill cranes serve as foster parents for the whoopers?

In 1975, the first whooping crane egg was placed in a sandhill nest. The sandhills accepted the egg as their own egg. Now about 17 whoopers live in the Rocky Mountains with sandhill cranes. They migrate with the sandhills and even eat the same food as the sandhills. Can you find the whooper in the photograph below?

Skill Building Activity

What foods do birds prefer?

A. Obtain these materials: 3 empty coffee cans, 6 plastic lids that fit the cans, can opener, scissors, wire, heavy string, mixed birdseed, sunflower seeds, baby powder.

B. Carefully remove the metal lids from both ends of the coffee cans. CAUTION: MAKE SURE THERE ARE NO ROUGH METAL EDGES. Use the scissors to cut a small hole shaped like a half moon in each of the plastic lids. CAUTION: USE SCISSORS CAREFULLY.

C. Place the cans on their sides. In the center of the first can, place some mixed birdseed. In the second can, place sunflower seeds. Inside the third can, sprinkle a thin film of baby powder. This will help you to tell if birds have visited this can.

D. Put the lids on each can. Place the "feeders" outdoors where birds are seen often. Use the string and wire to hang the feeders on low tree branches or on buildings. Hang all the cans in the same location.

  1. Predict which feeder will attract the greatest number of birds.

E. For a few days observe the birds that visit the feeders. Record your observations onto a chart.

  2. From which feeder did the birds take the most food?

  3. Was your prediction correct?

  4. Did the same kinds of birds visit each feeder? Why or why not?

  5. Did any birds visit the feeder that has no food? That feeder was the *control* in this experiment. The results from the control are used to compare what happened at the other feeders.

Scientists now keep a close watch on the whooping cranes. Some birds have been fitted with radio transmitters. From the radio signals, scientists are able to track the cranes' every move.

Thanks to the efforts of many scientists, there is more hope now for the whooping cranes than there was in the late 1930s. The work scientists have done with the cranes shows some of the ways scientific investigations are carried out. You have seen how a scientist asks questions and keeps careful records of observations. By observing the same subject over and over again, a scientist notices when changes take place. The observations lead to experiments. But experiments don't always show the results a scientist predicts. The scientist must then ask some new questions!

A scientist studies the world and the way things work. When scientists get involved in solving problems, they follow the steps you see outlined below. You can follow the same steps in your own investigations.

Ask Questions Make Observations → **Come Up With Ideas**

Answer Question and Then Ask Another Question

Test the Idea or Hypothesis

Record Results Make Conclusions ← **Carry Out an Experiment**

OCEAN FRONTIERS

UNIT 1

CHAPTER 1

THE OCEAN

1-1.

The Ocean Bottom

In 1622, the *Santa Margarita* sank off the coast of Florida during a storm. Today, divers have recovered gold and jewels from the shipwreck. In order to locate the ship, they studied the ocean bottom. When you finish this section, you should be able to:

☐ **A.** Describe and compare the three main parts of the ocean bottom.
☐ **B.** Describe the structure of the ocean floor.

Many people think that the ocean bottom is completely flat. Some areas are flat like plains on land. However, the ocean bottom has high and low places. These are similar to the mountains and valleys found on land.

The ocean bottom is divided into three main parts. The first part is called the **continental** (kahn-tih-**nen**-tul) **shelf**. The *continental shelf* starts where the part of the land we live on ends. It is part of the continent, but it is covered with water. The continental shelf is the shallowest part of the ocean. Its average depth is about 60 meters (200 feet).

At the end of the continental shelf, the land plunges downward sharply. This part of the ocean bottom is called the **continental slope**. The ocean may be 3,050 m (10,100 ft) deep at the bottom of the *continental slope*. Why do you think the word *slope* is used to describe what occurs?

The third part of the ocean bottom, called the **ocean floor**, begins where the continental slope ends. The *ocean floor* covers most of the ocean bottom. Where the ocean floor is flat, it is called the **abyssal** (uh-**bis**-ul) **plain**.

At one time, scientists thought the whole ocean bottom was smooth and flat. Today we know there is a huge chain of mountains on the ocean bottom. This mountain chain is called the **mid-ocean ridge**. The *mid-ocean ridge* is about 65,000 kilometers (40,000 miles) long and runs through every ocean on the earth.

Look at the map on top of page 12. It shows what the Atlantic Ocean would look like with all the water removed. Find the *abyssal plain* and the mid-ocean ridge. Can you find the crack in the center of the mid-ocean ridge? It is 13 to 48 km (8 to 30 mi) wide and more than 1.6 km (1 mi) deep in some places.

Continental shelf:
Part of the ocean bottom near land.

Continental slope:
Part of the ocean bottom where the continental shelf plunges downward sharply.

Ocean floor:
Part of the ocean bottom that lies at the bottom of the continental slope.

Abyssal plain:
Flat part of the ocean floor.

Mid-ocean ridge:
Mountain chain on the ocean floor.

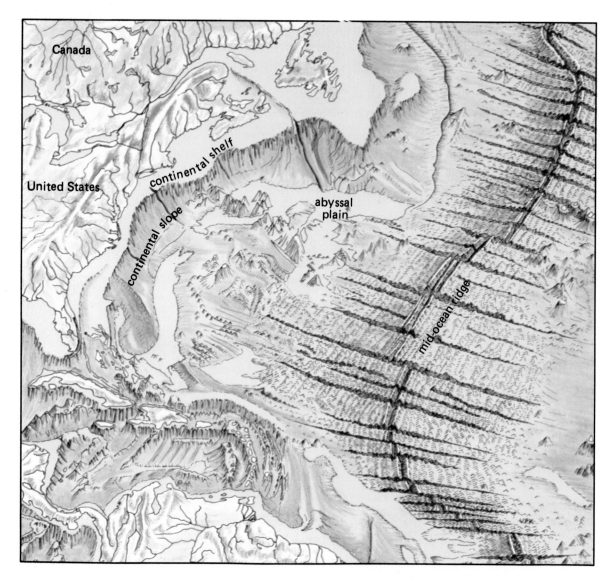

Canada

United States

continental shelf

continental slope

abyssal
plain

mid-ocean ridge

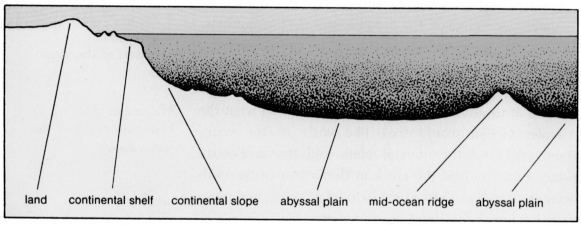

land   continental shelf   continental slope   abyssal plain   mid-ocean ridge   abyssal plain

Look at the map at the bottom of page 12. It shows what the ocean bottom would look like if it were cut exactly in half from left to right. You are now looking at the ocean bottom from the side instead of overhead. This type of map allows you to clearly see where the high and low places on the ocean floor are.

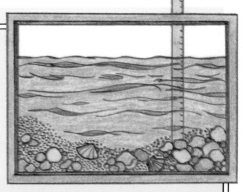

ACTIVITY

Measuring the "ocean bottom"

A. Obtain these materials: small aquarium, pebbles, gravel, water, ruler.

B. Your teacher will help you make a model of the ocean bottom. Use gravel and pebbles to show the three parts of the ocean bottom. Gently add the water to the aquarium.

C. Make a graph like the one shown.

D. Make measurements of the ocean bottom. Hold a ruler straight in the water at one end of the "ocean." Measure in cm how deep the "ocean" is.

E. On your graph, make an X above trial 1 opposite the number that shows the distance between the bottom and the water surface.

F. Repeat steps D and E nine times, taking measurements from one end of the aquarium to the other.

G. Draw a line connecting the X's on your graph.

   1. Label your graph to show the ocean parts.

   2. From your graph, how deep are the model ocean's floor and continental shelf?

   3. Imagine that a ship sank on the edge of the continental shelf near the continental slope. From your graph, make a hypothesis about where the wreckage might be found.

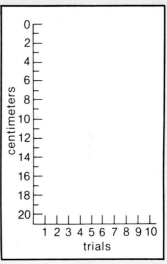

The structure of the ocean bottom is always changing. But it is hard to see these changes over a short period of time. Most changes take place over millions of years. Forces within the earth can push parts of the ocean bottom upward to form land. Some areas of land were once part of the ocean bottom. Ocean plant and animal remains have been found on land. This shows that this land was once part of the ocean bottom.

Section Review

Main Ideas: The continental shelf begins at the point where the land meets the ocean. At the end of the continental shelf, the ocean bottom plunges downward, forming the continental slope. At the bottom of the continental slope, the ocean floor begins. The abyssal plain and mid-ocean ridge form the ocean floor.

Questions: Answer in complete sentences.

1. Describe three parts of the ocean bottom.
2. Below is a cross section of the ocean bottom. It shows the area between the Hawaiian Islands and the California coast. Identify parts A–D.
3. On the diagram below, which letter is best described by each of the following definitions?
   (1) the part of the continent covered by water
   (2) a mountain chain on the ocean floor
   (3) the flat part of the ocean floor

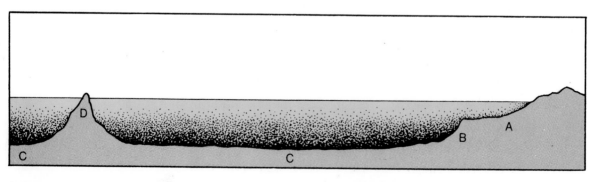

Salts and Sediments

Do you know how to do any magic tricks? This student is doing one that you may wish to try. The egg placed in one container sinks. The egg placed in the magic container floats. What do you think is so special about the water in the magic container?

Before the trick was performed, salt was dissolved in the water of the magic container. Adding salt made the water like ocean water. When you finish this section you should be able to:

☐ **A.** Explain what causes ocean water to be salty.
☐ **B.** Describe how materials are carried to the ocean bottom.
☐ **C.** Describe what causes submarine canyons.

Ocean water is very different from ordinary drinking water. One difference is that ocean water contains salt. You might wonder how much salt ocean water contains. One kilogram (about 35 ounces) of ocean water contains about 27 grams (less than an ounce) of table salt. The rest is water and other materials. The amount of salt varies slightly in different parts of the ocean. It is the amount of salt in water that determines how well objects float. The floating egg trick works because a lot of salt was dissolved in the water.

Besides salt, ocean water contains other materials. You may wonder how these materials got into ocean water. These materials actually came from the land and are called *minerals*. First rain falls onto the land. Some of this rainwater eventually flows into streams and rivers.

15

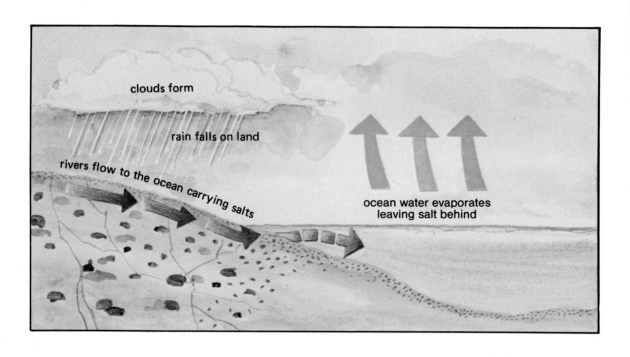

clouds form

rain falls on land

rivers flow to the ocean carrying salts

ocean water evaporates
leaving salt behind

**Sodium chloride:
A salt.**

Rivers flow from mountain lakes to the oceans. As the rivers flow over the land, they carry materials from the land. Some of these materials are salts. The salts are dissolved in the water. One kind of salt that rivers carry is **sodium chloride** (so-dee-um **klor**-ide). The salt you use on food is *sodium chloride*. When a river empties into an ocean, the salt mixes with the ocean water. The picture shows salt from a river mixing with ocean water.

Ocean water is heated by the sun. As ocean water is heated, it evaporates. This means that the water changes from a liquid to a gas. What happens to the salt in this evaporating water?

Study the above picture. Notice the order of events. Start by looking at the clouds. First rain falls on the land. Water then flows toward the ocean. Along the way it picks up salts that are found in the earth. Water containing salts eventually reaches the ocean. Arrows in the diagram show water evaporating from the ocean. Salts are left behind in the ocean. Evaporated water from the ocean can form clouds, which may pass over land. Rain falling from the clouds begins the sequence again.

Each time this sequence of events takes place, salts from the land are brought to the ocean. This process has been taking place for millions of years. This explains why the ocean is salty. Ocean water at the equator is less salty than some other parts of the ocean. This is because there is more rainfall over the equator. Ocean water at the poles is even less salty than at the equator. This is because the melting ice at the poles is mostly fresh water. As the ice melts, fresh water mixes with the salty ocean water, making it less salty.

Salts are not the only materials carried to the oceans by rivers. Rivers also carry sand, mud, clay, and rocks. These materials are called **sediments** (sed-uh-ments). *Sediments* settle to the bottom in still water. Most sediments settle close to the shore and form beaches. Other

Sediments: Sand, clay, and other materials that settle in water.

ACTIVITY

What happens when salt water evaporates?

A. Obtain these materials: 2 small, clean plastic bowls labeled A and B, 2 containers, water, salt.

B. In one container, dissolve 30 g of salt in 200 ml of water.

C. In bowl A, pour the salt water to a depth of 4 or 5 cm. This is the experiment.

D. Pour the same amount of plain, unsalted water into bowl B. This is the control.

  1. Why is a control necessary?

E. Place both bowls in the same warm place.

  2. Predict what both bowls will look like in two days.

F. Observe the bowls for the next two days.

  3. How do your results compare with your predictions?

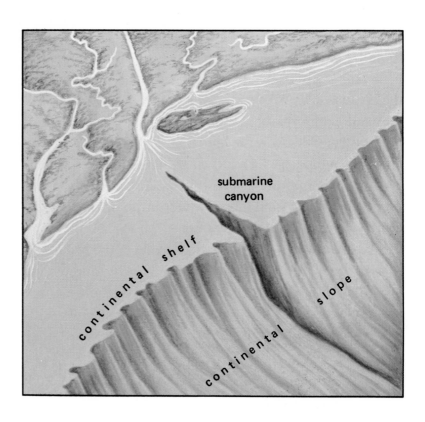

submarine
canyon

continental shelf

slope

continental

**Submarine canyon:
A groove cut in the
continental shelf and
slope.**

sediments are carried farther out. They settle on the continental shelf. Sometimes the sediments on the shelf move or slide. They slide down the continental slope. This movement makes deep cuts in the shelf and slope. These cuts are called **submarine canyons** (**sub**-muh-reen **kan**-yunz). Look at the diagram. Can you find the *submarine canyon*? Some of this sediment stays at the bottom of the slope. Some of the sediment moves farther out and settles on the abyssal plain.

Another type of sediment on the ocean bottom comes from plants and animals. When animals and plants die, their remains settle to the ocean bottom. They become part of the layers of sediment on the ocean bottom.

Some sediments are brought to the ocean floor by wind. Rock particles that are blown out to sea settle on the ocean surface and eventually sink to the bottom of the ocean.

Sediments are deposited very slowly on the ocean bottom. In fact, sediments carried to the ocean cause an increase of only 10 to 20 centimeters (4 to 8 inches) every thousand years! Plant and animal remains and other sediments account for another 2 to 3 cm (about 1 in.) every thousand years. In spite of this slow buildup of sediments, some parts of the ocean have thick layers of sediment. Sediments slide down the continental slope during underwater landslides. Millions of tons of sediments can be dumped over large areas of the abyssal plain. In this way, thick layers of sediments build up on the ocean floor.

Section Review

Main Ideas: Salts and sediments are carried from land to the ocean by streams and rivers. This is why ocean water is salty. This sequence of events has taken place for millions of years. Sediments carried to the ocean can slide over the continental shelf. This causes submarine canyons to form on the ocean floor.

Questions: Answer in complete sentences.

1. What causes submarine canyons to form?
2. Explain the sequence of events that causes the ocean to become salty.
3. Explain why some parts of the ocean are saltier than others.
4. How do each of the following get to the ocean floor?
   a. mud and clay from rivers
   b. animal remains
   c. plant remains
   d. rock particles
5. Is the buildup of sediment on the ocean floor a fast or slow process? Explain.

1-3.

Changes in the Ocean Floor

These students are using a special globe to figure out the answer to a riddle. The riddle is: "Mt. Everest is about 8,848 m (29,028 ft) high. It is the tallest mountain on land, but not the tallest mountain in the world. What is the tallest mountain in the world?"

The globe they are using is different from most globes. It has a surface that shows the bumps, ridges, and smooth spots on the ocean's bottom. Looking at the earth's surface under the ocean may provide them with the answer. When you finish this section, you should be able to:

- ☐ **A.** Explain the major cause of changes in the ocean floor.
- ☐ **B.** Describe three effects of the spreading out of the ocean floor.
- ☐ **C.** Explain what causes ocean valleys to form.

The students noticed that parts of the mid-ocean ridge extended above sea level. One part of a ridge in the Pacific Ocean was higher than any other. Using the library, they were able to discover the name of the tallest mountain in the world. It is Mauna Kea, the highest peak in the state of Hawaii. Measured from its underwater base, the mountain is 9,600 m (32,000 ft) high. How do such tall mountains form from the ocean floor? The answer can be explained by the changes that take place on the ocean floor.

Scientists think it is very hot inside the earth. It is believed to be so hot there that rock within the earth can melt, or become **molten** (**mol**-ten). This hot, *molten* rock in the earth can move up toward the earth's surface under the giant crack in the mid-ocean ridge. When the molten rock breaks through the surface, it forms new ocean floor on both sides of the crack. The new ocean floor pushes against sections of the old floor. Many scientists think that the old floor on both sides of the crack moves. Therefore, scientists say the ocean floor is spreading away from the crack.

Molten: Melted by heat.

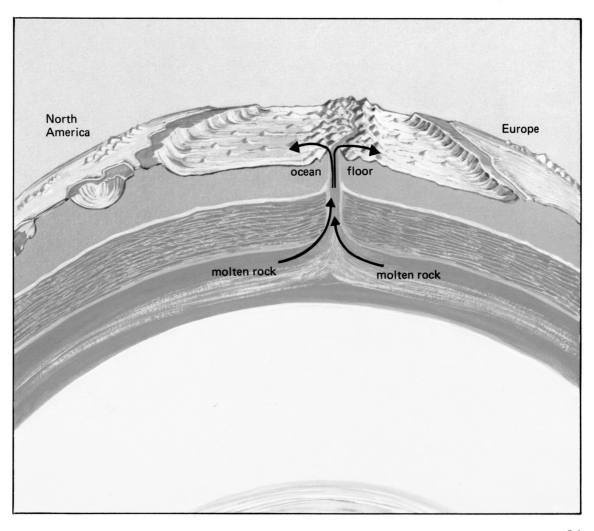

Scientists believe that the idea of sea-floor spreading explains changes in the earth's surface. They believe that the Atlantic Ocean is getting wider by 3 cm (about 1 in.) each year. Thus, the continents of Europe and North America are moving apart.

As the Atlantic Ocean floor spreads and the land moves apart, what do you think is happening to the Pacific Ocean? The Pacific Ocean is getting narrower. As the Pacific narrows, its ocean floor moves downward under the land that borders the ocean. Deep ocean valleys called **trenches** are formed. *Trenches* are some of the deepest places in the oceans. The drawing below shows how trenches are formed.

Trenches: Deep ocean valleys.

Look at the world map on page 23. The red lines show where most ocean trenches are located. In which ocean do you see most of the ocean trenches?

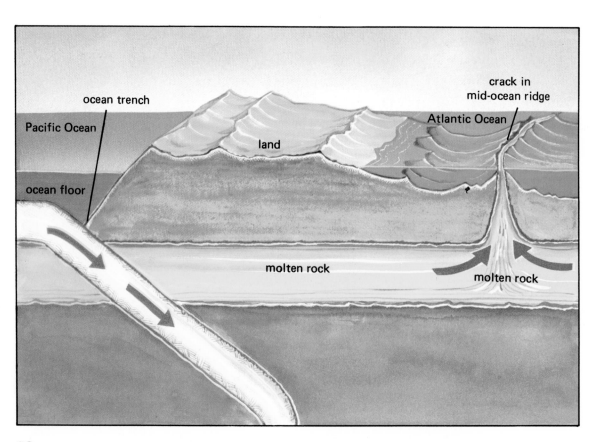

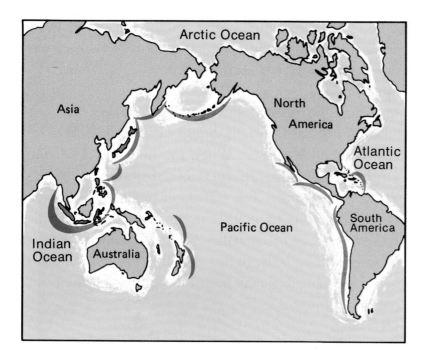

The molten rock that pushes up under the mid-ocean ridge causes the ocean floor to spread. However, it also forms mountains as it cools and hardens. Sometimes these mountains are so high they stick out of the water. We call them islands. The Azores (**ay**-zorz) are a group of islands in the North Atlantic Ocean. The Azores are really the tops of mountains that are part of the mid-ocean ridge.

Did you know that Hawaii is also part of a ridge in the ocean? Like the Azores, Hawaii consists of many islands that are the tops of underwater mountains.

This photograph shows the Kilauea volcano in Hawaii. It erupted in 1983. Molten rock poured down its slope. Scientists believe that this liquid rock comes from a vast underground chamber. When the liquid is forced upward, it bursts through the tops and sides of volcanoes. This action changes the surface of the earth. The very same thing happens at many places along the parts of the mid-ocean ridge. Scientists study the changes that occur on volcanoes on land. In this way, they can get some idea of the changes that may occur at locations on the ocean bottom.

Section Review

Main Ideas: Changes in the ocean floor are caused by molten rock. This liquid rock pushes upward through the mid-ocean ridge, cools, and forms a new part of the ocean floor. Mountains are gradually built up along the ridge. The ocean floor spreads apart and deep ocean trenches form as the ocean floor moves.

Questions: Answer in complete sentences.

1. What causes the major changes in the ocean floor?
2. What are three effects of changes in the ocean floor?
3. Where are deep ocean valleys located? What causes them?
4. Look at the world map at the top of page 23. What is meant by the red lines along the west coast of South America?
5. Study the photograph of one of the Azores Islands on page 23. What evidence is there that the mid-ocean ridge is a place that undergoes change?

CHAPTER REVIEW

Science Words

Select the definition from column B that goes best with each word in column A.

Column A	Column B
1. Continental shelf	a. Sand, clay, and other materials that settle in water
2. Trenches	
3. Sediments	b. A salt
4. Continental slope	c. Deep ocean valleys
5. Mid-ocean ridge	d. Flat part of the ocean floor
6. Sodium chloride	e. Part of the ocean bottom near land
7. Ocean floor	
8. Submarine canyon	f. Groove cut in continental shelf and slope
9. Abyssal plain	g. Mountain chain on the ocean bottom
	h. Sloping part of the ocean bottom
	i. Part of the ocean bottom that begins where the continental slope ends

Questions: Answer in complete sentences.

1. How do sediments from the land reach the ocean floor?
2. Scientists predict that the mid-ocean ridges will be the location of many earth movements and volcanoes in the future. What have you learned that would support that prediction?
3. Where is the most likely place on the ocean bottom to find a mountain? Where would you find a submarine canyon?
4. Explain how the movement of water from land to ocean causes ocean water to become salty.
5. How do scientists know that the ocean bottom is changing?
6. How are the mountains and plains of the United States like the ocean floor?

CHAPTER 2

OCEAN MOVEMENTS

2-1.

Currents

How does throwing bottles into the ocean help scientists learn about the ocean? A few years ago, students dropped 2,000 bottles into the ocean west of San Diego, California. Each bottle contained a brightly colored postcard. It asked the finder to let scientists know when and where the bottle came ashore. In this way, scientists could learn more about ocean currents. When you finish this section, you should be able to:

☐ **A.** Explain how wind causes currents.
☐ **B.** Describe the location and direction of major currents.
☐ **C.** Explain what causes deep ocean currents.

Five days after the bottles were dumped into the ocean, the first bottle was found. A boy found a bottle while fishing in Bahia de Todos Santos, a bay in Mexico. Other bottles have since been found in the United States, Mexico, and the Philippines. This shows that the ocean can carry objects over great distances. Objects may be carried by ocean **currents**. A *current* is water that moves in a certain direction.

Right now, as you are reading your book, the earth is spinning. You don't feel the spinning because the movement is slow. However, the spinning causes the air around the earth to move. Moving air creates wind. The wind moves over the ocean surface and pushes against the water. The water moves with the wind.

Current: Water that moves in a certain direction.

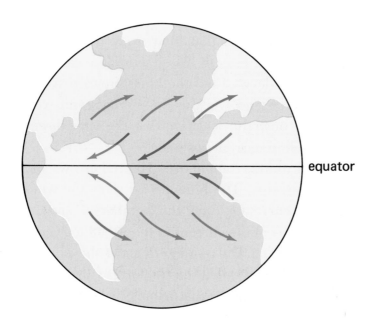

equator

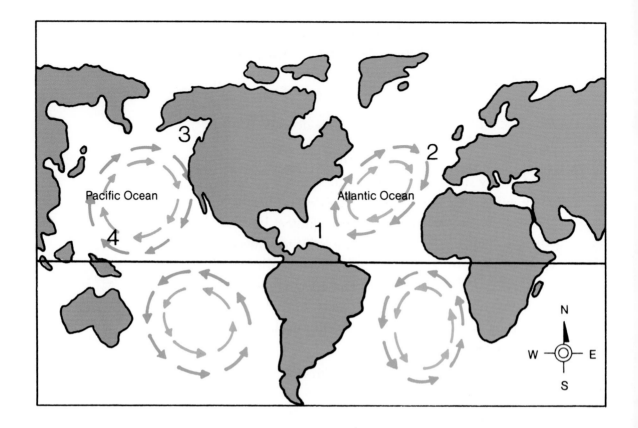

Trade winds: Winds that blow from east to west toward the equator.

Westerlies: Winds that blow from west to east away from the equator.

As they blow toward the equator, the winds move from east to the west. These winds are called **trade winds**. Look at the diagram at the bottom of page 27. Find the equator. Find the red arrows that show the blowing *trade winds*. Winds that blow away from the equator move from west to east. These winds are called **westerlies** (**west**-ter-leez). Find the blue arrows that show the blowing *westerlies*. As the trade winds and westerlies blow, they push the ocean water in the same direction. A giant, circling current results.

Look at the diagram above. The red arrows show the circling currents. The blue arrows show the winds that cause the currents. Find the numbers *1* and *2*. They show the part of the current in the Atlantic Ocean called the Gulf Stream. The numbers *3* and *4* show a current in the Pacific Ocean called the California Current. Why do you think it was given that name?

The currents you just read about are on the ocean surface. Other currents are below the surface. They are caused by the sun. The heat from the sun warms the ocean water. The sun does not evenly heat all the ocean water. At the equator, ocean water is warm. Where do you think ocean water is cold?

Cold water moves to the bottom of the ocean. You can think of it as slowly sinking to the bottom. The cold water at the North and South Poles sinks to the ocean bottom. The cold water slowly moves toward the equator. Warm water near the equator moves toward the poles to replace the sinking cold water. The movement of the cold and warm waters causes deep currents. The currents circle between the poles and the equator.

You know the amount of salt in ocean water is not the same all over. How does the sun's heat cause the water in some places to be saltier? The more salt in the water, the heavier the water is. Heavy water sinks to the ocean bottom. When it meets less salty water, the less salty water moves over it. A circling current forms. For example, the water of the Mediterranean Sea is saltier than the Atlantic Ocean. Where these two bodies of water meet there is a deep current. The saltier, heavy water moves along the ocean bottom. The less salty water moves over the heavier water into the Mediterranean Sea.

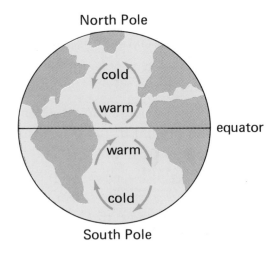

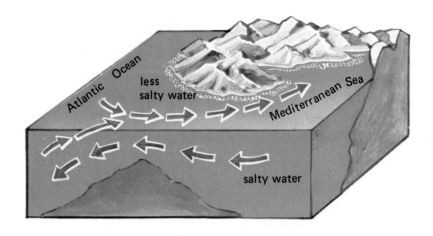

Currents at the ocean's surface and deep ocean currents are different in another way. Usually the deep ocean currents move more slowly than currents at the surface. It takes about 30 years before they circle up to the equator. It takes the same amount of water in the Gulf Stream only a few years to complete a circle of the ocean.

Section Review

Main Ideas: Currents are caused by the movement of wind at the ocean's surface. Deep ocean currents can be caused by the uneven heating of ocean water by the sun. The different amounts of salt in different parts of the ocean also cause deep ocean currents.

Questions: Answer in complete sentences.

1. Explain what causes a current at the ocean's surface.
2. Describe the location and the direction of movement of: **a.** the Gulf Stream **b.** the California Current.
3. The oceans of the earth are unevenly heated by the sun. Explain how this causes deep ocean currents.
4. Some parts of the ocean are saltier than other parts of the ocean. Explain how this can cause deep ocean currents.

As a wave moves toward land, it undergoes many changes. The wave rises up and water breaks and tumbles into the shore. Surfers make use of the force of this moving water and ride the waves as they move toward the shore. In this section, you will learn about waves and their effects. When you finish this section, you should be able to:

☐ **A.** Explain how wind causes waves.
☐ **B.** Identify the parts of a wave.
☐ **C.** Explain how waves can affect shorelines.

Surfers can tell something about the speed and direction of a wave as it moves toward the shore. They try to choose waves that will give them a long, smooth ride. What is it that makes the water move and form waves?

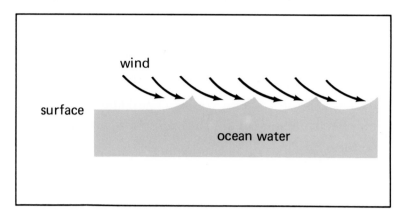

Waves form because of forces that act on the ocean water. You can experiment with the forces that cause waves by using a basin of water. You can use your hand to push the water and make waves. By dropping an object into the water, small waves can also be made. You can gently push the basin of water back and forth to create waves. Without forces acting on the water, the surface of the water would be almost as smooth as a mirror.

Like the basin of water, the ocean also has forces acting on it. Ships that travel across it push against water and make waves. The forces of earthquakes under the ocean also create waves.

In the last section, you learned how wind causes currents. Wind also causes waves. As wind moves over the water, it pushes against the surface. This movement causes part of the water to rise. The wind then pushes on the raised water and a wave is created. As the wind continues to blow, more waves are made.

What does a wave look like? A wave has two parts. The highest point of the wave is called the **crest**. The lowest point is called the **trough** (trof). The height of a wave is the distance from its *crest* to its *trough*. The length of a wave is the distance from its crest to the crest of the next wave. Waves move in the same direction as the wind. The size of a wave depends on the strength of the wind.

Crest: The highest point of a wave.

` · **The lowest**
` **ve.**

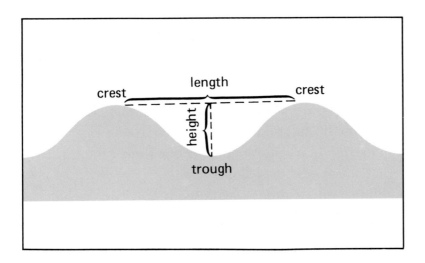

As a wave moves into shallow water near the shore, its trough rubs against the ocean bottom. The rubbing causes the trough to slow down. However, the crest still moves quickly. It gets higher and leans forward. The crest may lean so far forward that it tumbles over, forming a white foam. The wave is then called a **breaker**. After a wave breaks against the beach, the wave moves back into the ocean. It moves under the waves coming in. As the wave moves back into the ocean, it carries sand from the beach. The force of waves striking the shore over a long period of time can reshape a beach area.

Breaker: A wave in which the crest has tumbled forward.

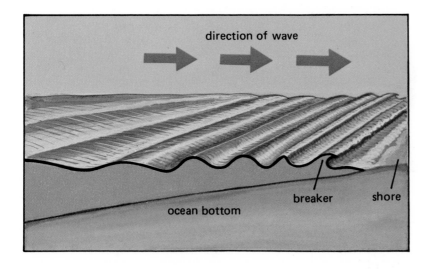

ACTIVITY

What are the effects of waves on the beach?

A. Obtain these materials: 2 blocks of wood, long tray (30 cm x 40 cm), milk container, sand, pebbles, water.

B. Place one block of wood under one end of the tray so that the tray is on a slope.

C. Fill that end of the tray with sand. Add some pebbles to the sand. Shape the sand and pebbles into a sloping "beach."

D. Fill your milk container with water. Gently pour the water into the tray at the other end. Stop pouring when the level of the water meets the beach.

E. Very slowly move the other block of wood toward the beach and then back 10 times. Wait a few seconds between each time.

F. Increase the force of your waves by pushing harder. Do this 10 times. This represents storm waves.

  1. How did the beach change?

  2. What caused the waves in this activity?

  3. What causes surface waves in nature?

  4. Carefully observe the beach. Where was some of the sand moved? Were any pebbles moved?

  5. A real sandy beach can be destroyed by a storm. Powerful waves can move sand back into the ocean. Make a hypothesis that explains why destroyed beaches are sometimes rebuilt by nature. Test your hypothesis using your equipment.

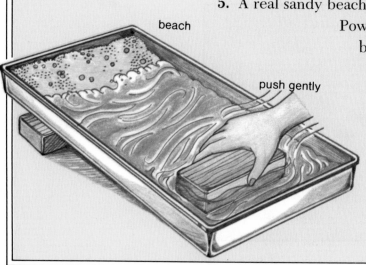

beach

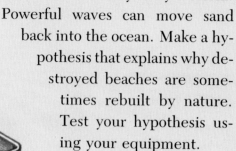

push gently

Even shores of rocks and mountain cliffs are changed by the action of waves. The pounding of the waves breaks rocks into small pieces. Water then pushes these pieces against even larger rocks. The mixture of water and small rocks crashing against a rocky shoreline eventually causes a change in the shoreline.

Can you explain how these unusual features were formed? Once these were part of the shoreline. Wave action wore away the cliff unevenly. Some rocks formed arches, while other rocks stuck up through the water.

Can you imagine a wave as high, or even higher than, your school building? The largest wave ever recorded was 64 m (210 ft) high. The wave was seen off the coast of Siberia on October 6, 1737.

Giant waves called **tsunamis** (tsoo-**nah**-meez) are caused by earthquakes or other movements of the ocean floor. These waves travel at speeds of several hundred kilometers per hour. The force of a *tsunami* can be so great that buildings near the shoreline can be destroyed. Scientists can track tsunamis. Warnings are sent to people to go to a safe place before these waves strike. These pictures show the damage caused by a tsunami.

Tsunami: Giant wave caused by movements at the ocean floor.

Section Review

Main Ideas: Wind causes waves by pushing against the surface of the water. When the crest of a wave tumbles into foam, a breaker forms. Breakers carry sand away from the beach. Over a long period of time, the force of waves can change the shape of a shoreline.

Questions: Answer in complete sentences.

1. Using the diagram on page 32, explain how wind causes waves.
2. Draw a labeled diagram that shows these wave parts: crest, trough, height, length.
3. Using the diagram on page 33, explain how waves can reshape the shoreline.

Both of these pictures were taken at the same place and on the same day. What is the major difference? As you can see, the water's edge might not be the best spot for a picnic. If you stayed long enough, your family and your picnic would float out to sea! The rise in water level is due to the *tide* coming in. When you finish this section, you should be able to:

☐ **A.** Explain what is meant by the word *tide*.
☐ **B.** Explain how the moon causes *tides*.
☐ **C.** Explain the effects of both the sun and the moon on *tides*.

These pictures show the shoreline of the Bay of Fundy in Canada. Twice in a 24-hour period water rises to the height you see in the bottom picture. In fact, these changes in water level occur all over the world at every shoreline.

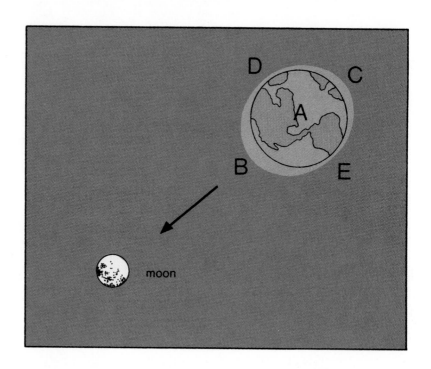

Tides: The rise and fall of ocean water.

The rise and fall of ocean water are called **tides**. When the water is at its highest level, we say there is a high *tide*. Which picture on page 37 shows the Bay of Fundy at high tide? When the water is at its lowest level, there is a low tide. Which picture shows the Bay of Fundy at low tide?

Tides occur along every ocean coast. The heights of the tides differ from one place to another. Tides are caused by the pull of the moon on the earth. Look at the diagram. The letter A represents the earth. The letters B, C, D, and E represent the oceans on the earth. The moon pulls on the ocean water at B, causing the water to bulge. The bulge creates a high tide on that side of the earth. The moon also pulls on the solid earth, shown as A. The moon pulls more on A than on C, causing another bulge. This bulge creates a high tide on the opposite side of the earth. The water at D and E flattens and low tides occur there. Because of the earth's spinning, the tides at B, C, D, and E will change. When the tides become high at D and E, there will be low tides at B and C.

ACTIVITY

How do tides affect water level?

A. Obtain some graph paper.

B. Scientists recorded the height of water in Boston Harbor for January 1.

Height of Water in Boston Harbor on January 1

time	1 A.M.	2 A.M.	3 A.M.	4 A.M.	5 A.M.	6 A.M.	7 A.M.	8 A.M.	9 A.M.	10 A.M.	11 A.M.	12 noon
height of water (meters)	2.0	1.7	1.6	1.9	2.4	2.9	3.4	3.8	4.0	3.7	3.3	2.7
time	1 P.M.	2 P.M.	3 P.M.	4 P.M.	5 P.M.	6 P.M.	7 P.M.	8 P.M.	9 P.M.	10 P.M.	11 P.M.	12 mid-night
height of water (meters)	2.2	1.6	1.2	1.3	1.6	2.1	2.6	4.6	3.4	3.5	3.2	2.8

C. Make a graph like the one below that shows how the height of water changed over 24 hours.

   1. At what time did the first low tide occur? The first high tide?
   2. How many hours passed between the first low tide and the first high tide?
   3. At what time did the second low tide occur? The second high tide?
   4. How many hours passed between the first and the second high tides? Between the low tides?

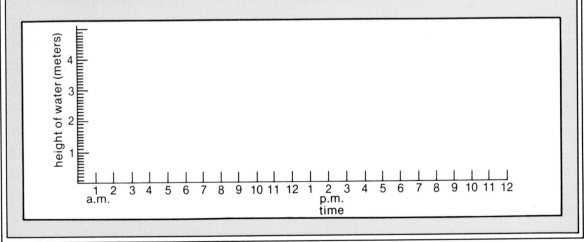

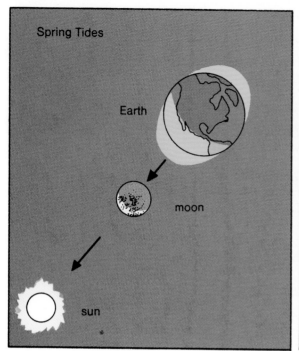

Spring Tides

Earth

moon

sun

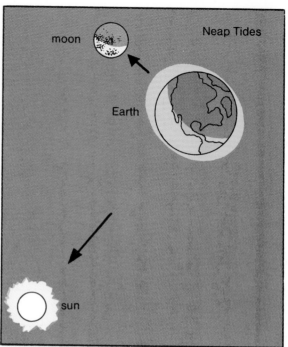

moon

Neap Tides

Earth

sun

Tides change from high to low every six hours. Within a 24-hour period a sequence would be high tide, low tide, high tide, and finally low tide. If you know when the last high tide occurred, you can predict when the next one will occur. For example, if a high tide occurred at 2 P.M., when would you expect the next high tide to occur?

There are certain times when the tides are very high and very low. These tides occur when the sun, earth, and moon form a straight line in space. At this time, both the sun and the moon pull on the earth. As a result, high tides are higher than usual, and low tides are lower than usual. This only occurs twice a month. These very high and very low tides are called **spring tides.**

When the earth, moon, and sun are at right angles to each other, low tides are not very low. High tides are not very high. The tides are not as great because the pull of the sun decreases the moon's pull on the earth. These are called **neap (neep) tides.** The diagrams show the posi-

Spring tides: Very high and very low tides.

Neap tides: Low tides that are not very low; high tides that are not very high.

40

tions of the earth, moon, and sun when *spring tides* and *neap tides* occur. Look at the positions of the earth, moon, and sun in each diagram. The arrows show the direction of the moon's pull and the sun's pull.

In some coastal areas of the world, spring tides can cause problems. Flooding may take place, especially if the weather is stormy. In the United States, flooding usually happens during the spring season.

Section Review

Main Ideas: This chart summarizes the types of tides.

Tide	Cause	Effect
every day tide	the pull of the moon on the oceans	high and low tides every 24 hours
spring tide	sun and moon in line with the earth	very high tides and very low tides
neap tide	sun and moon at right angles to the earth	high tides that are not as high; low tides that are not as low

Questions: Answer in complete sentences.

1. Explain what tides are.
2. Using a diagram, explain how the moon affects the rise and fall of ocean water.
3. Using a diagram, explain how the moon and sun together affect the tides.
4. What do you think would happen to the tides if the earth had no moon?
5. Use the diagrams on page 40 to answer this question: Why are neap tides not as large as spring tides?

CHAPTER REVIEW

Science Words

A. What term best fits each definition given?
   1. Winds that blow from east to west toward the equator.
   2. Winds that blow from west to east away from the equator.
   3. Water that moves in a certain direction.
   4. The highest point of a wave.
   5. The lowest point of a wave.

B. Unscramble the letters to find the correct terms.
   6. The D I E T is the rise and fall of ocean water.
   7. The S I S M A N U T are giant waves caused by underwater earthquakes.
   8. A R E R A K B E is a wave in which the crest has tumbled forward.
   9. Very high and very low tides are called G N I P S R tides.
   10. P N E A tides are low tides that are not very low and high tides that are not very high.

Questions: Answer in complete sentences.

1. Compare the direction and location of the trade winds and westerlies.
2. How do trade winds and westerlies cause ocean currents?
3. Describe the movement of deep ocean currents as they move from the polar regions to the equator.
4. The tides rise and fall in a regular pattern every 24 hours.
   a. How much time will pass between two high tides?
   b. How much time will pass between a high tide and a low tide?
   c. How many high tides will occur in a 24-hour period?
   d. How many low tides will occur in a 24-hour period?
5. When are high tides very high and low tides very low? Draw the positions of the earth, sun, and moon.

CHAPTER 3

OCEAN EXPLORATION

Do you eat a kind of food that is made from seaweed? Do you brush your teeth with sea plants? The answer is probably yes! These are just two examples of products the ocean can provide us with. When you finish this section, you should be able to:

3-1.

Ocean Resources

43

☐ **A.** Give examples of four kinds of resources that we get from the ocean and explain their uses.

☐ **B.** Explain how fresh water can be made from salt water.

Agar: A tasteless, odorless material made from seaweed.

Diatoms: Tiny ocean plants.

Commercial ice cream and toothpaste are made from substances that come from sea plants. Ice cream is thickened with a material called **agar** (ah-gar). *Agar* is a tasteless, colorless material made from seaweed. Toothpaste also contains an ocean product. It has gritty material in it that rubs food particles from your teeth. This gritty material consists of the remains of tiny ocean plants called **diatoms** (**dy-uh-tahmz**). In the ocean, *diatoms* are a main food source for ocean animals. When diatoms die, their remains settle to the ocean bottom. The diatom material in your toothpaste is millions of years old. It is obtained by mining land that was once an ocean bottom. Agar and diatoms are only two of the many products that the ocean provides for us.

The ocean is also a rich source of food. However, only ten percent of our food supply comes from the ocean.

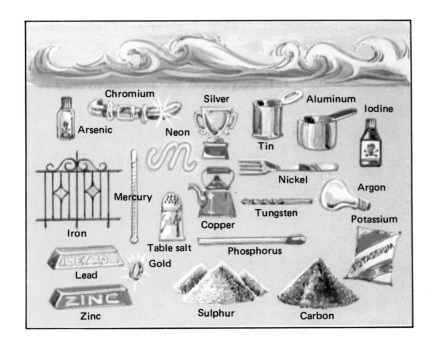

On land, people have learned to farm to supply the food they need. New crops are grown each year and new animals raised to replace what has been used. People hunt for food in the ocean. They take food from the ocean but do not replace it. Scientists believe we can learn to farm in the ocean. We can grow new ocean plants or crops each year and raise ocean animals. Ocean farming would increase the amount of food we get from the ocean. Also, we would be able to replace the food we take from the ocean. Ocean farming has been tried in different countries in order to feed hungry people. It is not an easy job. What problems would it cause?

Ocean water contains many materials also found on land. These materials are dissolved in the water. You have learned about a dissolved salt. Can you name it? Look at the drawing. The words you see are names of other materials dissolved in ocean water. The drawing also shows how the materials may be used. It is very expensive to get some of these materials out of the water. However, as we use up the supplies of these materials from the land, the ocean will be our only source.

Fossil fuels: Fuels formed from remains of plants and animals.

Petroleum: A fossil fuel in liquid form.

Natural gas: A fossil fuel in gas form.

The largest supply of **fossil fuels** (**fah**-sil **fyoo**-ellz) on earth may lie under the ocean bottom. *Fossil fuels* are formed from the remains of plants and animals that lived very long ago. These remains settled on the ocean bottom and were covered with layers of other sediment. The layers of sediment pushed down on the remains. After millions of years the remains changed to a liquid called **petroleum** (peh-**troh**-lee-um). *Petroleum* is a fossil fuel found under the ocean bottom. It is used to make gasoline and heating oil. Another fossil fuel is **natural gas.** *Natural gas* also is used to heat homes. Natural gas and petroleum are usually found together. Find the gas in the picture below. Between which layers is it found?

The picture on the right shows what is used to drill under the ocean bottom for fossil fuels. Scientists decide where to drill. Drilling is difficult and expensive. Sometimes there are accidents and oil gets into the ocean water. However, when the supply from the land is used up, the ocean may be the only source of fossil fuels. There is a limited amount of fuels in the ocean as well. We will soon have to find other sources of fuels.

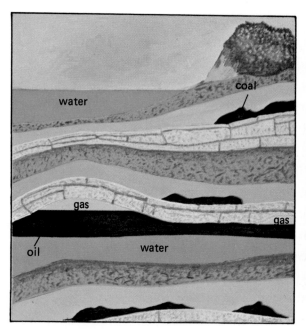

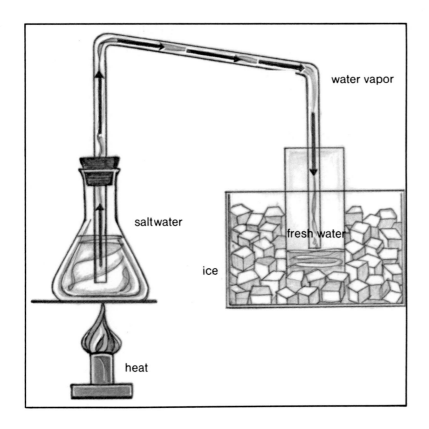

water vapor

saltwater

fresh water

ice

heat

The ocean can also provide us with water that we can drink. Scientists have found several ways to remove salt and other materials from sea water.

Salt can be removed from saltwater by **desalination** (dee-sal-ih-**nay**-shun). The diagram shows how *desalination* works. It is something that can be done in a class-**room.** Saltwater is heated. The steam it produces goes through a tube. The steam is then cooled. It forms fresh water. The salt stays behind.

This idea is used in many desalination plants. They are large buildings near the ocean. Ocean water is pumped into large tanks. The water is heated until it becomes steam. The steam is cooled into fresh water.

This process is necessary in areas where fresh water is scarce. Fresh water is needed for drinking, farming, and industry. A place like Key West, Florida, is such an area. It has a new type of desalination plant as shown in the

Desalination: The process of removing salt from ocean water.

photograph. It uses very powerful filters to get salt out of the ocean water. This plant can produce up to 12 million liters (3 million gallons) of fresh water a day. Filtering does not cost as much as heating the water does. It also uses less energy.

Section Review

Main Ideas: In the future, we will be more dependent on the ocean for its many resources. It is a source of food, fossil fuels, minerals, and fresh water.

Questions: Answer in complete sentences.

1. Name four resources we get from the ocean.
2. Providing food for all the people in the world is a difficult problem. Explain how ocean farming would help.
3. What is desalination?
4. Explain the sequence of steps that occurs during desalination.
5. What is the main idea shown in the picture at the top of page 45?

One of the most feared ocean animals is the great white shark. This animal can grow to a length of 9 m (about 30 ft). Fortunately, the great white shark spends most of its time far away from people. Great white sharks feed on fish by attacking them with powerful jaws. The shark's jaw contains rows of razor-sharp teeth. The great white shark is only one of the many forms of ocean life that usually remain hidden in the ocean's waters. When you finish this section, you should be able to:

☐ **A.** Describe the forms of life found at three ocean locations.
☐ **B.** Explain how sea animals depend on one another and on plants for food.
☐ **C.** Explain the sequence of events that occurs in an ocean food chain.

Some living things in the ocean are much larger than the great white shark. The whale shark, for example, can grow to over 15 m (about 50 ft) in length.

Did you know that the largest animal in the world lives in the ocean? The blue whale can grow to a length of 30 m (about 100 ft). The ocean is also the home for some plants and animals that are so tiny that they can be seen only with a powerful microscope. Although life in the ocean comes in many shapes and sizes, most living things seem to be concentrated in three ocean areas. These areas are the surface, just below the surface, and the bottom of the ocean near the shore.

Thousands of tiny plants and animals float on the surface of the ocean. They are called **plankton** (**plank**-tun). *Plankton* are so tiny they cannot be seen with the naked eye. Plankton live on the ocean surface, where there is sunlight, rather than on the ocean bottom. Tiny shrimp-like animals called **copepods** (**koh**-peh-podz) eat plankton. A *copepod* is as small as the head of a pin. Even big animals, such as some whales, eat plankton, too.

On the ocean bottom near the shore, there are many

Plankton: Tiny plants and animals on the ocean surface.

Copepods: Tiny shrimplike animals.

49

plants and animals. Here, sunlight reaches the bottom and many plants are able to grow. Why do you think there is little plant growth in the deeper parts of the ocean?

A great variety of animals live in the water near the shore. Crabs, lobsters, and shrimps move along the ocean bottom looking for food. Some fish swim along the bottom, too. They all eat plankton that fall from the surface. They also eat parts of other ocean animals. The starfish uses its long arms to pry open clams and scallops. The **sea anemone** (uh-**nem**-uh-nee) sits on the ocean bottom waiting for a fish to touch its poisonous arms. The *sea anemone*, shown in the picture on the right, looks more like a plant than an animal.

Most fish live in the deeper water, just below the ocean surface. Fish eat other fish to stay alive. Large fish eat smaller ones, which eat smaller ones, which eat still smaller ones. The small fish eat copepods and plankton. For example, sharks may eat codfish, which eat herring, which eat copepods, which eat plankton. This eating pattern is called a **food chain**. A *food chain* can be described as who-eats-whom.

Sea anemone: An ocean animal.

Food chain: A pattern of who-eats-whom.

Each food chain is like a pyramid. Many organisms are at the bottom of each food chain. Only one animal species is at the top of each food chain. Each animal feeds on the plants and animals below it on the pyramid.

In the ocean there are few places for fish to hide. Therefore, many fish have coloring to protect them. From above, ocean water looks blue. Many fish are blue on top. From below, the water looks white, and many fish have white bellies. The stingray is a fish whose color matches the ocean bottom, where it lives. Look at the picture below. Can you find the stingray buried in the sand?

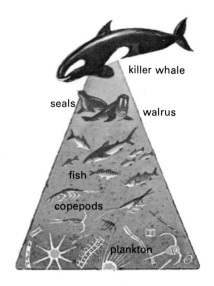

Section Review

Main Ideas: Most ocean plants and animals are found in three main areas. They depend on one another for food. The picture shows an ocean food chain.

Questions: Answer in complete sentences.

1. Give three examples of living things found on the ocean bottom near the shore.
2. What types of living things would you expect to find floating on the ocean's surface?
3. What types of living things would you expect to find in deep water?
4. What is meant by the term "food chain"?
5. Place these animals in the correct sequence for a food chain: copepods, plankton, shark, codfish.

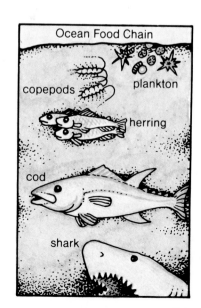

3-3.

The Ocean in Danger

One morning in March, 1980, the *Amoco Cadiz*, a giant tanker carrying crude oil, was sailing off the northern coast of France. At 10:45 A.M. the ship's steering equipment broke down. The giant tanker became impossible to control. Within only 12 hours the ship was torn apart by powerful waves. The tanker broke apart, pouring out 69 million gallons of crude oil. Can you guess how this affected the ocean? When you finish this section, you should be able to:

☐ **A.** Explain what pollution is.
☐ **B.** Describe how human activity affects the ocean and living things in it.

Pollution: The adding of harmful materials to the environment.

Sewage: Waste materials carried by sewers and drains.

The spreading oil slick from the sinking tanker eventually reached and covered 160 km (about 100 mi) of the French coastline. Animals and plants in the area were coated with a thick layer of oil. Even sea birds floating on the water were affected. Hundreds of people worked hard to clean the oil from the birds' feathers. Unfortunately, very few of the birds survived.

There are many substances other than crude oil that are accidentally dumped into the ocean. Some substances are deliberately added to the ocean. These substances, whether harmful or harmless, are not normally found in the sea.

The cause for the addition of these substances is human activity. In some places along the shoreline, the ocean has become a place to dump garbage. Some industries produce wastes that eventually reach the ocean. Many people are careless and do not think about the effect that these substances will have on the ocean. The addition of harmful materials to the environment is called **pollution** (poh-**loo**-shun).

Pollution of the ocean is often caused by the dumping of **sewage** (**soo**-ij) into the water. *Sewage* is waste material carried by sewers and drains. Sewage contains germs that cause disease in ocean plants and animals. To pre-

vent pollution, many cities have sewage-treatment plants like the one shown above. At these plants, the harmful materials are removed from the sewage.

Pollution can also be caused by chemicals in the water. Some chemicals are carried to the ocean by rivers. For example, **pesticides** (**pes**-tih-sydz), chemicals sprayed on crops, run off the land into rivers. The *pesticides* are carried to the ocean. They are harmful to the living things there. What do you think happens to the plants and animals as a result?

Pesticides: Chemicals sprayed on crops.

Some plants and animals will die. For those living things that survive, chemicals enter their bodies. If humans and other animals eat food from the ocean, these harmful substances affect them, too. To prevent this type of pollution, laws have been passed to limit the amount and kinds of chemicals used for spraying crops.

Since early times, people have depended on the ocean for food. Today, people in many parts of the world still depend almost totally on fish and shellfish. At the same

ACTIVITY

Can you remove oil from water?

A. Obtain these materials: cotton, motor oil, pan, paper, spoon, water.

B. Fill the pan with water.

C. Pour some oil into the water.

    1. Did the oil mix with the water?

D. Try to remove the oil from the water with a spoon, the cotton, and the paper.

    2. Were you able to get the oil out of the water?

    3. As a result of what you have learned in this activity, how would animals be affected by an oil spill?

    4. Using what you have learned in this activity, suggest a way to clear up an oil spill.

Species: All of the same kind of living thing.

time that food is being removed from the ocean, harmful materials are being added to it. We add garbage, sewage, oil, and chemicals to the very same waters that provide us with food. Ocean pollution is a threat to fish, to birds that feed on fish, and to humans.

Ocean pollution not only affects individual animals and plants. It can affect entire **species.** *Species* is the name for all of the same kind of living thing. Entire species could disappear because one of their major food sources dies from pollution.

Here is an example that will help you understand why. Imagine that chemicals dumped into a river are carried to the ocean. If the chemicals kill the plankton, the copepods that feed on the plankton will lose their food supply. Many copepods will die. Since copepods are an important part of the herring's diet, the herring could also die. In the food chain, plankton is eaten by copepods, which are eaten by herring. If one species is harmed by chemicals, so are all the others.

The eastern brown pelican is a species that was in danger from pesticide pollution. This bird is also part of an ocean food chain. Through the food chain, pesticides entered the bodies of these birds. As a result, the pelicans laid eggs with very thin shells. The eggs would crack and the unhatched pelican chicks would die. This situation received the attention of concerned scientists. Laws were passed against the use of certain pesticides. Now there are more brown pelicans than before.

Some animals are in danger for a reason other than pollution. Blue whales are in danger of becoming **extinct** (ek-**stinkt**). An animal is *extinct* when there aren't any left. Blue whales have been hunted for many years. They are hunted for their meat, bones, and baleen.

Extinct: Does not exist anymore.

The graph below shows the number of blue whales killed since 1930. How many were killed in 1930? How many were killed in 1980? The number of whales killed each year has decreased. There are two reasons for this. Because so many were killed between 1930 and 1940, there were fewer left to be killed later. Also, it is now against the law for Americans and Europeans to hunt blue whales.

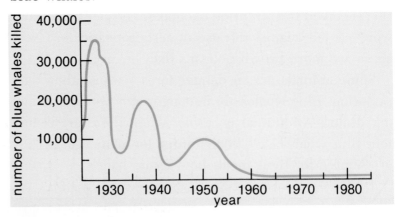

Section Review

Main Ideas: Human activity has resulted in ocean pollution. Pollutants such as sewage, oil, and chemical pesticides affect ocean food chains. This may cause some species to become extinct. Overhunting by humans has also threatened many species.

Questions: Answer in complete sentences.
1. How are pollutants added to the ocean?
2. Explain how these pollutants are harmful to ocean water: **a.** sewage **b.** chemical pesticides **c.** oil.
3. Explain how pollutants affect food chains.
4. What threatened the population of the blue whale? What was the effect of laws that were passed?
5. How are sewage and pesticide pollution reduced?
6. Study the graph above. How many blue whales were killed in 1930, 1950, and 1980? What conclusions can you make from these numbers?

Exploring the Ocean Bottom

Have you ever swum underwater? Were you able to breathe? Without air from special equipment, you cannot stay underwater very long. Equipment used by divers allows them to stay underwater for almost an hour. This allows scientists to explore the ocean bottom. When you finish this section, you should be able to:

☐ **A.** Describe two pieces of equipment people use to explore the ocean.

☐ **B.** Explain how sound is used to determine the shape of the ocean bottom.

☐ **C.** Explain how scientists gather sediments and what information they can learn from them.

For thousands of years people have been diving into water to gather shellfish, sponges, and other living things. The amount of time humans could spend underwater depended on how long the divers could hold their breath.

During the 1800's, the first diving suits were invented. These suits allowed a person to spend much more time underwater. An air hose was connected to the diving suit. The opposite end of the air hose was connected to

Aqualung: An air tank worn on a diver's back.

an air supply on board a ship. However, there was danger in using this equipment. The hoses would often tangle and break, cutting off the diver's air supply. People risked using these diving suits to search shipwrecks for treasure. The first person to use diving gear for scientific study was the nineteenth-century French scientist Henri Milne-Edwards.

In 1943, the **aqualung** (ak-wuh-lung) was invented. The *aqualung* is an air tank worn on the diver's back with a hose from the tank to the diver's mouth. The aqualung allows divers to explore underwater for long periods of time. Look at the picture of the diver on page 57. Can you locate the parts of the aqualung? What do divers wear to open their eyes safely and see underwater?

Even with an aqualung and a face mask, a diver can only swim to a certain depth. After a depth of more than 133 m (439 ft), the water presses against the diver so much that it can crush the diver. In order to explore greater depths, **bathyscaphes** (bath-ih-scafs) were invented. A *bathyscaphe* is an underwater ship. It can carry people and equipment to a depth of 3,600 m (about 12,000 ft). The bathyscaphe in the picture is called *Alvin*.

Finding out what the ocean floor looks like is difficult. To map the surface of the ocean bottom, an **echo sounder** is used. This instrument uses sound, which travels through water. When sound hits the bottom of the ocean, it bounces back to the ship. The time it takes for the sound to hit the ocean bottom and return to the ship is measured. Scientists can figure out how far the sound traveled if they know how long it took to return. Therefore, they know how far down the bottom is. They can map the high and low places on the ocean bottom.

Look at the boats pictured below. Each boat is using an echo sounder. With your finger, follow the sound waves sent out from the boat on the left. Continue to the place where the sounds hit the ocean bottom. Now follow the path of the sound bouncing back. Now look at the boat in deeper water, as shown on the right. Would it take more or less time for the sound to bounce back to that boat?

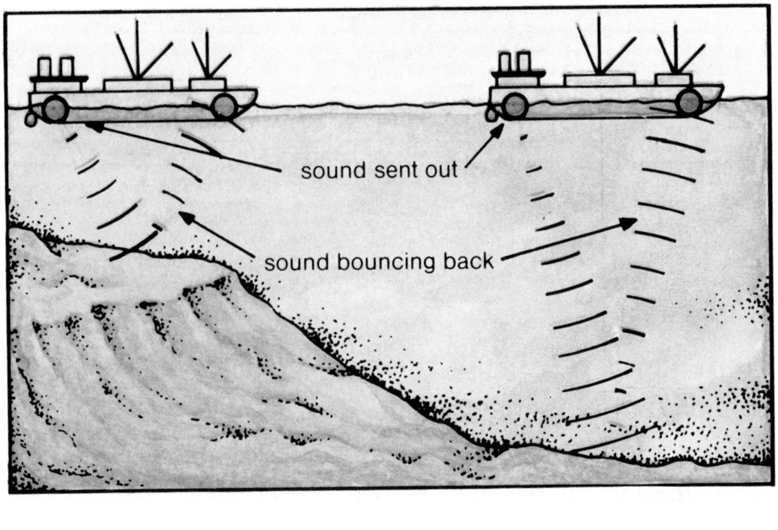

sound sent out

sound bouncing back

ACTIVITY

Making observations from an echo sounder chart

A. Study the chart below and answer these questions:
1. At what depth is the underwater mountain?
2. How high is the mountain?
3. How deep is the deepest part of the ocean shown on the chart?

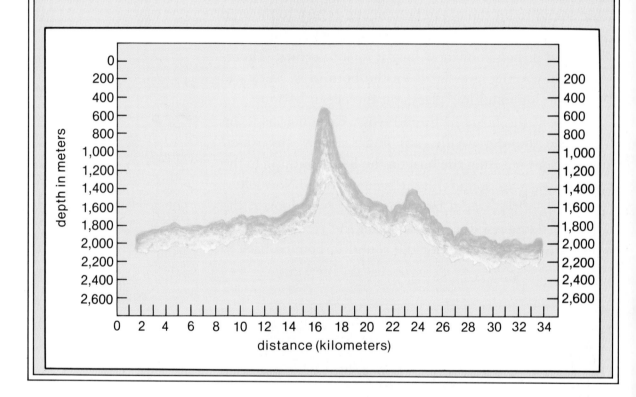

The layers of sediments on the ocean bottom built up over a very long period of time. Studying them can provide information about the history of the earth. They contain the remains of plants and animals that lived in the ocean long ago. When they died, they sank to the bottom and became covered with sediment. Even changes that take place on land are recorded in the ocean sediments. Dust from volcanoes sometimes reaches the oceans and filters through the water. Eventually some of it is added to the sediment. Sediments carried to the ocean from streams and rivers on land also tell us what the soil on the earth's surface was like in the past.

Scientists get samples of sediment by drilling a long hollow tube into the ocean bottom. The tube is then brought to the surface of the water. The hollow part contains a sample of sediment from the ocean bottom. Scientists remove the core of ocean sediment from the tube. They do this just like you would remove the core of an apple. The core is carefully sliced in half lengthwise.

The layers of sediment in a core are like clues for a detective. Here is a diagram of sediment layers in a core. Which layer do you think formed first? If you think it is the bottom layer, you are right. The only way for it to be where it is is that it reached the ocean floor first. Everything that fell on it had to have settled from the ocean at a later time. Which layer formed last?

Imagine that the C and F layers in the core sample are sediments from the dust of two different volcanoes. Which volcano was the first to burst? Which of the volcanoes probably erupted for the longer time?

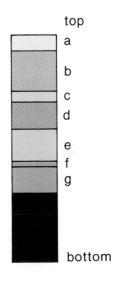

top
a
b
c
d
e
f
g
bottom

Section Review

Main Ideas: Divers use equipment such as the aqualung and bathyscaphe to explore the underwater world. The ocean bottom can be mapped, using an echo sounder. Sediment samples from the ocean bottom are studied to learn about changes that have taken place on earth.

Questions: Answer in complete sentences.

1. What is an aqualung?
2. What is a bathyscaphe? Why is it used?
3. Explain how an echo sounder is used to make a picture of the ocean bottom.
4. What can scientists learn from studying the sediments of the ocean bottom?

People in Science

Eugenie Clark

Dr. Eugenie Clark is a famous marine biologist. She has spent most of her life studying sharks. As a young girl, Dr. Clark spent long hours at the New York Aquarium. She also read everything she could on sharks and other fishes. She studied about marine animals in college. Later she became a college teacher.

As founder and director of the Mote Marine Laboratory in Florida, Dr. Clark did experiments on shark behavior. Later she began a worldwide study of sharks. This involved diving into oceans where sharks live.

She has studied the behavior of the great white shark. This is one shark that attacks humans. After 26 years of research on sharks, Dr. Clark has found that most sharks, unless threatened, prefer to escape rather than attack anything as large as a human.

CHAPTER REVIEW

Science Words Define each of these words:

1. pesticides
2. echo sounder
3. food chains
4. sewage
5. pollution

What word best fits each of the blanks?

6. A fossil fuel is formed from the remains of _____ and _____.
7. Two fossil fuels are _____ and _____.
8. Desalination is the process for removing _____ from ocean water.
9. _____ are tiny plants and animals on the ocean surface.
10. Tiny shrimplike animals are called _____.

Questions: Answer in complete sentences.

1. What are the four important resources that the ocean provides?
2. Describe the causes of ocean pollution.
3. This is an example of an ocean food chain: plankton → copepods → cod → seal → shark. How would the copepods and seals be affected if the cod became extinct? Explain your answer.
4. How is an echo sounder used to map the ocean bottom?
5. Which living things in each pair would be the highest in the ocean's pyramid of life? Give a reason for each of your choices. **a.** pelican, fish **b.** plankton, fish **c.** seaweed, fish **d.** seaweed, pelican **e.** seal, fish.
6. How can ocean water be changed into fresh drinking water?
7. What devices help scientists explore the ocean?

How does temperature cause ocean currents?

A. Obtain these materials: 1 large beaker, 1 small beaker, potholder, ice water, hot water, blue food coloring, red food coloring.

B. Pour about 2 cups of hot water into a large beaker. CAUTION: USE A POTHOLDER WHEN POURING HOT WATER. Add 2 or 3 drops of red food coloring to the hot water and stir.

C. Pour about 1/2 cup of ice water into a small beaker. Add 2 or 3 drops of blue food coloring and stir.

D. Using the potholder, as shown below, hold the beaker of hot water on a slant. Very slowly and carefully, add the cold water to the hot water. Let the cold water trickle very slowly down the inside of the large beaker of hot water.

    1. What happened to the cold water?

    2. Which is more dense, cold water or hot water? Explain.

E. Pour about 2 cups of ice water into a large beaker. Add 2 or 3 drops of blue food coloring and stir. Pour about 1/2 cup of hot water into a small beaker. Add 2 or 3 drops of red food coloring and stir.

F. Hold the beaker of cold water on a slant and very slowly and carefully pour the hot water into the cold water. CAUTION: USE A POT-HOLDER WHEN POURING HOT WATER.

    3. What happened to the hot water?

    4. How does this experiment show how temperature causes deep ocean currents?

Marine Biologist ▶

A **marine** (muh-**reen**) **biologist** is a scientist who studies the ocean's living things. *Marine biologists* are especially interested in ocean food chains. Anything that harms a species in the ocean will probably affect many food chains. By studying ocean species, marine biologists can help to prevent species from becoming extinct. They study science for many years and are usually expert divers and swimmers.

◀ Salvage Diver

A **salvage diver** is a person who finds sunken ships and brings valuable objects to the surface. Much time is spent studying old records to locate shipwrecks. Once located, the area around the ship must be carefully studied. Water currents could cause the sunken ship to move while divers are working on or near it. Great skill and patience are needed for this dangerous work.

SOUND

UNIT 2

CHAPTER 4

HEARING SOUND

4-1.

How Sounds Are Made

The crowd has quieted down. The runners are down at the starting line. They strain to hear the voice of the starter. "Ready. On your mark. Get set." The sharp sound of the starter's whistle rings in their ears. They leap from the starting line. When you finish this section, you should be able to:

☐ **A.** Explain what causes sound.

☐ **B.** Describe the relationship between movement and sound.

The sound made by the whistle needs **energy** (eh-ner-jee). *Energy* is the ability to do work. Energy causes objects to move. When you pick up a book, you use energy to move it. The starter used energy to say,

Energy: The ability to do work.

ACTIVITY

Observing the cause of sound

A. Obtain a plastic ruler.

B. Take turns with a partner in this activity. One of you should put your ear against the desk top in order to listen. The other should place the ruler so that half of it extends over the edge of the desk.

C. With one hand, hold the ruler flat against the desk top. With the other hand, lightly hit the free end of the ruler.

D. The listener should describe the sound produced by the ruler.

   1. What did it sound like?

   2. What caused the sound?

   3. What do you notice when the ruler stops?

   4. Where did the energy to move the ruler come from?

E. Changing the length of the ruler that extends over the desk changes the sound.

   5. Make a hypothesis about what will happen to the sound when the length of the ruler is made longer and shorter.

   6. Do an experiment to check your hypothesis.

   7. Copy the chart shown. Record your data.

   8. What conclusions did you reach?

Length	How Sound Changed
shorter	
longer	

"Ready, on your mark, get set." Energy was stored in the starter. This energy was changed to sound energy when she blew the whistle.

Sound is one of many forms of energy. Light, heat, and electricity are some other forms. Energy can be changed from one form to another. You have observed many energy changes. For example, when you use a toaster, electrical energy is changed to heat energy.

Sounds are produced when energy causes an object to **vibrate** (**vi**-brayt). *Vibrate* means to move back and forth quickly. If you strike a drum with your hand, you use energy. The energy causes the drumhead to move. It moves back and forth quickly. These vibrations cause

Vibrate: To move back and forth quickly.

70

sound. When the drumhead stops vibrating, the sound also stops.

Look at the pictures on page 70. What sounds would you hear if you were there? What do you think is vibrating to cause the sounds?

The woodpecker's beak moves back and forth against the tree. That causes a tapping sound. The jackhammer vibrates as it digs into the ground. When you speak or sing, your throat vibrates. Place your hand on your throat and hum. What do you feel?

Many objects vibrate so quickly that their motion can't be seen. The effects of the motion can be seen by using a table tennis ball and a thread. If a vibrating object touches the ball, the ball will bounce away.

The metal object in the photographs below is a **tuning** (**too**-ning) **fork**. A *tuning fork* is used to tune musical instruments. It has two prongs. When the prongs of a tuning fork are hit, they vibrate. A musical tone can be made when they are struck with a rubber hammer. Energy to produce sound comes from the person striking the fork. In the picture on the left, the table tennis ball is not vibrating. In the picture on the right, the tuning fork has been struck. What happened to the ball? What caused it to move?

Tuning fork: A device used to tune musical instruments.

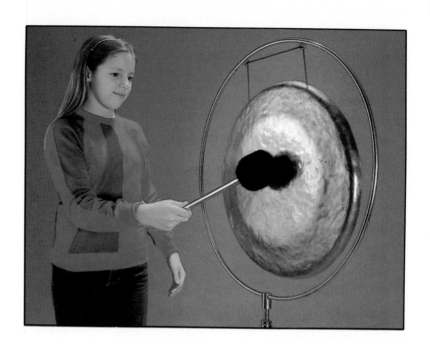

Section Review

Main Ideas: Energy is the ability to do work. It causes objects to move. Sound is a form of energy produced when an object vibrates. Energy is the source of all vibration.

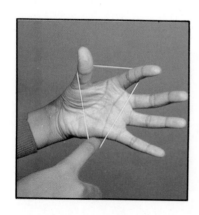

Questions: Answer in complete sentences.

1. Explain how sounds are produced. Use the words *energy* and *vibrate* in your explanation.
2. Study the picture of the rubber band. In this position no sounds come from the rubber band. What could you do to make sound come from it?
3. What one word best describes the motion of a rubber band when it is producing sound?
4. We can't see rapid vibrations, but we know they exist. Describe how the photographs on page 71 show that they exist.
5. Look at the picture of the gong above. What source of energy will make the gong ring?

These students are rehearsing for a concert. Notice the different types of instruments they are using. Each instrument works differently. Each instrument produces a different sound. When you finish this section, you should be able to:

☐ **A.** Name the three types of musical instruments.
☐ **B.** Explain how sound is produced by each type of instrument.
☐ **C.** Classify instruments by their vibrating parts.

One group of musical instruments is the **stringed instruments**. Some examples are the harp, violin, and guitar. Musicians produce sounds on *stringed instruments* by plucking or stroking the strings. Each stringed instrument produces a special sound. The thick strings on an instrument produce lower sounds than the thin strings.

How tight or how loose a string is will change the sound, too. Tight strings produce higher sounds. Loose strings produce lower sounds. How can musicians get

Stringed instrument: An instrument with one or more strings.

different sounds from a stringed instrument? The thickness and tightness of the strings cause different sounds. The tightness of the strings can be changed by twisting the tuning pegs at the end of a guitar's neck.

Suppose you have two strings of the same thickness but of different lengths. The longer string will produce a lower sound than the shorter string. Here is how a musician can make the same string produce different sounds. The top photo shows a guitar string being plucked. A low sound is produced. In the bottom photo, the same string is pressed tightly against the wood. Pressing the string against the wood shortens its length. Now when the string is plucked, a higher sound is made.

Wind instruments are a second type of musical instrument. They are made of either wood or metal. For this reason, they are known as woodwinds or brass. Let's look at each kind of *wind instrument*.

The photograph and diagram below show a woodwind called the clarinet. It is a hollow tube through which air can flow. On the mouthpiece, there is a thin piece of wood called a reed. Blowing through the mouthpiece will cause the reed to vibrate. These vibrations are carried through the hollow tube. They produce sound. Holes on the sides of the tube allow different sounds to be made. As a player's fingers cover and uncover these holes, high and low sounds can be made.

Saxophones, oboes, and bassoons are other instruments that have reeds. When the musician blows across a reed, it starts to vibrate. The vibrating reed causes the column of air in the instrument to vibrate. The vibrating air makes a sound.

Wind instrument: An instrument made of a hollow tube through which air can flow.

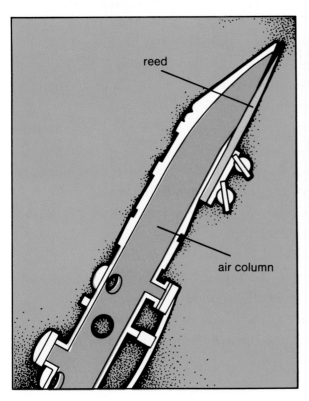

reed

air column

Brass wind instruments are usually made of the metal brass. To play a trumpet, musicians press their lips against the mouthpiece. When musicians blow, their lips vibrate. Their vibrating lips cause the air column in the trumpet to vibrate. That makes a sound. Pressing the valves at the top of the trumpet changes the length of the air column. Changing the air column changes how high or low the sound will be.

ACTIVITY

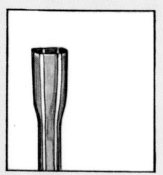

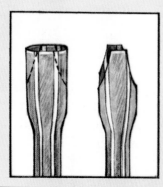

How can you change the sound of a musical instrument?

A. Obtain these materials: 4 drinking straws, scissors, small glass of water.

B. Flatten about 3 cm of one end of the straw. Rub the scissors 2 or 3 times across both sides of this end. Make a cut on each side of the flattened end. CAUTION: BE VERY CAREFUL WHEN USING THE SCISSORS. This is the reed part of the instrument.

C. Moisten the straw and blow through it. The end of the straw should vibrate and make a sound. You may have to try this a few times.

   1. What caused the sound when you blew through the straw?

   2. Would the length of the straw affect the sound of your instrument? Make a hypothesis.

D. Make several straw instruments, each of a different length. Try each one.

   3. Did you feel the vibrations of the straw?

   4. How were the sounds of longer instruments different from the sounds of shorter instruments? Compare your results with your hypothesis.

   5. How are your instruments like woodwind instruments?

Violin

Banjo

Cello

Saxophone

Tuba

Oboe

Look at the picture above. Which instruments are woodwinds? Which are brass? Which are stringed instruments?

Can you think of an instrument that is not played by plucking strings or blowing through an air column? How about drums and cymbals? These are examples of **percussion** (per-kuh-shun) **instruments**. *Percussion instruments* produce musical sounds when hit. They are hit either by hand or by some other part of the instrument. They may be made of a solid material or materials stretched over a container. A cymbal is made of solid metal. A drum is a container with material stretched over

Percussion instrument: An instrument that produces a musical sound when hit.

77

it. Both drums and cymbals cause vibrations when they are hit.

Bands and orchestras use several types of drums. A drummer can change how high or low the drum sounds by turning knobs. A tight drumhead vibrates faster than a loose one. It also makes a higher sound. The sound of a kettledrum can be changed before or while it is being played. Look at the kettledrum on the left. Before it is played, the tightness of the drum can be changed by turning the knobs at the top. The pedal at the base can be used to tighten the drumhead while it is being played.

Section Review

Main Ideas: Classifying musical instruments.

Type of Instrument	Example	What Vibrates	What Causes Vibration
1. String	Violin	Strings	Plucking or stroking strings
2. Wind			
a. Woodwind	Clarinet	Reed, Air Column	Blowing across reed
b. Brass	Trumpet	Lips, Air Column	Blowing into mouthpiece
3. Percussion	Drum	Drumhead	Hitting drumhead

Questions: Answer in complete sentences.

1. Name three main types of musical instruments.
2. Give an example of each type of these instruments. How is sound produced by each type of instrument?
3. What are two types of wind instruments?
4. For each type, tell what part vibrates.
5. Tell what type of instrument each of these is: **a.** clarinet **b.** trumpet **c.** cymbal **d.** drum **e.** violin **f.** tuba **g.** banjo **h.** harp

Both the radio and the lamp in the photograph below are turned on. The radio is sending out sound energy. The lamp is sending out light energy. Anyone standing nearby can hear the radio and see the light. What would happen if the radio and the lamp were covered? When you finish this section, you should be able to:

☐ **A.** Explain how sound travels.
☐ **B.** Compare how sound energy and light energy travel.

If you covered the radio and lamp with a box, you would notice two things. First, the sound would not seem as loud. Second, you could not see the light from the lamp through the box. Both the sound and light are changed by an object placed in their paths. The box allows some sound to pass through. But no light can pass through the box.

What would happen if the box had holes in it? You could see light passing through the holes. The sound would be louder because it would pass through the holes.

Both sound and light energy spread out from a source. The sound energy spreads out from the speaker in the radio. The light energy spreads out from the light bulb. In what direction does the energy spread out?

How does sound spread from its source? A school basketball game is being played. The referee blows his whistle to call a foul. The players hear the whistle. They stop playing. The fans hear the whistle, too. Those sitting near the court hear the sound. So do those sitting high up in the bleachers. The source of the sound is the vibrating air passing through the whistle. The sound spreads out in all directions. No matter what the source of the sound, it will spread out in all directions. But when a barrier is placed in front of the source, the sound is stopped. This is why the whistle cannot be heard as well outside the gym. A barrier also keeps unwanted noise from being heard inside the recording room above.

Light also spreads out in all directions. When a lamp is turned on in a dark room, light reaches all parts of the room. Some light reaches the ceiling, floor, and walls. What would happen if there were a barrier in front of the light source?

The fact that both sound and light energy spread out in all directions is important. If they didn't, you could not light a room by turning on an overhead light. You wouldn't hear a radio that was in the corner of a room. This spreading out of energy can also be a problem. It could be a problem if you wanted a lot of light or sound to reach a certain spot. Look at the photos below. They show how sound and light can be aimed.

There are many ways to direct sound energy and light energy. Flashlights, car headlights, and spotlights all aim light. This is done by bouncing the light energy off a shiny surface. This causes most of the energy to leave in one direction instead of spreading out. When you cup your hands over your mouth to shout, you send sound energy in one direction.

Sound and light both spread out in all directions. But they travel at different speeds. Light always travels at the same speed through air. It travels at 300,000 km/sec (186,000 mi/sec). The speed of sound in air depends on the temperature and moisture of the air. The speed of sound in dry air at 0° Celsius (32° Fahrenheit) is 330 m/sec (about 1,100 ft/sec).

The speed of sound is often compared to the speed of a jet plane. Some jets travel at the same speed as sound. Others travel at twice the speed of sound.

Jets that travel faster than the speed of sound cause **sonic booms** (sah-nik boomz). These are very loud sounds. *Sonic booms* that reach the ground can cause buildings to vibrate. They can vibrate so much that glass and walls may crack.

Sonic boom: Loud sound produced when a jet is moving faster than sound.

Supersonic: Faster than the speed of sound.

A jet that flies faster than the speed of sound is called **supersonic** (soo-per-**sah**-nik). A *supersonic* jet has been made that carries many people. This jet is called the *Concorde*. The *Concorde* can fly from London to New York in just over three hours. It would take a regular jet almost seven hours for the same trip.

Section Review

Main Ideas: Comparing Sound and Light

	Sound	Light
Difference:	Travels at 330 m/sec	Travels at 300,000 km/sec
Likenesses:	Both forms of energy Both spread in all directions Both may be aimed	

Questions: Answer in complete sentences.

1. Describe how sound and light travel.
2. Name two things that sound and light have in common.
3. What is one way in which sound differs from light?
4. Give an example of a way sound can be aimed. Explain how your example works.
5. Can light be aimed? Explain how.
6. At a night launching of a space rocket, which would you notice *first* at blastoff, the roar of the engines or the light from the exhaust? Explain.

CHAPTER REVIEW

Science Words: Unscramble the letters to find the correct terms. Then write their definitions.

1. RYGENE
2. USSIONCREP TENMSTRUIN
3. DOWINDOW
4. GUNTIN ROFK
5. NIWD RUSTMINETN
6. DEGSTRIN TUSRMINENT
7. TRASBEVI
8. NOSCI MOBO

Questions: Answer in complete sentences.

1. A musician plucks a guitar string and a sound is produced. What happens to this string? What is the source of energy?
2. What type of instrument is each of the following: **a.** drum **b.** banjo **c.** clarinet? How is each used to produce sound?
3. Look at the photograph of the girl with the gong on page 72. What type of instrument is the gong? Give a reason for your answer.
4. When a rocket is launched, both sound and light are produced. What are two things that these forms of energy have in common?
5. Match the cause in the first column with its effect in the second column.

Cause	Effect
1. vibrating object	**a.** produces sonic boom
2. tightened strings on guitar	**b.** produces sound
3. jet traveling faster than sound	**c.** produces lower sound
4. loosened drumhead	**d.** produces higher sound

CHAPTER 5

SOUND WAVES

5-1.

Sound and Matter

The dolphin shown on page 85 was part of an experiment. A scientist covered its eyes. But this did not keep the dolphin from "talking." Microphones placed in the water picked up its sounds. This experiment shows that sound can travel through water. When you finish this section, you should be able to:

☐ **A.** Explain how *sound waves* travel.

☐ **B.** Explain and give examples of matter through which sound travels.

☐ **C.** Compare how sound travels through different types of matter.

Sound energy moves from place to place. Vibrations travel from the dolphin through the water. When you hear a bird's song or a friend's voice, you hear vibrations that travel through air.

Sound travels in **waves**. A *sound wave* is a vibration that moves through matter. Think of this. Pretend you have dropped a pebble into a quiet body of water. You can see ripples spreading out. Sound travels through air much like ripples move through water. A sound wave starts where the vibration is produced. It spreads in all directions. But sound waves are not exactly like waves

Sound wave: A vibration that moves through matter.

produced in water. Instead of an up-and-down motion, sound waves travel back and forth. Compare a sound wave to the movement of a coiled spring. Look at the picture below. If you push the end of a spring, you cause a wave to move through it. The spring's coils do two things. They bunch up together and then spread out. The bunching up and spreading out travels from one end of the spring to the other. Sound waves travel like that, too.

When you hear a bird's song, you hear sound waves that have traveled through air. Air is made of particles. The vibrations made by the bird cause the air particles to bunch up together. Then those air particles spread out.

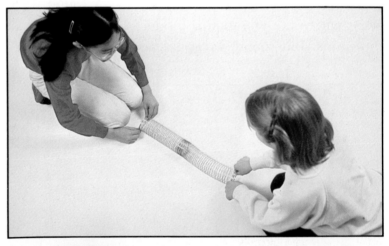

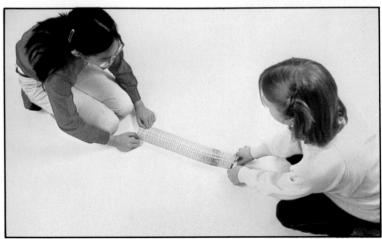

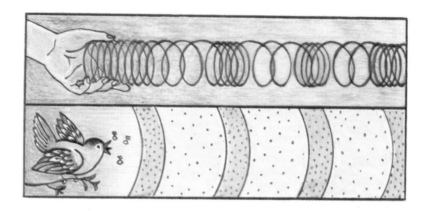

Now those air particles next to them bunch up. When those particles spread out, the next group bunches together, and so on. This bunching and then spreading out of air particles describes how a sound wave travels.

Most of the time you hear sound waves that travel through air. But you can also hear sounds in water. Try tapping two stones together underwater. The vibrations caused by the stones make the water particles vibrate. The sound wave moves through water instead of air.

Matter through which sound can travel is called a **medium**. Air and water are **media**. Solids are also good sound *media*. Test this yourself. With one finger, tap very gently on your desk. What do you hear? Now place

Medium: Matter through which sound can travel.

Media: More than one medium.

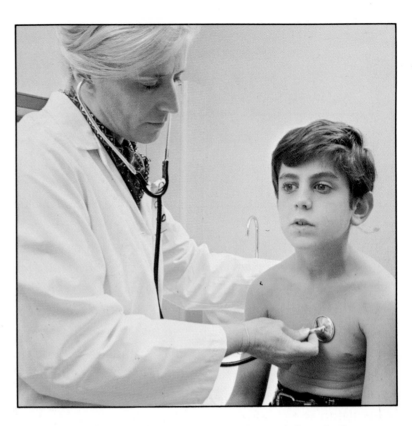

Stethoscope: An
instrument used to hear
heartbeats.

your ear on your desk top. Gently tap the desk again. What difference do you notice?

The wood on your desk is a good *medium* for sound. When you tapped, sound waves traveled through the wood to your ear. Wood is a solid. Solids carry sounds very well. Long ago, Native Americans would put their ears to the ground. They could find out if buffalo were near. Why do you think that worked?

Has your doctor ever listened to your heartbeat with a **stethoscope** (**steth**-uh-skope)? Sound travels very well through a *stethoscope*. When the round disc on its end is placed on your chest, the disc vibrates as your heart beats. The vibrations send sound waves through the air in the rubber tubes to the doctor's ears. The sound of your heartbeat is heard by the doctor. The air in the tubes contains many gases. Gas is a medium for sound.

What would happen if there were no matter for sound waves to travel through? This question was studied by Robert Boyle during the 1600's. He did something to find out if sound could travel without air. Boyle placed a bell, which could be rung, under a sealed glass jar. He rang the bell. The sound was loud enough to be heard through the glass. Then, using a pump, he removed the air inside the glass jar. He created a **vacuum** inside the jar. Space that does not contain matter is called a *vacuum*. He rang the bell again. What do you think happened? Although Boyle could see the bell vibrating, he could not hear a sound. With no air inside the jar, no air particles could vibrate. Boyle concluded that sound cannot travel in a vacuum. Since then, other scientists have done Boyle's experiment and had the same result.

Vacuum: Space that does not contain matter.

ACTIVITY

How does sound travel in different media?

A. Obtain these materials: ticking watch, meter stick.

B. Place your ear flat against one end of the meter stick. Have your partner hold the ticking watch against the other end.
   1. What did you observe?

C. Now put the meter stick down. Have your partner hold the watch one meter away from your ear.
   2. What did you observe?
   3. What were the two different media?
   4. What difference did you notice in steps **B** and **C** above?
   5. Write a short paragraph that sums up how sound travels in different media.

Sound travels at different speeds in different media. Look at the chart below. What is the speed of sound in water, in wood, and in steel? Sounds travel faster in solids than in liquids. Sounds travel slowest in gases.

Medium	Speed of Sound
air	344 m/sec (1,135 ft/sec)
water	1,450 m/sec (4,790 ft/sec)
wood	3,050 m/sec (10,100 ft/sec)
steel	5,002 m/sec (16,500 ft/sec)

Lightning and thunder occur at the same time. However, light travels much faster than sound. The light reaches your eyes before the sound reaches your ears. The longer it takes for you to hear thunder after a flash of lightning, the farther away the storm.

Section Review

Main Ideas: Sound travels in waves as it moves through matter. Sound cannot travel in a vacuum. Media through which sound travels can be solids, liquids, or gases. Sound waves travel fastest through solids and slowest through gases.

Questions: Answer in complete sentences.

1. Compare the movement of a sound wave to pushing or pulling a coiled spring.
2. Give three examples of media through which sound can travel.
3. Can sound travel through a vacuum? Explain your answer.
4. Look at the chart above. In which medium does sound travel the fastest? Which is the slowest?
5. Look at the picture on page 88. At what place is the sound of the heartbeat traveling through a solid? At what place is it traveling through gases?

Do you yell and cheer at school basketball games? Have you noticed the many kinds of sounds that you hear? Some are louder than others. Sounds can be low or high. When you finish this section, you should be able to:

Different Sounds

☐ **A.** Explain what causes sounds to be loud or soft.

☐ **B.** Explain what causes sounds to be low or high.

☐ **C.** Describe how loud noises affect people.

When you cheer at a basketball game, the sound of your voice is louder than when you whisper. The loudness or softness of a sound is called its **intensity.** Sounds that are loud have a high *intensity.* Soft sounds have a low intensity.

When you cheer, the sound you produce has a lot of energy. This energy is carried by air particles over long distances. When you whisper, the sound has less energy. Air particles still carry your voice, but over a shorter distance. The intensity of a sound depends on how

Intensity: The loudness or softness of a sound.

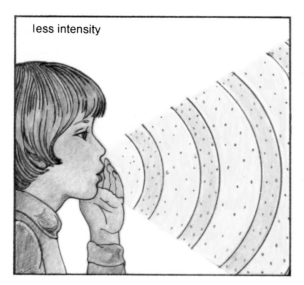

less intensity

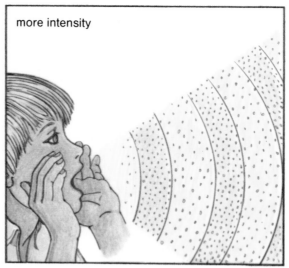

more intensity

strongly an object vibrates. Strong vibrations make large sound waves. Large sound waves make intense or loud sounds. Soft sounds are made when an object does not vibrate strongly. The sound waves are smaller. They make less intense, or softer sounds.

Sounds differ in another way. They can be high or low. The highness or lowness of a sound is called **pitch**. The sounds produced by a flute have a high *pitch*. Sounds from a tuba have a low pitch.

The pitch of a sound depends on how fast the object vibrates. The number of vibrations per second can be

Pitch: The highness or lowness of a sound.

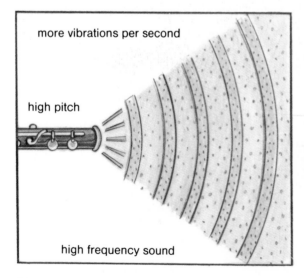

more vibrations per second

high pitch

high frequency sound

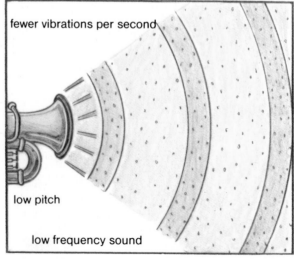

fewer vibrations per second

low pitch

low frequency sound

counted. This is called **frequency**. Something that vibrates very fast makes a high-pitched sound. Humans can hear sounds that have a *frequency* of 15 to 20,000 vibrations per second. Do you know where middle C is on a piano? It has a frequency of 256 vibrations per second. Higher notes have a higher frequency.

The boy in the picture is blowing air into the bottles. Each bottle produces a different pitch. That is because the air column in each bottle is different. When the boy blows into the air column above the water, it vibrates. Look at the bottle with the most liquid. Its air column is shortest. This makes its pitch higher. The frequency in this bottle is higher. Which bottle would have the lowest pitch? If you said the one without liquid, you are right. It also has the lowest frequency.

Frequency: The number of vibrations made in one second.

93

ACTIVITY

Changing pitch and intensity

A. Obtain these materials: 6 bottles of the same size, water, grease pencil, a ruler or wooden stick.

B. Number the bottles 1 through 6 and line them up in a straight row.

C. Add water to the bottles, putting the least in bottle 1 and the most in bottle 6.

D. Tap each bottle gently with the stick to create a different pitch. Adjust the amount of water in each to create the notes of a musical scale.

1. Which bottle had the most air?

2. Which bottle produced the highest pitch?

3. Write a conclusion that explains the relationship between the amount of air in the bottles and pitch.

4. What can you do to change the intensity of the sounds you create?

Can a sound be low-pitched and loud? Can a sound be low-pitched and soft? The answer is yes. Choose a piano key that has a low pitch. If you hit this key hard, the intensity is high. It sounds loud. If you hit the same key gently, the intensity is low. It sounds soft. On a piano, how could you make a high-pitched sound with high intensity?

We are usually more aware of sound intensity than sound pitch. Sound intensity can be measured with a sound-level meter. The picture below shows a sound-level meter. Intensity is measured in units called **decibels** (des-ih-belz). The higher the *decibel* number, the louder the sound. Look at the chart below. It lists kinds

Decibel: Unit of measurement of sound intensity.

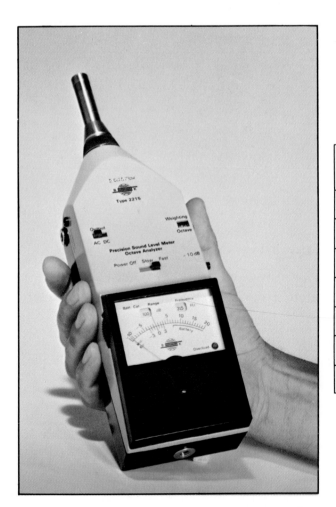

Cause	Decibel Level	Effect
Jet plane engine	160	Damage to hearing
Thunder	110	
Traffic	80	Annoying
Vacuum cleaner	60	
Automobile	45	
Whisper	15	Acceptable
Breathing	0	

of sounds. It also lists their decibel numbers. Which sound has the lowest intensity? Which sound has the highest intensity? Which sound measures 45 decibels? What is the decibel level of a whisper?

Sounds at readings near 0 can barely be heard. Sounds between 60 to 100 decibels are annoying to people. Sounds above 130 decibels can be dangerous. Constant listening to such loud sounds can cause hearing damage. Do you listen to loud sounds often?

Section Review

Main Ideas: Sounds can change in pitch and intensity.

Type of sound	How sound is made	Effect
low intensity	less energy	Sound doesn't travel far.
high intensity	more energy	Sound travels farther.
low pitch	lower frequency	Sound is lower.
high pitch	higher frequency	Sound is higher.

Questions: Answer in complete sentences.

1. Explain what causes a sound to be loud or soft.
2. What is pitch? How is the frequency of a sound related to pitch?
3. How can you make a low-pitched sound that has a high intensity? How can you make a low-pitched sound with low intensity?
4. Give two examples of sounds that measure over 100 decibels.
5. What can constant listening to sounds of high intensity do to people?

Mark is bouncing a ball against the wall. As soon as the ball hits the wall, it bounces right back. Sound bounces off objects in the same way that Mark's ball bounces off the wall. When you finish this section, you should be able to:

☐ **A.** Describe two effects that can occur when sound waves strike an object.
☐ **B.** Describe how sound affects people.

When we say that a sound is **reflected** (re-**flek**-ted), we mean that a sound wave has bounced off an object. What would happen if the ball struck the wall at an angle? The tennis ball would be *reflected* in the way shown in the top drawing. Sound waves behave in the same way. The bottom drawing shows how sound waves would be reflected from a wall.

Reflected: Bounced off of something.

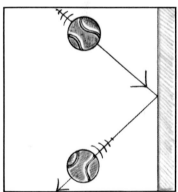

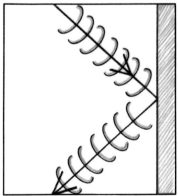

Echo: A sound reflected from an object.

A sound that is reflected from an object like a wall is an **echo** (eh-ko). You must stand at least 9 m (30 ft) from the wall to hear an echo. This allows time for the sound to hit the wall and be reflected before the next sound is heard. If you are closer, the echo will not be heard as a separate sound. It will mix with other sounds being made. Sometimes, the sound is reflected from many objects. Many echoes are heard.

Lazzaro Spallanzani was an Italian scientist. He lived in the eighteenth century. He wondered how bats could fly in the dark and not bump into anything. He did experiments to find out. He covered a bat's ears. The bat bumped into things as it flew. He felt that the bat's ability to fly at night had something to do with sound. But the bat did not seem to make noises when it flew. Actually, bats do make sounds. As a bat flies, it makes **ultrasonic** (ul-truh-**sah**-nik) sounds. These are sounds that are too high to be heard by the human ear. The sounds are reflected from objects. The echoes are heard by the bat.

Ultrasonic: Sound frequency that is higher than 20,000 vibrations per second.

98

The bat can tell where the objects are when it hears the echoes. So the bat can fly in darkness without bumping into the objects. The chart below shows the range of sound heard by humans and other animals.

Hearing Ranges of Animals	Vibrations per Second
Dog	15 to 50,000
Crocodile	20 to 5,000
Human	15 to 20,000
Porpoise	150 to 150,000
Robin	250 to 21,000
Bat	1,000 to 120,000
Moth	3,000 to 150,000

Look at the chart. Find the range of sound heard by humans. Find the range for bats. Notice that we can hear sounds produced by just 15 vibrations per second. Bats cannot. But above 20,000 vibrations per second, we cannot hear. Those are vibrations in the ultrasonic range.

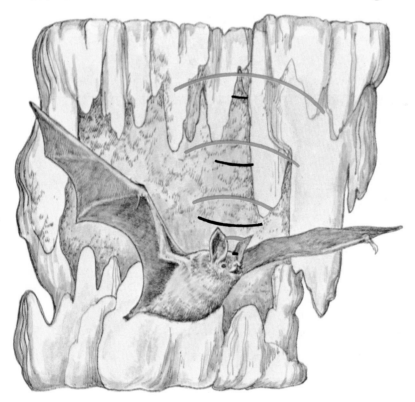

Acoustics: The study of sound and how it affects people.

Acoustics (uh-**koo**-sticks) is the study of sound and how sound affects people. People who plan buildings like concert halls study *acoustics*. They try to keep down noise pollution. Noise is a form of pollution when it disturbs people in their daily activities. There are many sources of noise pollution in our lives. Radios, traffic, airplanes, and machines all produce loud noises. These noises may even be harmful. There are several ways to control noise pollution. One is to stop the source of the noise. Another is to put up sound barriers. The barrier is placed between the source of the noise and the people nearby. This is sometimes done at airports. The noises made by machines can be reduced, too. The noisy parts are covered with something that takes in the sound.

Noises may also be caused by echoes. Echoes are helpful to a bat. But echoes can disturb people. Echo sounds can mix with other sounds. Mixing makes these other sounds unclear. Probably there is a place in your school where echoes occur. Do you know where? Echoes occur in large, empty rooms, such as gyms. They occur in rooms without drapes or rugs.

There are ways to control echoes. Certain materials used on walls, ceilings, and floors stop sounds from being reflected. These materials **absorb** (ab-**sorb**), or take in, the sound. Soft materials, such as cloth drapes and rugs, *absorb* sound. Materials with tiny holes, such as cork, break up sound waves. The sound waves cannot be reflected. Ceiling tiles are often made of materials with tiny holes. People help absorb sounds, too. When a large room is filled with people, echoes are not heard. Look at the picture on page 100. How can the room be changed to prevent echoes?

Absorb: To take in.

Section Review

Main Ideas: Sound may be reflected or absorbed. Reflected sound can cause echoes. People study acoustics to control echoes and noise.

Questions: Answer in complete sentences.

1. Study the picture on page 98. Then answer the following questions:
   a. How would the time between the sound and the echo change if the girl were farther away from the wall? (Use the words *reflect* and *echo* in your answer.)
   b. What is the source of the sound? In which direction is it traveling?
   c. What is the medium for the sound waves?
   d. What is reflecting the sound waves?
2. What are some ways in which the echoes in a large room can be reduced?
3. Explain how bats can fly at night and not bump into things.
4. Using the chart on page 99, answer these questions: What is the range of sounds heard by a moth? How is this range different from a dog's?

5-4.

Sound Messages

Diane went to the phone. She dialed several numbers. A moment later she heard a ring. Then she heard a clear, familiar voice. "Bonjour," said the voice. "Hello, Grandma," said Diane. "I'm leaving for the airport now. I'll see you in Paris in just a few short hours!"

The world is a much smaller place since the telephone was invented. When you finish this section, you should be able to:

☐ **A.** Describe the events that occur when you use a telephone to send and receive messages.

☐ **B.** Use a diagram to explain how a changing pattern of electricity can cause a phonograph speaker to produce sound waves.

The sound energy of spoken words can be changed into electrical energy. That energy can travel through wires across the country. And it takes less time than it takes for you to read this sentence.

People have always wanted to send messages to others who were not close by. A messenger traveled on horseback for days to bring a letter. But on May 24, 1844, Samuel Morse changed all that. He sent a message through wires using a **telegraph** (**tel**-uh-graf). The *telegraph* could not send the sound of a person's voice. Instead it sent a pattern of electrical current that stood for the letters and numbers. A person sending a message would first write it out. Then a telegraph operator would change each letter in the message into a code. The code was made up of clicks and pauses that the operator would tap out on the telegraph. The machine sent out a pattern of electric current that was like the pattern of the clicks and pauses.

When the current reached a telegraph station, it was changed back into the clicks and pauses. The receiving telegraph operator would then write out the message. The telegraph produced many changes. People could now send messages in a matter of minutes, instead of weeks. That was great, but something was missing. It was the sound of the human voice.

Telegraph: A device for sending messages using a code.

"Mr. Watson, come here; I want you." Those seven words made up the first voice message carried by a telephone. Alexander Graham Bell spoke those words in 1876. Mr. Bell's chat with Mr. Watson took place over the distance between two buildings. Now we use the telephone to send voice messages from city to city and from country to country.

In a telephone, sound waves in the air are changed into a pattern of electrical energy. The electrical energy is sent through wires. Modern telephones come in all shapes and sizes. All of them work in about the same way.

The part of the telephone you speak into is called the **transmitter** (trans-**mit**-ter). Inside the *transmitter* is a metal disc. When you speak, the metal disc vibrates. It vibrates in the same pattern as your voice does. This pattern is carried by the electricity in the telephone wires. The electricity travels through the wires to the telephone **receiver** (ri-**see**-ver). The *receiver* is the part of the telephone through which you hear. At the receiver, the electricity goes to a second metal disc. It vibrates, too. The original sound is then heard by the listener.

Just a year after Mr. Bell spoke to Mr. Watson, something else happened. Thomas Edison made the first phonograph.

For Edison's phonograph, sounds were recorded on a record. The record was a cylinder. It had grooves on it.

Transmitter: The part of the telephone you speak into.

Receiver: The part of the telephone through which you hear.

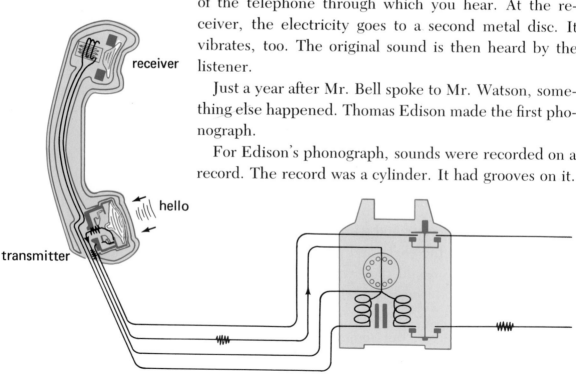
receiver

hello

transmitter

In the grooves was tinfoil. The singer sang into a horn. The vibrating horn caused a needle to vibrate. The vibrating needle moved through the grooves. It made a pattern on the tinfoil. To play the record, it was placed on a phonograph. A needle on the phonograph moved through the grooves on the record. The pattern on the tinfoil caused the needle to vibrate in the same pattern. These vibrations caused the phonograph speaker to vibrate in the pattern of the real voice.

To make a record today, a spiral-shaped groove is cut into a flat disc. Sound waves cause a needle to move from side to side in the groove. The needle cuts a pattern along the walls of the groove. The disc is covered with metal. The metal disc is made into a mold. The mold stamps the pattern onto plastic records. A record is placed on a record player. As it spins, a needle moves through the groove. The needle picks up the pattern of vibrations that is cut into the groove. The pattern travels through a wire to a speaker. In the speaker the pattern changes back to sound. Then the music is heard.

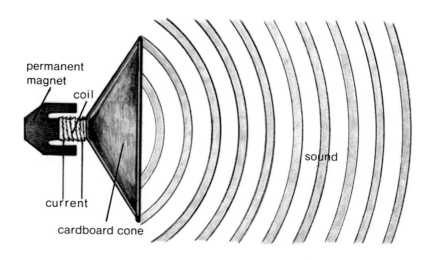

permanent
magnet

coil

current

cardboard cone

sound

The telephone receiver and the speaker of a phonograph work the same way. Look at the diagram above. Sound waves in air can be produced by electricity that moves through a wire. Notice the current flowing through the wire. In a phonograph, the vibrations of the needle change the current. In a phone, the sound vibrations that enter the transmitter change the current. When the current is strong, the magnet pulls very hard. The speaker cone moves back and forth, since the elec-

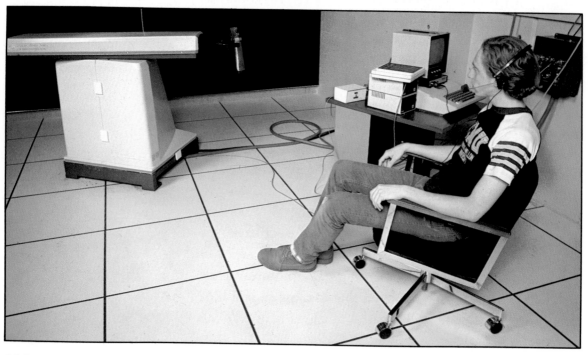

ACTIVITY

Can you make a working model of Edison's phonograph speaker?

A. Obtain these materials: a phonograph, an old unneeded 33-RPM record, paper of various thicknesses and sizes, scissors, tape.

B. Make 2 or 3 paper cones of various sizes. Have your teacher place a sewing needle through the end of the cone.

C. Lightly hold the cone so that the needle is on the grooves of a turning record.

  1. What did you hear?
  2. What is causing the cone to vibrate?
  3. Make a hypothesis to explain how speeding up the record changes the sound from your speaker cone. Test the hypothesis. Write your conclusion.

tric current keeps changing. The movement of the speaker cone produces sound waves in the air in front of it. Those sound waves travel to your ear.

Telephones and phonographs have come a long way since Bell and Edison. All ways of sending messages have improved. Telephone messages between distant countries used to travel through wires under the ocean. Now the sound waves are changed and transmitted by satellites in space. The photograph shows a satellite. It makes voices sound very clear even over long distances.

Phonographs have also improved greatly. Speakers have become more powerful. At the same time they have gotten smaller. Tape recorders that pick up the slightest change in sound are used. Even computers can be made to "hear" sound. There are computers that work only when given a command from one person's voice, like the one on page 106.

Section Review

Main Ideas: A telephone changes sound waves into electrical energy. It also changes electrical energy back into sound waves. A phonograph changes the vibrations on a phonograph record into sound waves in air.

Questions: Answer in complete sentences.

1. What is a telephone transmitter? What does it do?
2. What is a telephone receiver? What does it do?
3. Explain each of the steps that happen as a telephone changes sound into electricity, then back into sound.
4. How were the sound waves from human voices recorded on Edison's phonograph?
5. How was sound produced when a record was played on Edison's phonograph?

People in Science

Cyril Harris

Cyril Harris is famous for his work in the field of acoustics. He is a physicist with a great interest in music. Many of the world's concert halls and theaters owe their fine sound to Dr. Harris. His job is to work with builders of music halls. Dr. Harris decides where the seats and stage should be to reduce the noise and echoes.

Dr. Harris grew up in Hollywood, California. His interest in sound started when he was very young. At the age of 12, he began building radios. Dr. Harris studied acoustics in college and has a Ph.D. in physics. He has taught acoustics for 30 years. Dr. Harris is an expert in reducing noise on city streets. He has also helped in the designing of hearing aids. Dr. Harris protects his own hearing by wearing ear plugs whenever he travels on planes or trains. He even wears them when he sleeps.

CHAPTER REVIEW

Science Words: Match the terms in column A with the definition in column B.

Column A	Column B
1. Sound wave	A. Bounced
2. Medium	B. Vibrations per second
3. Vacuum	C. Loudness or softness
4. Intensity	D. A vibration that moves through matter
5. Pitch	E. Space without matter
6. Frequency	F. A reflected sound
7. Decibel	G. Matter through which sound can travel
8. Echo	H. The part of the telephone you speak into
9. Reflected	I. Unit of sound intensity
10. Transmitter	J. Highness or lowness

Questions: Answer in complete sentences.

1. What are two things that can happen when sound waves strike an object?
2. How is a sound wave like a coiled spring?
3. Robert Boyle did an experiment using a bell placed in a vacuum. What was the hypothesis that he was testing? What were his results?
4. The moon does not have any air. If one of two astronauts on the moon's surface struck a rock with a hammer, would the other astronaut hear it? Explain.
5. A person at a baseball game sees the bat hit the ball before hearing the sound. Explain why this is so.
6. Lazzaro Spallanzani experimented with the night flight of bats. What were his results?
7. Can a sound get louder without changing its pitch? Explain.

Studying the vibration of strings

A. Obtain these materials: 3 guitar strings of different thicknesses, 3 metal screw eyes, board at least 15 cm by 60 cm, 2 15-cm lengths of wood molding, set of masses.

B. Insert the 3 screw eyes at the edge of the board so that they are equal distances apart. Attach the guitar strings to the screw eyes. Stretch them over the lengths of molding as shown.

C. Stretch 1 string over the board. Add masses to it until you get it tight enough to produce a tone when plucked. CAUTION: KEEP YOUR HEAD AWAY FROM THE STRING AS YOU TIGHTEN IT. It may snap. Add 100 g to the string to increase its tightness. Pluck the string. Add another 100 g. Pluck again. Add a third 100-g mass and pluck.

    1. Record your observations.

D. Remove 100 g at a time. Pluck the string each time.

    2. Record your observations.

    3. Write a conclusion based on 1 and 2 above.

E. Now attach 2 other strings to the board. Place a *total* of 300 g of mass on each string. Pluck each string.

    4. Record your observations.

    5. Write a conclusion for this investigation.

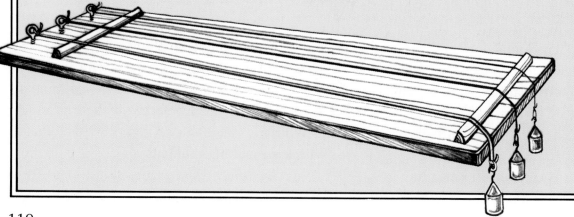

CAREERS

Sonar Operator ▶

How do ships stay clear of other ships? The **sonar operator** listens to sound waves that travel through the ocean. The *sonar operator* also studies pictures of the sound waves on a screen. The sonar operator can tell the difference between the sounds made by ship engines and those made by whales. By sending out sound waves the specially trained sonar operator can tell what objects are in the water by their echoes.

◀ Piano Technician

When a famous player strikes the keys of a grand piano, will lovely music result? That might depend on the work of the **piano technician** who tuned the piano. Pianos are instruments that have many parts. Changes in weather may change the length of the strings inside the piano. This changes the pitch that is heard. Specially trained *piano technicians* tighten or loosen the strings. They also replace broken piano keys.

SENSING AND MOVING

UNIT 3

CHAPTER 6

YOUR SENSES

6-1.

Sense Organs

Being good at a sport takes a lot of effort. Whether leaping, throwing, passing, or catching, you must be able to control the movements of your body. Knowing how your body works will help you to control it. When you finish this section, you should be able to:

- ☐ **A.** Describe some parts of a cell.
- ☐ **B.** Describe how cells, tissues, and organs work together in body systems.
- ☐ **C.** Describe what the nervous system does.
- ☐ **D.** Trace the path that messages of odors take from the nose to the brain.

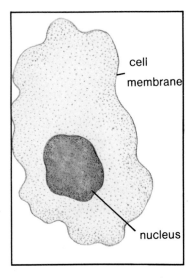

Every living thing is made of one or more **cells (selz)**. The *cell* is a tiny living part of a plant or animal. Most cells are smaller than the period that ends this sentence. Your body is made of almost 3 trillion (3,000,000,000,000) cells.

Each of your cells has an outside covering called a **cell membrane (mem-**brayn). Inside the cell is a **nucleus (nyoo-**klee-us), which is round in shape. The *nucleus* controls all the activities of a cell.

Each cell is able to produce more cells that are just like it. Food and oxygen are carried to the cells through the blood. Cells are able to use the food and oxygen to produce energy for your body. The blood also carries waste products away from the cells.

Using microscopes, scientists have found that cells have different shapes and sizes. They have also found that cells doing the same job are usually found together. **Nerve cells** have the job of carrying information, or messages, from parts of the body to the brain. The picture below shows a *nerve cell* as seen under a microscope.

Cell: Tiny living part of the body.

Cell membrane: Outside covering of a cell.

Nucleus: The part of the cell that controls its activities.

Nerve cell: Cell that carries information.

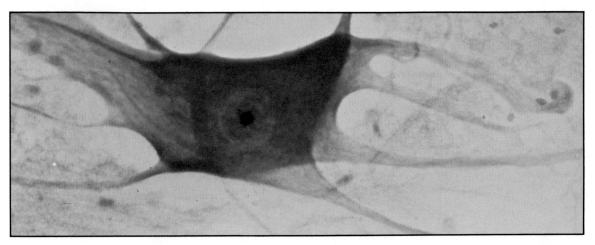

Tissue: Group of cells that works together.

Organ: Group of tissues that works together.

Body system: Groups of organs that work together.

Nervous system: The system that controls all other systems in the body.

Sense organs: Parts of the body that are sensitive to smell, taste, hearing, sight, and touch.

Besides nerve cells, the body has muscle cells, blood cells, bone cells, and other types of cells. Groups of cells working together to do one kind of job form **tissue** (tish-oo). For example, nerve cells join together to form nerve *tissues*. Certain tissues work together to form an **organ** (**or**-gun). The heart is an *organ* made of various tissues. Some tissues that make up the heart are blood, muscle, and nerve tissue.

Organs work with other organs to form a **body system** (**sis**-tum). The body has many systems. Systems enable us to move, eat, and get rid of wastes. Each *body system* is composed of organs, which are composed of tissues, which are composed of cells.

There is one system that controls all other body systems. It is called the **nervous** (**nerv**-us) **system**. The brain is the major organ of the *nervous system*. This system also consists of nerves that carry information to and from the brain. A third part of the system, the **sense organs**, receives the information that is carried along the nerves to the brain. Through the *sense organs*, the body knows, or senses, what is going on around it. These parts of the body respond to smell, taste, hearing, sight, and touch. Let's examine the nose, which is the organ for the sense of smell.

Contained in the nose are many nerve cells. These cells respond to odors. You can smell the odor of food

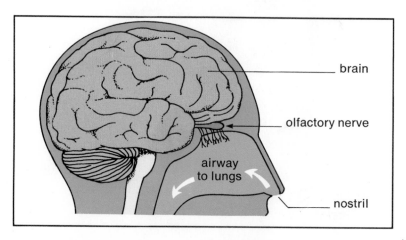

cooking even when it is cooking in another room. How does the smell message get to your brain? When you breathe in, air enters your nose. On its way to your lungs, the air passes nerve cells in your nose. These nerve cells are branches of one main nerve called the **olfactory** (ol-**fak**-tore-ee) **nerve**. The *olfactory nerve* carries smell messages from your nose to your brain. The drawing on page 116 shows how.

How might your sense of smell be a safety device for your body? Suppose your olfactory nerve picked up the smell of smoke in a building on fire. It would send the smell message to your brain. Your brain would send back a message that causes you to leave the building. So your sense of smell acts as a safety device for your body.

Your brain may receive a smell message that it understands as pleasing. Then it sends a message to other parts of your body to cause you to move closer to the smell. The smell of freshly baked cookies might cause such a response.

Olfactory nerve: The nerve that carries smell messages to the brain.

Section Review

Main Ideas: The body is composed of living cells. Cells, tissues, and organs work together in body systems. Information is received by the sense organs and carried by the nerves to the brain, which is the major organ of the nervous system.

Questions: Answer in complete sentences.

1. What parts make up a body system?
2. What is the olfactory nerve?
3. What three parts does the nervous system consist of?
4. Make a diagram of a living cell and label its parts.
5. While sitting in the living room, you smell dinner cooking in the kitchen. How does your brain receive the smell message?

Nervous System
Controls other body systems
Receives and transmits information
Enables us to smell, touch, taste, hear, and see
Causes muscles to move

ACTIVITY

How quickly does your nose detect an odor?

Seconds	Number of people
15	
30	
45	
60	
75	
90	
105	
120	
135	
150	
165	
180	

A. Obtain these materials: graph paper, pencil.

B. Your teacher will pour some perfume into a saucer. Half the class will observe. Half the class will record data. Then you will switch roles.

C. As an observer, shut your eyes when the teacher tells you to do so. Raise your hand when you first notice the odor. Keep your hand raised until it is counted.

D. Prepare a data chart, like the one shown, for your work as a recorder. Over one row, write "Seconds." Over the other row, write "Number of people." Count and record the number of people who have their hands raised at each 15-second interval.

E. Prepare a graph, like the one shown, using the data from your chart.

    1. With what sense organ was the odor detected?

    2. How long did it take the first observer to notice the odor?

    3. Why did observers take different amounts of time to detect the odor?

    4. Write a paragraph that sums up the results shown in the chart and on the graph.

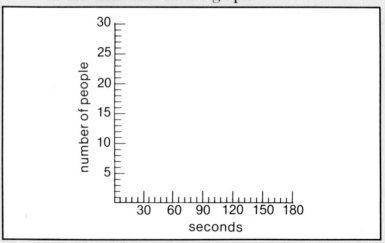

This girl has just tasted the lemon. How do you think it tasted? The expression on her face should tell you the answer. You probably have bitten into a lemon. How would you describe its taste? When you finish this section, you should be able to:

☐ **A.** Identify four basic taste areas of the tongue.
☐ **B.** Explain how the brain receives taste messages.
☐ **C.** Describe how the senses of taste and smell work together.

There are four basic tastes that most people recognize. They are sweet, sour, salty, and bitter. Many foods have just one taste. A lemon, for example, tastes sour. Some foods combine two or more of the basic tastes. Barbecue sauce has both a sweet and a sour taste. Other foods have tastes that seem to be neither sweet nor sour, neither salty nor bitter. Pepper and other spices are examples of such foods.

The sense organ for taste is the tongue. In the tongue are groups of nerve endings called **taste buds**. When you chew food, tiny bits of it enter the *taste buds* through openings in the tongue. Taste buds for each of the four tastes are located in different areas of the tongue.

Taste buds: Groups of cells on the tongue that are sensitive to taste.

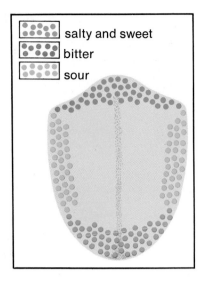

salty and sweet
bitter
sour

Taste nerves: Nerves that carry taste messages to your brain.

Taste buds that respond to sweetness are on the tip of the tongue. Some of the taste buds for saltiness are also there. Along the sides of the tongue are taste buds for sourness. Those for bitterness are at the back of the tongue.

The sense of taste is part of the nervous system. When food enters the taste buds in the tongue, **taste nerves** pick up the messages. The *taste nerves* send the messages from the taste buds to the brain. The brain responds with a sweet, sour, salty, or bitter taste.

Look at the photographs of the boy eating. Each food has one or more taste. What taste messages are being sent to his brain about each food?

The senses of smell and taste affect one another. When you chew food, odors from the food reach the olfactory nerve in the nose. While you are tasting the food, you are also smelling the food. Often you are smelling food when you think you are tasting it. That's why food seems tasteless when you have a cold. With a cold, passages in your nose are closed. Food odors cannot reach the olfactory nerve. Because you cannot smell it, food is less tasty.

ACTIVITY

How can you test your sense of taste?

A. With a partner, obtain these materials: blindfold, paper, 2 paper cups with water, pencil, 10 tooth-picks.

B. Your teacher will give you five food samples, each in a numbered paper cup. Decide who will be the taster. Make a chart like the one shown to record the taster's observations.

C. Blindfold the taster. The taster should hold his or her nostrils closed.

D. With the flat end of the toothpick, pick up a small amount of one food sample. Place the food sample on the taster's tongue.

E. Tell the taster to spread the sample around with the tongue. Then ask the taster to identify the type of taste and name the food.

F. Repeat steps **D** and **E** with each food sample. Have the taster drink some water after each sample to clear the taste buds. Use a new toothpick each time.

G. Switch places with the taster. Repeat the activity with your partner recording.

1. Were there any food samples the tasters could not identify? Make a hypothesis that explains why the tasters had trouble identifying those foods.

2. Were these food samples easy to identify? Explain.

3. Would the results be the same if the tasters had their eyes open? Why were the tasters asked to wear a blindfold?

4. Why were they asked to hold their nostrils closed?

5. Write one paragraph summarizing the data in your chart. Use the words *taste buds*, *taste nerves*, and *brain* to explain the results.

Food Sample	Food Identified
1.	
2.	
3.	
4.	
5.	

Since smell and taste work together, it is possible to fool the brain by smelling one food while eating another. What would happen if you ate a slice of raw potato while smelling an apple? Which food would you taste? The potato slice would taste like an apple. The brain picks up the smell message more quickly than the taste message. The odor from the apple is picked up before the taste of the potato. So the potato tastes like an apple.

The sense of smell can be a safety device for you. If food is spoiled, your sense of smell will detect the odor on the first bite. If the odor from the food is very bad, you will notice it as you bring the food to your mouth.

Section Review

Main Ideas: The sense of taste is a function of the nervous system. Taste buds and taste nerves are located in the tongue, a sense organ. They pick up and send taste messages to the brain, which interprets, or explains, the messages. Messages of taste often work with messages of smell.

Questions: Answer in complete sentences.

1. What are the four basic tastes? In what sense organ are they found?
2. When you bite into food, you know before you chew it how it tastes. Why?
3. Look at the drawing of the tongue on page 120. Where are the taste buds located for: a. saltiness, b. bitterness, c. sourness, d. sweetness?
4. Why does food seem tasteless when you have a head cold?
5. Trace the route of taste from the first bite of food to the brain's response.
6. Look at the photographs on page 120. Name each food and the part of the tongue that tastes it.

How would you like to baby-sit for this infant? She is certainly making a big fuss! Do you think you ever cried like this? When babies cry, they are trying to tell adults something. If you baby-sit, you know you can find out what babies need by listening to their sounds. When you listen, you hear. Your sense of hearing is one of the ways you receive information. When you finish this section, you should be able to:

- ☐ **A.** Describe the parts of the ear.
- ☐ **B.** Describe how sound messages travel from the outer ear, through the head, and to the brain.

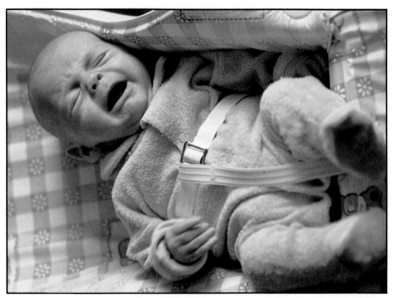

Our sense of hearing tells us what is happening outside our bodies. A baby's cry, the ringing of a doorbell, and the honking of a car horn all tell us something different. But not everybody has a good sense of hearing. Some people need hearing aids to pick up sound. Hearing aids make sounds louder. They are very small, as you can see from the photograph on the right.

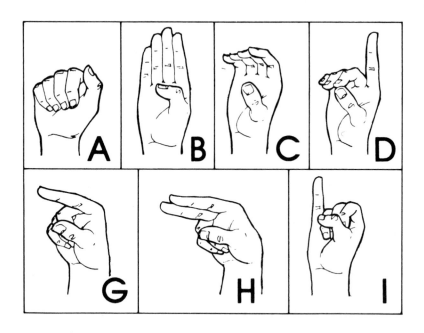

Some people who do not hear sound have learned to understand finger spelling. This method makes use of the fingers to form the letters of the alphabet. Whole conversations of words and phrases are spelled out. Sign language is different from finger spelling. It makes use of hand and arm gestures that stand for words and phrases. Lipreading makes use of the sense of sight, rather than the sense of hearing. This skill requires people to watch the shapes and movements of the lips of those speaking. It is possible, then, for people without the sense of hearing to understand the sounds around them.

People who do have the sense of hearing are not able to hear all sounds. Many sounds made by animals are out of the range of human hearing. There are, however, a great many sounds that people can hear. You have already learned how sound is made.

Vibrate: To move back and forth.

A sound is made when something **vibrates** (vi-brayts). When something *vibrates*, it moves back and forth. A vibrating object makes the air around it vibrate. The sound vibrations travel in all directions. How do sound vibrations in the air become sounds you hear?

ACTIVITY

Are two ears better than one?

A. With a partner, obtain these materials: blindfold, paper, pencil.

	Right	**Wrong**
Ears uncovered		
Right ear covered		
Left ear covered		

B. Make a chart that is organized like the one above. Use it to record your data. Have your partner sit down. Place the blindfold on your partner.

C. At a distance of about 3 m from your partner, clap your hands. Ask your partner to point to where the sound came from. Repeat this 10 times. Try several different locations, including some that are near your partner's head.

    1. How many correct responses did your partner make?

D. Now have your partner press a cupped hand tightly over the left ear. Repeat step **C.**

    2. How many correct responses were made?

E. Now have your partner uncover the left ear and press a cupped hand tightly over the right ear. Repeat step **C.**

    3. How many correct responses were made?

F. Switch places with your partner and then repeat the activity.

    4. Write a sentence that sums up the results of having both ears uncovered.

    5. Having two ears may be a safety device for humans. Explain.

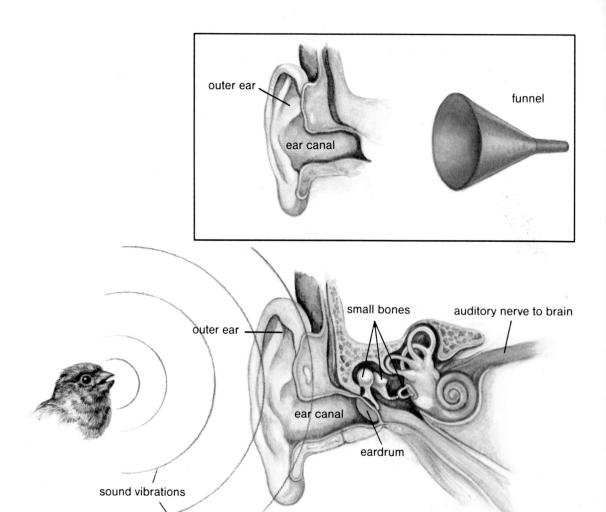

outer ear

ear canal

funnel

outer ear

small bones

auditory nerve to brain

ear canal

eardrum

sound vibrations

Sound vibrations are picked up by one of your sense organs, the ear. Let's trace the path of a sound message from the air to your brain.

The ear you see when you look in a mirror is not your whole ear. It is the part of your ear called the **outer ear**. Your *outer ears* gather sound vibrations. Your outer ears work like funnels. They direct the sound vibrations into another part of your ear called the **ear canal**. Your *ear canal* is a narrow tube that begins at the inner side of the outer ear. The ear canal carries the sound vibrations into your head.

Outer ear: The part of the ear that gathers sound vibrations.

Ear canal: A narrow tube inside the ear that carries sound vibrations into the head.

At the end of your ear canal is the **eardrum**. The sound vibrations that have traveled through the ear canal then strike the *eardrum*. The eardrum also starts to vibrate. The vibrations from your eardrum pass along to nearby bones. These bones are very tiny. They begin to vibrate.

Around the small bones are nerve cells. The nerve cells carry the message about the vibrations to one main nerve. This nerve is called the **auditory** (aw-dih-tore-ee) **nerve**. The *auditory nerve* carries the sound message to your brain. When the brain receives the message, you know you have heard a sound.

Eardrum: The part of the ear at the end of the ear canal.

Auditory nerve: The nerve that carries sound messages to the brain.

Section Review

Main Ideas: Sound is picked up by the outer ear and sent to the eardrum, which vibrates. Nerve cells carry the vibrations to the auditory nerve, which carries them to the brain.

Questions: Answer in complete sentences.
Use this information to answer questions 1–6:
Anne Marie is outside roller skating. She hears her mother call, "Anne Marie, come in for dinner."

1. How did the sound vibrations reach Anne Marie?
2. What parts of Anne Marie's ears gathered the sound vibrations?
3. After the vibrations were gathered, they were directed into a narrow tube. What is that tube called?
4. Vibrations traveled along the narrow tube to the eardrum. What happened to Anne Marie's eardrum when the sound vibrations struck it?
5. Where did the sound message go from her eardrum, and how did it get there?
6. When did Anne Marie actually hear the sound of her mother's voice?

6-4.

Sight

This baseball pitcher is throwing a curve ball. It takes great skill to send a baseball curving toward home plate. Seconds after this photograph was taken, the batter swung at the curve ball and hit it out of the ball park. The batter's eyes provided him with the information he needed to hit that home run. It takes almost perfect vision, or eyesight, to hit a curve ball with a bat. When you finish this section, you should be able to:

- ☐ **A.** Trace the path of light through the parts of the human eye.
- ☐ **B.** Compare nearsightedness with farsightedness.
- ☐ **C.** Compare some parts of the eye to parts of a camera.

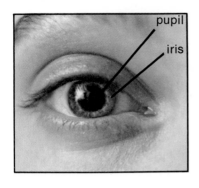
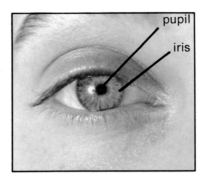

Your eyes are the sense organs for sight. When you see an object, such as a baseball, your eyes receive the light reflected from or given off that object. Eyes provide the brain with the information needed to see. Like the ears, the eyes have parts. The colored part of the eye is called the **iris** (**eye**-rus). In the center of the *iris* is an opening called the **pupil** (**pyoo**-pul). The *pupils* look like black dots. Light enters the eyes through the pupils.

When the light is dim, the pupil appears larger than when the light is bright. But it is not the pupil that changes size. It is really the iris that changes size by opening and closing. In dim light, the iris opens to let more light enter the eye. In bright light, the iris closes a little to stop too much light from entering. If too much light enters, parts of the eye can be damaged.

After light enters your eye, it passes through a part of the eye called the **lens** (**lenz**). When the light passes through the *lens*, a pattern appears on the back of the eye. The pattern is an upside-down picture of the object you are looking at.

On the back of the inside of the eye are nerve cells. These nerve cells carry the message about the pattern to one main nerve. This nerve is called the **optic** (**op**-tik) **nerve**. The *optic nerve* carries the sight message from the inside of your eye, or sense organ, to your brain. The brain changes the upside-down pattern so that you see the object right-side up.

When the lens of the eye forms a pattern, or image, on

Iris: The colored part of the eye.

Pupil: The opening in the center of the iris.

Lens: The part of the eye that changes light from an object into a pattern.

Optic nerve: The nerve that carries sight messages to the brain.

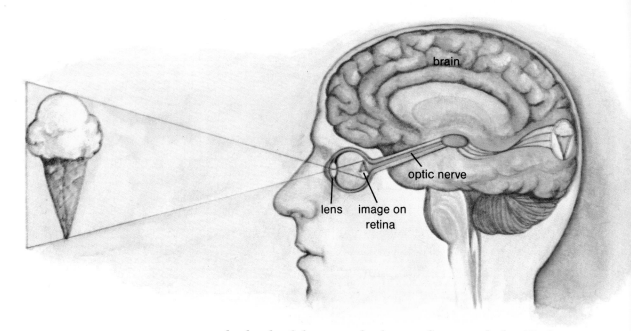

brain

optic nerve

lens

image on
retina

the back of the eye, the lens is focusing light. To focus an image of an object means to make it sharp and clear. The lens becomes thinner to focus light coming from far objects. It becomes thicker to focus light coming from near objects.

If you wear glasses, your vision problem may be **nearsightedness**. *Nearsightedness* is difficulty in seeing objects that are far away. Objects far away are not clear because the images are not focused on the back part of the eye, which is called the **retina** (**reh**-tih-nuh). They are focused, instead, in front of the *retina*. That's why objects far away look fuzzy to nearsighted people.

**Nearsightedness:
Difficulty in seeing
faraway objects.**

**Retina: The back part of
the eye, where images
are focused.**

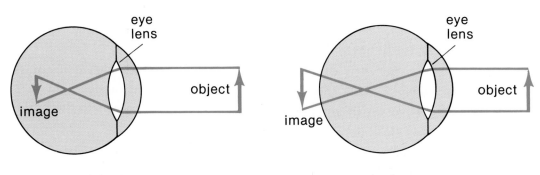

eye
lens

object

image

nearsightedness

eye
lens

object

image

farsightedness

ACTIVITY

Observing changes in your eyes

A. Obtain these materials: mirror, paper, pencil.

B. Look at your eyes in the mirror. Draw a picture of the iris and pupil of one eye. Try to draw the picture the same size as your eye. Label the iris and the pupil.

C. Look at this diagram of pupil sizes. Find the dark circle closest in size to your pupil. Write down the letter of the dark circle. Under it, write "Normal Light."

```
•      •      •
A      B      C

•      •      •
D      E      F

●      ●      ⬤
G      H      I
```

D. Your teacher will dim the lights in your classroom. Look again at your eyes in the mirror.
   1. What difference do you observe?

E. After 10 seconds, write down the letter of the circle closest in size to your pupil. Under it write "Dim Light." Your teacher will put the lights on. After 10 seconds, look at your eyes again.
   2. What do you observe now?

F. Write down the letter of the circle closest in size to your pupil. Under it write "Normal Light."
   3. Write one paragraph summing up the results. Include a sentence that answers: How does the amount of light in a room affect the size of the pupils of the eyes?

Many adults have a vision problem called **farsightedness**. *Farsightedness* is difficulty in seeing objects that are close. Here, too, the image of the object is not focused on the retina. It is focused behind the retina. Both nearsightedness and farsightedness can be corrected. Eyeglasses cause the light reflected from the object to fall directly on the retina.

Farsightedness: **Difficulty in seeing objects that are close.**

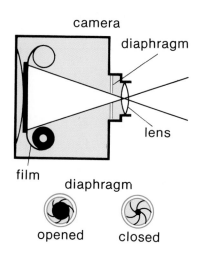

camera
diaphragm
lens
film

diaphragm

opened   closed

Diaphragm: Part of a camera that controls how much light enters.

If you have used a camera, you know that at the front of the camera is a clear, glass part. Light passes through this glass to the film inside the camera. Can you guess its name? If you said "lens," you are right. It does the same job for a camera that your own lenses do for your eyes. Light from the object being photographed passes through the camera. When it reaches the film, it causes chemicals on the film to react. An image is formed on the film. It is the picture you see when the film is developed. Camera film is a little like the retina of the eye.

The part of the camera that controls how much light enters is called the **diaphragm** (**dy**-uh-fram). The *diaphragm* is like the iris of the eye. If the light going through the diaphragm is too much or too little, the picture will be either washed out or too dark.

Section Review

Main Ideas: The eye is a sense organ. Parts of the eye are the iris, pupil, lens, retina, and optic nerve. Light from an object passes through the lens and focuses upside down on the retina. Sight messages are then carried to the brain by the optic nerve. The brain makes the image of the object right-side up.

Questions: Answer in complete sentences.

1. Define each of the following: iris, pupil, lens, retina, and optic nerve.
2. Your eyes receive the image of a tree upside down. Why do you see the tree right-side up?
3. Where is the image focused in the eye of a near-sighted person?
4. Which parts of a camera can be compared to the iris and the lens in the human eye?
5. In a dark room, what happens to your pupils and irises? Why?
6. In the bright sunlight, what happens to your pupils and irises? Why?

This student can't see. But he is reading. The book he is reading is printed in a special system that does not use ink. The system consists of raised dots, which stand for words and numbers. The student is reading by feeling the shapes of the words. Through his fingertips, he receives and sends information to his brain. When you finish this section, you should be able to:

☐ **A.** Describe the skin as a sense organ.
☐ **B.** Locate some sense receptors in the skin.
☐ **C.** Explain how touch messages are carried to the brain from the skin.

The system the young man is using to read is called the Braille system. The raised dots of the Braille system allow those without the sense of sight to make use of their sense of touch. Touch is the sense that lets us know when we have made contact with a person or an object. When

6-5.
Touch

we touch, we learn the shape and hardness of an object. A great deal of human activity depends on touching. What activities do not depend on a sense of touch? Reading Braille and many other activities are possible because the skin is sensitive to touch.

Your skin is a sense organ. It is the largest sense organ of the body. The skin can pick up messages about heat, cold, pain, touch, and pressure. In the skin are many nerve cells. These nerve cells are called **receptors** (ree-**sep**-torz). Each *receptor* senses only one kind of message. In the skin are receptors for heat, cold, pain, touch, and pressure.

Look at the girl in the picture. What messages is her skin picking up about the rabbit? The receptors in her skin are picking up messages about touch, pressure, and perhaps heat from the rabbit's body.

Receptors are not evenly spread out over the skin. Some places have more receptors than others. The skin is

Receptors: The nerve cells in the skin.

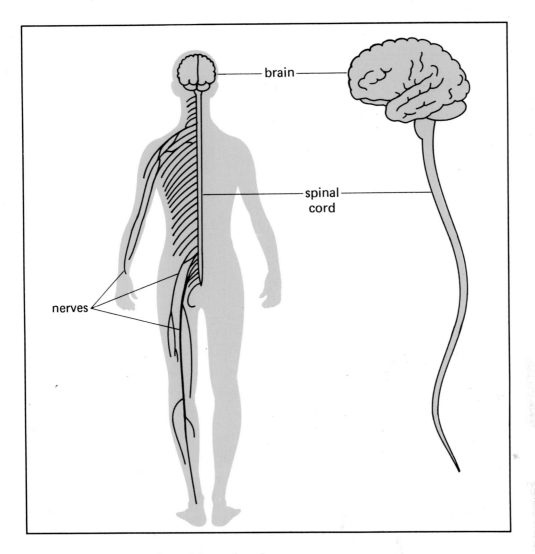

brain

spinal cord

nerves

more sensitive in the places that have more receptors and picks up more messages there. The skin is less sensitive in places that have fewer receptors and does not pick up as many messages there. Some receptors are deeper within the skin than others.

Your fingertips are more sensitive than the back of your hand. There are more touch receptors there. Touch receptors lie close to the skin's surface. Pressure receptors lie deep within the skin. If you press lightly against your skin, you will feel only touch. If you press hard enough, you will cause the pressure receptors deep within the skin to react. Then you will feel pain.

ACTIVITY

Using your touch receptors

A. Obtain these materials: paper clip, ruler.

B. Choose a partner. Decide who will be tested first. Make a chart like the one shown. Write your observations when you are the tester.

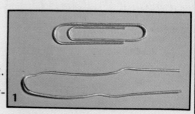

Location	1 end	2 ends	1 end	2 ends	1 end	2 ends	1 end	2 ends
finger palm hand (back) arm								

C. Unbend the paper clip and reshape it as shown in photograph 1. The ends of the clip should be about 1 cm apart. The person being tested should roll up a sleeve. Eyes should be closed.

D. Gently touch one end of the clip to the person's finger as shown in photograph 2. Then touch two ends (photograph 3). Repeat 3 times.

   1. Did your partner feel one end or two ends?

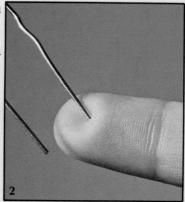

E. Repeat step **D** on the palm of the hand, back of hand, and arm.

   2. Did your partner feel one end or two ends?

F. Switch places with your partner and repeat the activity.

   3. Where on your body did you and your partner feel the correct number of paper-clip ends?

   4. Where do you think the largest number of touch receptors are located in the body?

   5. Write a paragraph that answers: Why are some parts of the body more sensitive to touch than some other parts? Use the term *touch receptors*. Refer to your chart.

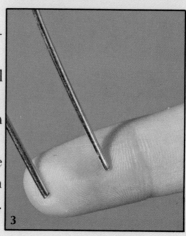

The receptors are the starting points for messages that go to your brain. Other nerves take the message from the receptors to the **spinal** (**spy**-nul) **cord**. The *spinal cord* is a large nerve that carries the messages about heat, cold, pain, touch, and pressure to your brain.

What happens in your nervous system when you touch a hot stove? The heat message is received by your sense receptors. The spinal cord carries it to the brain. At the same time, the spinal cord sends a message to the muscles of your hand. You move away from the hot stove. The response happens before you have a chance to think about the heat. The swift response is called a reflex. It is a safety device against injury to your body.

Spinal cord: A large nerve that carries messages to the brain.

heat receptor in finger

message of heat

brain

muscle cells

message to move finger

spinal cord

Section Review

Main Ideas: Your skin is the sense organ for touch. Touch receptors in the skin gather messages about touch, heat, cold, pain, and pressure. The messages are carried to the spinal cord, a large nerve, which carries them to the brain.

Questions: Answer in complete sentences.

1. What are sense receptors?
2. Imagine you have fallen and scraped your knee. How does the message get from your knee to your brain?
3. Which part of the hand is most sensitive? Why?
4. Rewrite this sentence so that it will be correct: The spinal cord is a touch receptor.
5. Compare the skin, in size, to other sense organs.
6. Some receptors lie deep within the skin. Which receptors lie the deepest?

CHAPTER REVIEW

Science Words   Define each of these words:

1. Cell
2. Cell membrane
3. Nucleus
4. Nerve cells
5. Tissue

What words best complete the sentences?

6. A _____ is a group of tissues that work together.
7. An organ is a group of _____ that work together.
8. A group of organs that work together is a _____ _____.
9. The body system that controls all the other systems is the _____ _____.
10. The nerve that carries smell messages to your brain is the _____.

Questions: Answer in complete sentences.

1. You are chewing on a piece of onion. How does your brain respond?
2. Name the parts of the body that make it possible for you to hear. Describe what each part does.
3. You walk into a very dark room. In about 10 seconds you see a pile of diamonds on a table.
   a. Explain why you couldn't see the diamonds when you entered the room.
   b. Explain how your brain received the message about the presence of the diamonds.
4. You reach into your pocket and pull out a coin. You know it's a dime without looking at it. How did information about the coin reach your brain?
5. Make a chart of the functions of the nervous system.
6. What are the five kinds of messages that can be picked up by receptors in your skin?

CHAPTER 7

BONES AND MUSCLES

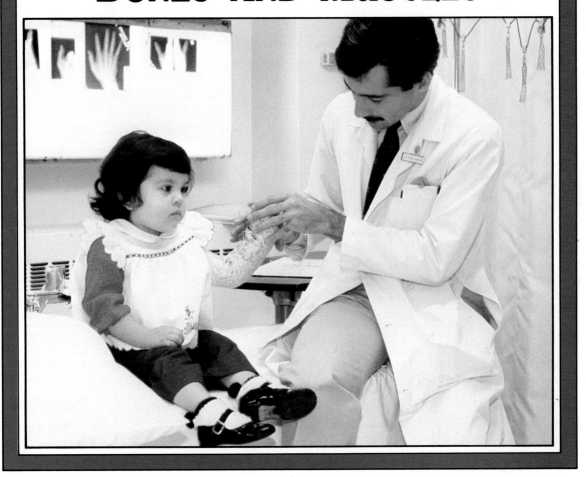

Have you ever broken a bone? The doctor is checking the plaster the broken bone is wrapped in. He wants to know if it is strong enough to keep the bone from moving. As the break in the bone heals, new cells grow. Eventually, the bone will be stronger than it was before the break.

7-1.

Bones

What are bones made of? When you finish this section, you should be able to:

☐ **A.** Describe what the *skeletal system* does.
☐ **B.** Identify some of the bones of the body.
☐ **C.** Identify the parts of the *backbone* from a drawing of one.

Although your bones are strong and hard, they are made of living tissue. All living tissue can be harmed. The bones of the body are harmed if they don't receive enough food. And they can be broken if they are hit hard enough.

Bones are made of living cells and blood *vessels* (**ves-sulz**). The blood vessels carry food to the cells and carry wastes away. Bones are also made of mineral matter. The chief mineral is *calcium* (**kal**-see-um). Calcium is needed for the growth of bones. Milk is a good source of this mineral. Treated with care, a bone is able to heal and repair itself.

The 206 bones in the human body make up the **skeletal system**. The *skeletal system* functions in four ways. One of its functions is support of the body. The bones support the body somewhat the way beams of a building support the whole building. They give the body its shape. Bones also protect the body organs that lie under them. Movement is another function of the skeletal system. Muscles attached to bones pull on the bones. Thus we are able to walk, lift, and sit. The fourth function is very important. The blood that flows through the body is made in the bones.

Certain substances are needed for a healthy, growing skeletal system, such as yours. Because milk contains calcium, it is a natural food for young people. You need *vitamin* (**vy**-tuh-min) D also. This vitamin is added to the milk you drink. Your body also produces vitamin D in the presence of sunlight. Calcium and vitamin D work together to keep bones healthy and growing straight.

Skeletal system: All the bones of the body.

Skeletal System
Support
Protection
Movement
Production of blood cells

140

The bones that make up the skeletal system are referred to as the skeleton. Inside your body is a skeleton that looks very much like the one in the drawing. You can find some of the bones in your body by gently pressing on the surface of your skin. All of the body's bones are not shown in the drawing of the skeleton. A front view of a skeleton cannot show all the bones in the back of the skeleton. How many bones can you count on the skeleton in the drawing?

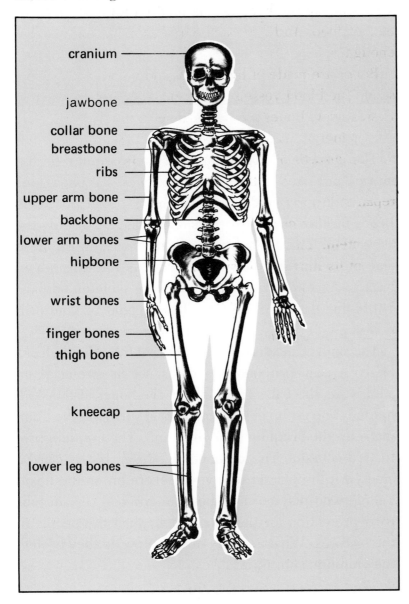

cranium

jawbone

collar bone
breastbone

ribs

upper arm bone

backbone

lower arm bones

hipbone

wrist bones

finger bones

thigh bone

kneecap

lower leg bones

The 206 bones in the skeletal system are of different shapes and sizes. There are round ones, flat ones, long ones, and short ones. Every bone has a special job. Many bones protect important parts of the body. To study the skeletal system, let us start with the bones in the head and end with the bones in the feet. As you learn about each bone, refer to the drawing of the skeleton on page 141 to find the bone. Also, locate each bone on your own skeleton.

The skull of an adult is very different from the skull of a baby. A newborn baby's skull is not as strong as an adult's. As the baby grows older, the bones of the skull harden. The group of skull bones that surround the brain make up the **cranium** (**kray**-nee-um). The *cranium* protects the brain. The cranium is strong, but it can be cracked if the person receives a severe hit on the head. People who play certain sports or work in certain jobs wear protection for the cranium. Look at the people in the pictures. What are they doing? How do they protect the cranium from injury?

Cranium: Group of skull bones that surround the brain.

Another bone that is part of the head is the **jawbone**. Touch your chin and move your hand up toward your ear. The bone you feel is your *jawbone*. The movement of the jawbone allows you to chew food and speak.

The structure shown on the left below is a large column of bones that goes up the center of your back. It is called the **backbone**. One end of the *backbone* is connected to the head. The other end is connected to the hipbones.

The backbone is actually made up of many small bones. Gently rub your backbone with one hand. Can you feel the small bones? They are called **vertebrae** (ver-tuh-bray). The backbone has 33 *vertebrae*.

Look at the drawing of one vertebra (**ver**-tuh-bra). Each vertebra has an opening through its center. The spinal cord passes through these openings. The spinal cord is protected by the vertebrae of the backbone.

Jawbone: A bone that is part of the head.

Backbone: A column of bones that extends up the center of the back.

Vertebrae: The small bones that make up the backbone, or spine.

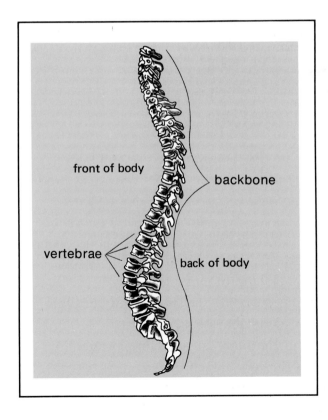

front of body

backbone

vertebrae

back of body

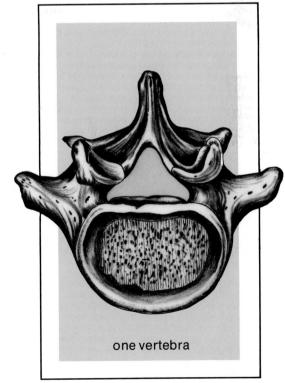

one vertebra

Ribs: Twelve pairs of bones that surround and protect the heart and lungs.

Connected to the backbone are twelve pairs of bones called **ribs**. The *ribs* extend around to the front of the body. At the front of the body, the upper seven pairs are connected to a bone called the breastbone. The ribs form a cage that protects the heart and lungs.

Attached to the bottom of the backbone are two large hipbones. These hipbones and the lower parts of the backbone form the **pelvis** (**pel**-vis). The *pelvis* helps bear the weight of the body.

Pelvis: The hipbones and lower parts of the backbone.

The upper parts of each leg and each arm have one large bone. The lower parts of your legs and arms have two bones. Your hands and feet have many small bones. Your hands have more bones than any other part of your body. Look at your hand. Each finger has four bones. Can you find the four bones?

Marrow: A soft substance in the hollow space of some bones.

Many bones are hollow inside. The hollow space is filled with a soft substance called **marrow** (**mar**-roh). There are two types of *marrow*. In young people, all marrow is red. As one gets older, red marrow is found in flat bones, such as ribs. The rest of the marrow is yellow. Blood cells are produced in red marrow.

Section Review

Main Ideas: The 206 bones of the skeletal system support, protect, and move the body. They also produce blood cells.

Questions: Answer in complete sentences.

1. How do bones support and protect the body?
2. How do bones help to move the body?
3. The cranium, jawbone, backbone, and vertebrae are parts of the skeletal system.
    a. Where in the body is each bone located?
    b. What is the job of each bone?
4. Look at the drawing on page 141. Locate the ribs. From their location, can you tell their function?

Have you ever looked at an X ray of any part of your body? The X-ray photograph on the left shows the bones of a young child's hand. The photograph on the right shows the bones of an adult's hand. There is a difference in the way the bones join, or come together, in each hand. Do you see what the difference is? When you finish this section, you should be able to:

☐ **A.** Explain the function of *cartilage*.
☐ **B.** Identify and compare the functions of *movable joints*.
☐ **C.** Explain the function of *ligaments*.
☐ **D.** Identify one type of *immovable joint*.

You can see that the spaces between the bones of the fingers are close together in the adult's hand. In the child's hand the spaces are farther apart. They are filled with a soft substance that does not show up on the X ray. Compare the wrist areas in the two X-ray pictures. The

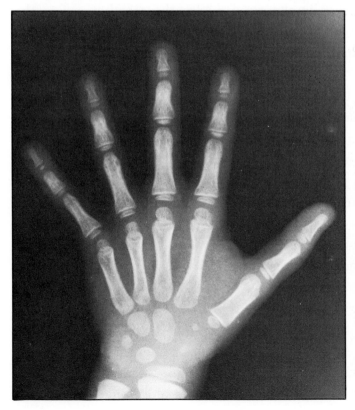

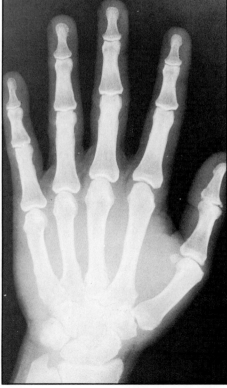

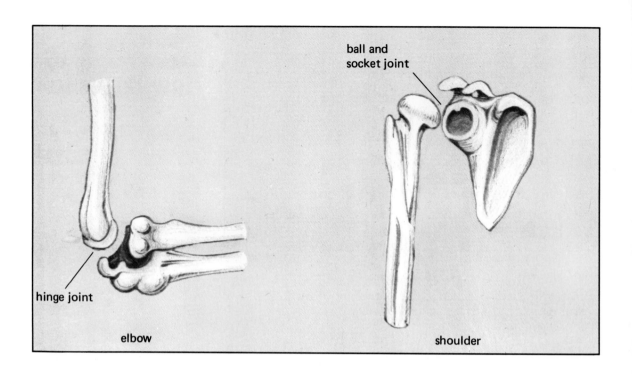

ball and
socket joint

hinge joint

elbow

shoulder

**Cartilage: A soft
substance that is found
where some bones
meet.**

**Joint: The place where
two bones meet.**

**Hinge joint: A kind of
joint where the bones
can move back and
forth or up and down.**

**Ball-and-socket joint: A
kind of joint where the
bones can move in many
directions.**

child's wrist is not yet solid bone. The same soft substance lies in the wrist where the arm bones join the
hand bones. There is a name for this soft substance. It is
the same substance that babies' bones are made of. It is
known as **cartilage** (kar-tih-lij). Most of your bones are
hard. However, you do have *cartilage* at the end of your
nose and in places where some bones meet. The place
where two bones meet is called a **joint**. At some *joints*,
the bones are able to move. The cartilage at the joint is
like a padding that keeps the ends of the bones from
rubbing together when they move.

You have three kinds of movable joints. One kind is
like the hinge on a door. It is called a **hinge joint**. The
bones at a *hinge joint* can move back and forth or up and
down. The joints in your elbows and knees are hinge
joints. So are the joints in your fingers and toes.

Another kind of movable joint is the **ball-and-socket
joint**. At a *ball-and-socket joint*, the end of one bone is
shaped like a ball. It fits into a curved space at the end of
the other bone. Bones at this kind of joint can move in

146

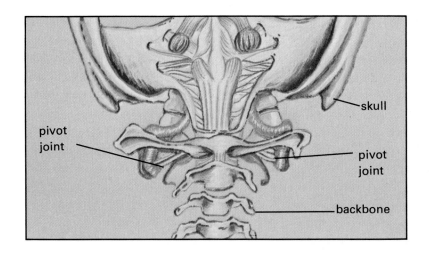

pivot joint

skull

pivot joint

backbone

many directions. The joints in your shoulders and hips are ball-and-socket joints.

A third kind of joint is the **pivot joint**. The bones at a *pivot joint* can move around and back. The joint where the head meets the backbone is a pivot joint.

What keeps bones from sliding off each other when they move? Bones at these three types of joints are held together by strong bands of material called **ligaments** (**lig**-uh-ments). *Ligaments* stretch across joints from the end of one bone to the end of the other. Ligaments hold the bones in place. Look at the drawing below. Can you find the joint, bones, and ligaments?

Pivot joint: A kind of joint where the bones can move around and back.

Ligaments: Strong bands of material that hold bones in place at joints.

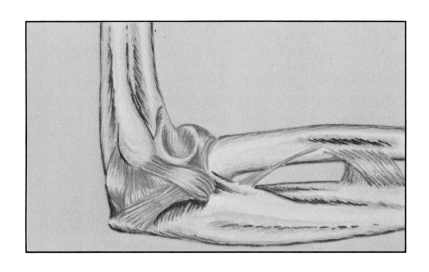

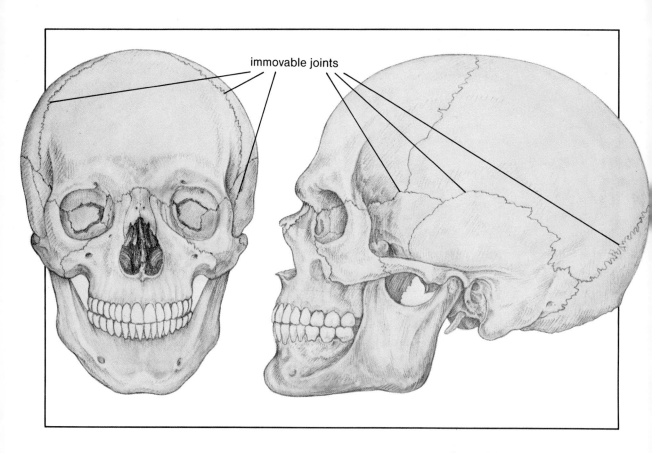

immovable joints

Dislocation: A bone forced out of its usual position in a joint.

Sometimes a joint receives a sharp blow when a person falls. When this happens, one bone is forced out of its usual position, or location, in a joint. This is called a **dislocation** (dis-loh-**kay**-shun). A dislocated bone usually can be pushed back into place by a doctor.

The body has three types of movable joints. It also has one type of joint that does not permit bones to move. The body's immovable joints are part of the skull. In this diagram of a skull, you can see crooked lines.

These are the places of immovable joints. Eight bones surround the brain. When you were very young, the joints were slightly movable. Then, the bones on either side of the joints moved slightly. This movement allowed your brain to increase in size. As you got older, the tissue at the joints was replaced by bone. Now that your brain is full size, there is no need for these joints to still be movable.

Section Review

Main Ideas: The places on the body where bones come together are joints. The body has three types of movable joints, where the bones are padded by cartilage and held in place by ligaments. Immovable joints are found in the skull.

Questions: Answer in complete sentences.

1. What is a joint?
2. List three types of movable joints. Give examples.
3. What is the difference between cartilage and ligaments?
4. Why do you no longer have movable joints around your brain?

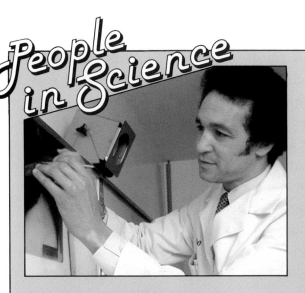

People in Science

Augustus A. White, III

Dr. White is a scientist and doctor whose work is the treatment of people with bone and muscle injuries. He is an **orthopedic** (or-thoh-**pee**-dik) surgeon.

Dr. White studied medicine at Stanford University in California and at the Karolinska Institute in Sweden. While a professor of medicine at Yale University Medical School, he set up a special laboratory to study how the muscles cause the bones of the body to move. Dr. White is a good athlete and is interested in sports and the injuries they cause. He is the author of over 100 books and articles. Much of his writing deals with how the bones of the spine move as people use their muscles to walk, run, and lift. Dr. White has won many awards for his work. Dr. White is now a teacher of doctors at Harvard Medical School.

7-3.

Muscles

You may be surprised to learn that you have all the muscles that this body builder has. They just do not look the same on you. The bulging muscles you see on the body builder lie near the surface of the body. There are many other muscles that lie deep within the body. When you finish this section, you should be able to:

☐ **A.** Describe the functions of the *muscular system*.

☐ **B.** Locate the muscles called the *biceps* and the *triceps*.

☐ **C.** Describe the difference between *voluntary* and *involuntary* muscles.

Make a guess about how many muscles there are in your body. More than 100? More than 200? Your body has more than 600 muscles! They make up a body system that is called the **muscular system**. The *muscular system* makes it possible for you to move from place to place. Some muscles cause organs of the body, such as the heart, to function. Muscles acting on the blood vessels move blood through the body. Food and wastes also are moved through the body because of muscles. Muscles even connect skin to bone and skin to skin.

As you read this book, muscles are pulling on the bones of your arms and hands so that you can hold the book and turn the pages. Some muscles are pulling on the book, turning its pages. Some muscles are pulling on other bones to keep you seated upright. The small muscles around your eyes make it possible for you to read.

As you read, your eyelids move. They move down over your eyes and then back up again. You are able to blink

Muscular system: All the muscles of the body.

Muscular System
Acts on bones to move body from place to place
Acts on lungs and other organs
Moves food through digestive organs
Moves blood through blood vessels

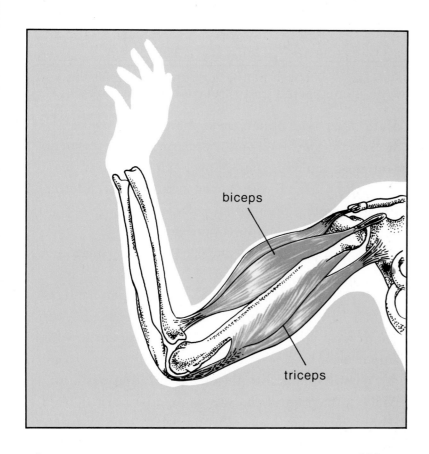

biceps

triceps

when you want. However, you cannot stop yourself from blinking forever. Blinking is a movement you cannot completely control.

Every movement you make is caused by muscles. Some muscles you can control. They are called **voluntary** (**vahl**-un-teh-ree) **muscles**. Your arm and leg muscles are *voluntary muscles*. You can move your arm and leg muscles when you want to. Look at the drawing above. It shows the muscles in the upper part of the arm. The muscle on the top side of the arm is called the **biceps** (**by**-seps). The muscle on the bottom side of the arm is called the **triceps** (**try**-seps). The *biceps* and *triceps* work together to move the arm. They are voluntary muscles. Can you find your biceps and triceps?

Look at the drawing again. What are the muscles attached to? Most voluntary muscles are attached to bones.

Voluntary muscles: Muscles that can be controlled.

Biceps: The muscle on the top side of the upper arm.

Triceps: The muscle on the bottom side of the upper arm.

ACTIVITY

How do a contracted and a relaxed muscle look?

A. With a partner, obtain these materials: 2 books.

B. Roll up the sleeve on your right arm. Put your arm on your desk top with your elbow resting on the surface. Rest the back of your lower arm on the tabletop. Observe your upper arm.

C. Make a diagram of your upper arm.

  1. Do you observe any muscles near the surface of your upper arm?

D. Have your partner put 2 books in your open hand, as shown in the photograph. With the books in your hand, raise your arm. Observe what happens to your upper arm.

  2. What happened to the shape of the upper arm?

E. Make a diagram of the way your upper arm looked when you lifted the books upward.

  3. Write a paragraph comparing how your upper arm looked at rest with how it looked as you lifted the books. Use these terms: *muscle system, voluntary, biceps*.

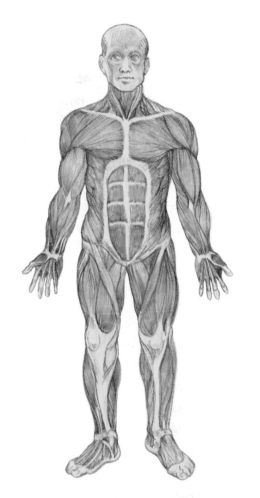
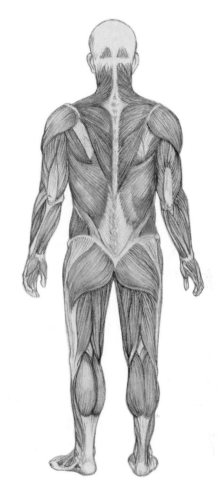

Some muscles are attached directly to the bones. Other muscles are attached to the bones by tough cords called **tendons** (ten-dunz). Through the *tendons*, the muscles control the movement of the bones. When the muscle contracts, or gets shorter, it pulls on the tendon. Then the tendon pulls on the bone.

When you want to move your arm, your brain sends a message to the muscle. The muscle shortens and becomes firm as the movement occurs. In other words, the muscle contracts. When you want to stop the movement, your brain tells the muscle to relax. When you contract your biceps, it bulges. As it shortens, it pulls the bones of the lower arm upward.

Look at the drawing above. It shows some of your body's muscles. Can you find the biceps and triceps?

Tendons: Tough cords that connect muscles to bones.

Involuntary muscles: Muscles, such as the heart, that cannot be controlled.

There are some muscles in the body that cannot be controlled. They are called **involuntary** (in-**vahl**-un-teh-ree) **muscles.** *Involuntary muscles*, unlike voluntary muscles, are not attached to bones. The heart, for example, is composed of involuntary muscles. When the muscle tissues in the heart contract, blood is forced out through blood vessels. You do not have to think about controlling this muscle. It contracts and relaxes on its own.

The stomach and intestines are also composed of involuntary muscles. When they contract and relax, food is mixed and moved through the body.

The muscles that help you breathe are both voluntary and involuntary. Try holding your breath for an instant. Notice that the muscles in your chest are not moving. You are controlling them. But for how long can you control them? Only for the short time that you can hold your breath.

Section Review

Main Ideas: Every movement made by the body is caused by muscles. Muscles work by contracting and relaxing. Voluntary muscles usually are attached to bones and can be controlled. Involuntary muscles are not attached to bones and cannot be controlled.

Questions: Answer in complete sentences.

1. What one word best describes the purpose of the muscular system?
2. What is the difference between the heart muscles and a leg muscle?
3. How would you describe what the biceps muscle of a weight lifter is doing as he holds up a bar?
4. Look at the drawing on page 153. Where are the tendons located? Answer in one sentence.
5. What is the difference between a tendon and a ligament?

Kinds of Muscles

It takes a lot of energy to do what this gymnast is doing. She can do it because her muscles are in good condition. Well-developed voluntary muscles allow her to turn, twist, and pull her body in the direction she wants it to go. Strong biceps and triceps give her the support she needs to stand on her hands. But she couldn't come down from that position if she didn't have strong abdominal muscles. Do you know where any of these muscles are located in your body? When you finish this section, you should be able to:

☐ **A.** Identify and describe three types of muscle cells.

☐ **B.** Explain why muscle cells need blood.

Even when the athlete on the bar rests, her muscles are not totally relaxed. Because of her work she always has good muscle tone, or a certain amount of muscle contraction. When a muscle is used often, plenty of blood flows through it. Anyone sick in bed for a long period of time loses muscle tone. Without exercise, people feel

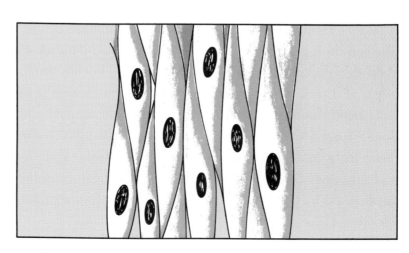

weak and tired because their muscles do not receive enough blood. In order to have good muscle tone, a large amount of blood must reach the muscle cells.

Every muscle in the body contains thousands of tiny cells. There are three types of muscles in the body. In each type, the muscle cells look different.

Smooth muscle: A type of muscle containing long, thin, and pointed cells.

One type of muscle is called **smooth muscle**. The cells of *smooth muscles* are long, thin, and pointed at each end. Look at the drawing above. It shows a group of smooth muscle cells. Do you see a dark area in the center of each cell? This area is the nucleus. You learned that the nucleus controls all cell activities. Each smooth muscle cell has one nucleus in its center. The muscles in your stomach are smooth muscles.

Cardiac muscle: A type of muscle that the heart is made of.

Another type of muscle is **cardiac (kar-dee-ak) muscle**. The word *cardiac* means of or near the heart. Your heart is made of *cardiac muscle*. Look at the drawing at the top of page 157. The cells of cardiac muscle branch out and weave together. Each cell has one nucleus.

Skeletal muscle: A type of muscle containing long, cylinder-shaped cells with stripes across them.

The third type of muscle is called **skeletal muscle**. The cells of *skeletal muscles* are long and cylinder-shaped, like straws. They have many nuclei. Look at the drawing at the bottom of page 157. These cells have dark and light bands across them. What other type of muscle has dark and light bands? The tongue and lips are skeletal muscles. So are the biceps and triceps.

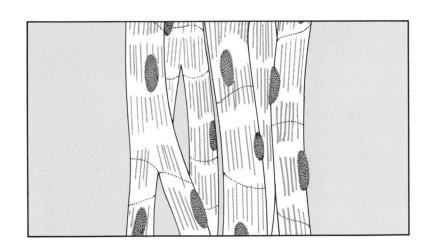

Some skeletal muscles are attached to bones by tendons. When the muscle contracts, the tendons and bones move, too. If you hold your hands palms down and wiggle your fingers, you will see the tendons on the backs of your hands move. The tendons are moved by the arm muscles pulling on the finger bones.

A lot of energy is needed for muscle cells to contract. The source of this energy is food carried to the muscle cells by blood vessels. The blood also carries oxygen to muscle cells. There, oxygen and food combine, energy is released, and waste products are formed. The blood carries the waste products away from muscle cells. Exercise keeps the blood supply in the muscle cells at a healthy level.

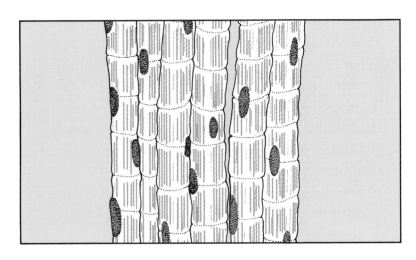

ACTIVITY

What can you learn about your muscles?

A. Obtain these materials: paper, pencil.

B. Draw a diagram showing the type of cells found in the stomach muscles.

   1. Are these cells parts of voluntary or involuntary muscles? Explain.

C. Draw the type of cell found in the heart.

   2. Are these muscles part of voluntary or involuntary muscles? Explain.

D. Draw a diagram showing the type of cells found in the front part of the upper arm.

   3. Are these cells from voluntary muscles?

E. Make a chart that sums up information on the stomach, heart, and front upper-arm muscles.

Section Review

Main Ideas: Your body has three types of muscle cells. All muscle cells produce energy by combining oxygen with food.

Questions: Answer in complete sentences.

1. Name the three types of muscle cells.
2. Why do your muscle cells need blood?
3. What type of muscle cells are described below?
   a. thin, long, and pointed at the ends
   b. striped and branched
   c. cylinder-shaped and striped, not branched
4. When are you likely to show the most muscle tone in your arms?
   a. waving goodbye
   b. hanging from an exercise bar
   c. combing your hair

CHAPTER REVIEW

Science Words: Select the definition in column B that best fits each term in column A.

Column A	Column B
1. Cranium	a. Where two bones come together
2. Vertebrae	b. Bones surrounding the brain
3. Cartilage	c. Strong bands holding bones in place
4. Ligaments	d. Bones of the backbone
5. Joint	e. Substance that pads bones

Give an example of each of the following:

6. Involuntary muscle
7. Voluntary muscle
8. Pivot joint
9. Ball-and-socket joint
10. Hinge joint

Questions: Answer in complete sentences.

1. Give one example of how a part of the skeletal system protects some part of the body.
2. Compare voluntary muscles and involuntary muscles:
   a. What is the main difference between these two kinds of muscles?
   b. Which kind of muscle is found in the arm?
   c. Which kind of muscle is found in the heart?
3. How do cardiac, skeletal, and smooth muscle cells differ from each other in appearance?
4. Compare the muscular system and the skeletal system:
   a. What is the main purpose of each system?
   b. How is the blood related to each system?
   c. How do the systems work together to move the body?

Exploring your eyes

Part I. Where is your blind spot?

The spot called the blind spot is the place where the optic nerve connects to nerve cells. To find your blind spot, do the following:

A. Obtain these materials: dark marking pen, white sheet of paper.

B. On the paper draw a cross and a dot as shown below.

C. Hold the sheet in front of your eyes. While staring straight ahead, close your left eye. Now, without turning your head, look at the cross. Move the paper back and forth and up and down. Keep your right eye focused on the cross and your left eye closed.

 ✛   ●

    1. What do you observe about the dot?

D. Repeat the activity. This time, close your right eye and look at the dot as you move the paper.

    2. What do you observe about the cross?

    3. Write a paragraph that sums up the results of the activity.

Part II. What is an afterimage?

Seeing an object after it has left your view is called the afterimage.

A. Obtain these materials: index card, pen, 1 m of string.

B. Make two holes on the card. Draw a bird on one side of the card. Draw a cage on the other. Pull the string through the holes in the card.

C. Hold the string at its ends. Have someone twist the card around and around so that it will spin quickly in front of your eyes.

    1. What did you observe?

    2. Can you explain why cartoon characters seem to move?

CAREERS

Physical Therapist ▶

Physical therapists help patients who have injured muscles, nerves, joints, and bones. They teach them exercises that gradually move injured tissues. They also teach people to use artificial limbs.

Physical therapists complete a 4-year college program of anatomy, biology, and chemistry. Patience and some strength are required. Physical therapists work in hospitals, nursing homes, and schools, and in industry.

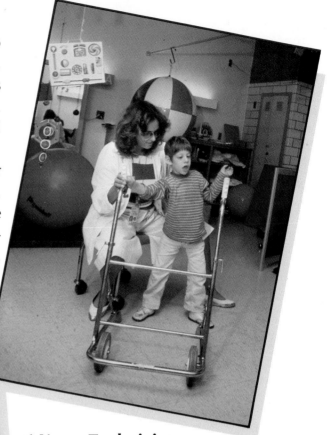

◀ X-ray Technician

X-ray technicians take pictures of parts of the body and develop X-ray film. X rays help doctors study injuries, such as broken bones, or illnesses, such as ulcers. Training can be done in a two-year college program. Students study chemistry, physics, and biology. X-ray technicians, also called radiologic (ray-dee-oh-**loj**-ik) technologists (tek-**nol**-oh-jists), work in hospitals, clinics, doctors' offices, and industry.

161

ELECTRICITY AND MAGNETISM

UNIT 4

CHAPTER 8

ELECTRICITY

8-1.

Static Electricity

This looks like a shocking experience! Actually, this person is very safe. If you comb your hair on a dry day, you may hear crackling sounds. Some strands of hair may stand up. Perhaps you've seen plastic sandwich wrap almost magically pulled to your hand. Each experience has the same cause—electricity.

When you finish this section, you should be able to:

☐ **A.** Describe what negatively and positively charged objects are.
☐ **B.** Describe what happens when charged objects are brought near one another.
☐ **C.** Give examples of *static electricity*.

When an object moves, energy is present. Energy is needed for hair to stand on end. A form of energy that can produce such movement is **electricity** (ih-lek-**tris**-ih-tee). *Electricity* can cause objects to move because it produces a **force**. A *force* is a push or a pull. Electricity causes a force that pushes the strands of hair apart.

These forces were observed many years ago. About 600 B.C., a Greek named Thales was looking at amber. Amber is a yellow material sometimes used in jewelry. When Thales rubbed amber with fur, some strange things happened. The amber pulled bits of feather and straw near it. Thales could not see how this happened.

Now we know more about matter than people did many years ago. Thales did not know what happened in the amber and the fur because they were changed by particles of matter smaller than the eye can see.

All matter, such as amber, fur, paper, and feathers, contains tiny electrical particles. These particles are called **charges** (**char**-jez). There are two types of *charges:* positive and negative. We can pull or rub negative charges off one object and place them on another. When an object gains or loses negative charges, the object is said to be electrically charged.

Rub a plastic comb with wool. Negative charges rub off the wool onto the comb. The comb is now negative. Then place the comb near a piece of paper. The negative charges in the paper move to the side of the paper away from the comb. This causes the side of the paper closest to the comb to become positive. The positive side of the paper is attracted to the negative comb.

Electricity: A form of energy.

Force: A push or a pull.

Charge: The electrical property of matter.

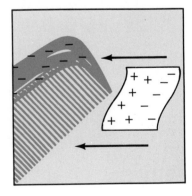

An object has the same number of positive and negative charges. The object may lose negative charges. It is left with a greater number of positive charges. The object is now positively charged. An object may gain negative charges. That object is said to be negatively charged.

Look at the photograph below on the left. The boy is holding two balloons. Both balloons have been given a negative charge. When two negatively charged objects are brought close to each other, what happens? They **repel** (rih-**pel**), or move away from, each other. The same thing happens when two positively charged objects are brought close together. The balloons move away from each other. The same or like charges repel each other.

Look at the photograph on the right. One balloon has been given a positive charge. The other has a negative charge. What happens when two objects with opposite charges are brought close together? The balloons move toward each other. They move this way because unlike charges attract each other.

When an object gains or loses negative charges, electricity is produced. It is called **static electricity**. Objects with *static electricity* may attract or repel each other.

Repel: To move away from.

Static electricity: A type of electricity produced when objects gain or lose negative charges.

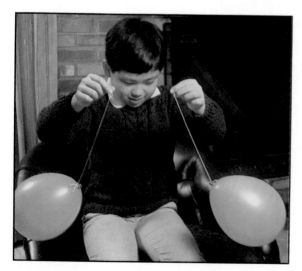

ACTIVITY

Producing a static electricity charge

A. Obtain these materials: plastic comb, paper, wood shavings from a pencil sharpener, piece of wool cloth 15 cm square.

B. Tear the paper into tiny pieces.

C. Rub the comb back and forth quickly with the wool.

D. Hold the comb about 2 cm above the pieces of paper.

1. What happened to the paper?

E. Repeat C and D above, but this time bring the comb near the pile of wood shavings.

2. What did you observe?

3. When you rubbed the comb with the wool cloth, which object received the extra negative charges?

4. When you brought the comb near the paper or the wood shavings, what happened to some of the negative charges that were part of the paper?

5. Explain why the objects were attracted to the comb.

They may also attract objects that do not have any static electricity.

Turn back to the photograph on page 164. The young woman received a static electricity charge from a machine. The machine was part of a science museum display. Negative charges spread out over her body. Each strand of her hair received a negative charge. What effect did those charged strands have on each other?

Electron: The smallest negative charge.

Think of paper moving onto a charged comb. Negative charges are moving from place to place. These negative charges are called **electrons** (ih-**lek**-trahnz). *Electrons* are tiny. To us, they are invisible. When you produce static electricity, you are really moving electrons from place to place. Rubbing certain objects across others can cause electrons to move from one object to another. When you walk across a rug, you may rub electrons from the rug onto your shoes. Then, when you touch a metal object such as a doorknob, what happens? You may see a spark or feel a mild shock. The electrons travel from your feet through your body. The electrons then travel from your fingers to the doorknob, which causes a spark.

Clouds can sometimes build up huge numbers of extra electrons. When this happens a giant spark jumps from cloud to cloud, or from a cloud to the ground. We call such a giant spark lightning. Lightning is made of billions of electrons moving from place to place.

Section Review

Main Ideas: All matter contains negative and positive charges. Like charges repel, and unlike charges attract. Negative charges can move from object to object, causing static electricity.

Questions: Answer in complete sentences.

1. When is an object said to be electrically charged?
2. How does a negatively charged object differ from a positively charged object?
3. Give an example of how you could take negative charges from one object and place them on another.
4. What happens when a negatively charged object is brought close to a positively charged object? What happens when two negatively charged objects are brought together?
5. How is lightning an example of static electricity?

Have you ever been at home when the electricity went off? Suddenly the lights go out. Heaters and fans stop. Everything gets very quiet. Can you think of other things that stop when the electricity stops? When you finish this section, you should be able to:

Current Electricity

☐ **A.** Describe the path that electricity takes when it is used.
☐ **B.** Compare materials that allow electricity to move through them easily with those that do not.

Static electricity is produced by rubbing certain objects across others. It can also cause sparks, or charges that move through the air. Even though it is interesting, static electricity is hard to put to use. The **appliances** you see in the photograph use a form of electricity that is different from static electricity. *Appliances* such as those in your home use electricity that moves through wires.

In 1729, an English scientist, Stephen Gray, discovered that metal objects could carry electricity from one place to another. Gray was able to get short "bursts" of electricity to move through metal wires. In 1800 an Italian scientist named Alessandro Volta, shown at right, invented a new device. It let electricity move through wires for a longer time. The modern form of Volta's device is called a dry cell, or battery.

Electrical appliance: A device that uses electricity.

169

Current electricity: The flow of negative charges, or electrons.

Circuit: The path through which current electricity flows.

Since Volta's time, other scientists have found ways of moving charges through wires for even longer periods of time. When electric charges move through wire, **current electricity** is produced. *Current electricity* is the flow of negative charges, or electrons. The electrons flow in a path called a **circuit** (ser-kut).

Look at the picture above on the left. It shows a *circuit*. There are four parts to this circuit. There is a source of electric charges (battery), a path through which the charges flow (wires), a switch, and a user of the electricity (light bulb). In a circuit, the current flows from the source through the wires, switch, to the user of the electricity, and then it returns to the source.

When all the parts of the circuit are connected so that the current can flow, the circuit is said to be closed. When any part of the circuit is not connected, the current cannot flow. The circuit is said to be open. The switch in a circuit is often used to open or close the circuit. The circuit is open when the switch is up. When do you think the circuit is closed? Look at the picture on the right. Is it open or closed?

ACTIVITY

Testing conductors and insulators

A. Obtain these materials: aluminum foil, door key, plastic button, battery, light bulb with socket, paper, pencil, 2 pieces of wire 30 cm long, rubber band, nickel, screwdriver.

B. Make a chart like the one shown.

Item Tested	Conductor	Insulator
aluminum foil		
door key		
paper		
nickel		
rubber band		
plastic button		
pencil		

1. Look at the items on the chart. Predict which ones will be insulators and which ones will be conductors. Record your predictions.

C. Connect the wire, light bulb, and battery as shown.

D. Hold the uncovered end of each wire to the aluminum foil.

2. What happened to the light bulb?

E. On your chart, check whether the aluminum foil is a conductor or an insulator.

F. Repeat steps D and E for each item on your chart.

3. Which items were conductors?

4. Which items were insulators?

5. Write a conclusion for this activity that compares your results with your predictions.

Conductors: Materials that allow current to flow through them easily.

Insulators: Materials that do not allow current to flow through them.

Some materials allow current to flow through them easily. These materials are called **conductors** (kun-**duk**-terz). Materials that allow little or no current to flow through them are called **insulators** (**in**-suh-lay-terz).

When people make circuits, they use *conductors* where they want electrons to move freely. Where they don't want electricity to move, they use *insulators*. The handle of a switch is made of an insulator. Can you think of a reason why?

Some materials allow very few electrons to move through them. Examples are paper, wood, rubber, and glass. They are good insulators. Can you find the insulators in the photograph? Other materials have some electrons that can be moved easily. Examples are copper, aluminum, silver, and gold. They are all metals. They are very good conductors. Copper wire is often used to wire buildings because it costs less than other metals.

Section Review

Main Ideas: Current electricity that flows through a closed circuit provides us with useful electricity. Conductors, such as metals, allow current to flow through them easily. Insulators do not.

Questions: Answer in complete sentences.

1. How is current electricity different from static electricity?
2. What is a circuit?
3. List the four parts of a circuit.
4. Compare an insulator with a conductor.
5. Identify the insulators and conductors below.
   a. rubber-soled shoes
   b. copper wire
   c. gold chain
   d. plastic switch handle

One Kind of Circuit

Ed can't get the bulbs to light. He thought that perhaps he hadn't connected the battery. He checked the battery. That wasn't the problem. What do you think might be causing his problem? When you finish this section, you should be able to:

☐ **A.** Describe a type of circuit in which there is only one path for charges to flow through.
☐ **B.** Make a circuit diagram and label its four parts.
☐ **C.** Identify and describe the jobs of two parts of a dry cell.

The bulbs are part of a circuit. They are the users of the electric current. The bulbs are connected one after another. The type of circuit in which the parts are connected one after another is called a **series circuit**. In a *series circuit* there is only one path through which the charges can flow. The charges flow from the source, through the wire and each bulb, and back to the source. If the circuit has a switch, the current flows through the switch, too.

If one bulb is loose or broken, the electricity does not flow. All the lights will go out. This happened to Ed's circuit. One loose bulb had broken the circuit because the bulbs were connected in a series circuit.

Series circuit: A circuit with only one path through which charges can flow.

173

Look at the pictures above. Both show a series circuit. How are the circuits different from each other? The amount of current flowing through both circuits is the same. When more bulbs are added to a series circuit, the light from each bulb is dimmer, because the users of the current must share the available current.

Scientists often make drawings or diagrams of a circuit. They use symbols to show the parts of the circuit. These symbols are shown on the chart in the margin. Scientists draw circuit diagrams in a boxlike shape.

The diagram below shows a series circuit. How many light bulbs are in the circuit? Is the switch open or closed? Can you point to the dry cell and wires?

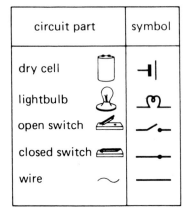

circuit part		symbol
dry cell		⊣|
lightbulb		
open switch		
closed switch		
wire		—

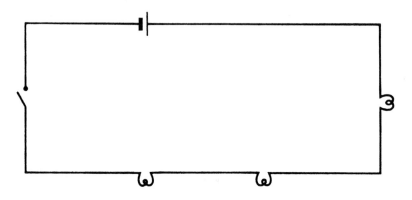

The source of the current shown in this section was a dry cell. Dry cells also provide current for radios and flashlights. Chemical reactions take place in dry cells. The reactions cause electrons to flow. Dry cells push these electrons through circuits. The parts of the dry cell that connect to circuit wires are called **terminals.** In a dry cell, electrons move to one *terminal*. The terminal they

Terminals: Parts of a dry cell to which wires are connected.

ACTIVITY

Exploring a series circuit

A. Obtain these materials: 1.5-volt dry cell, 2 light bulbs in sockets, screwdriver, switch, 4 pieces of wire 30 cm long.

B. Connect a series circuit as shown.

  1. Predict what will happen when you close the switch. Record your prediction.

C. Close the switch and then open it.

  2. Write down what you observed.

D. Unscrew 1 light bulb.

  3. Predict what will occur when you close the switch. Record your predictions.

E. Close and open the switch.

  4. Write down your observations.

  5. Draw and label a circuit diagram for this circuit.

  6. Write a summary for this experiment that compares your predictions with your results.

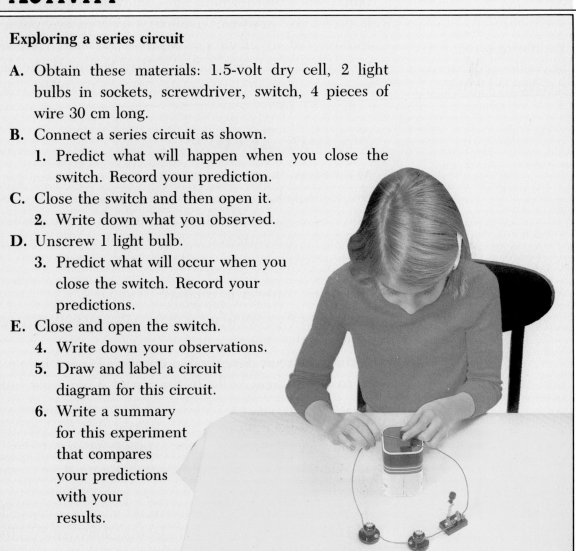

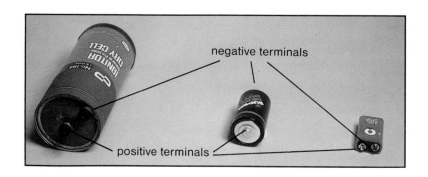

negative terminals

positive terminals

Negative terminal: Part of the dry cell that has extra electrons.

Positive terminal: Part of the dry cell that has a shortage of electrons.

move to has extra electrons. It is called the **negative terminal**. The other terminal has a shortage of electrons. It is called the **positive terminal**. Electrons are pushed through the circuit by the *negative terminal*. They are pulled to the dry cell at the positive terminal. The picture above shows the terminals of three types of dry cells.

Section Review

Main Ideas: In a series circuit, there is only one path through which the charges can flow. Charges always flow from the negative terminal of a dry cell to the positive terminal. Circuit diagrams show the source of electricity and the parts through which the electricity flows.

Questions: Answer in complete sentences.

1. In what type of circuit is there only one path through which the charges can flow?
2. In the circuit described in question 1, what happens to all the light bulbs in the circuit if one light bulb goes off?
3. Draw a diagram of a series circuit that has one dry cell, four light bulbs, and a closed switch.
4. What happens at the negative terminal of a dry cell?
5. What happens at the positive terminal of a dry cell?
6. Describe the direction of electron flow between the terminals of a dry cell.

Becky is having a problem with her lamp. One of the bulbs isn't lit. Do you think the light bulbs in Becky's lamp are connected in a series circuit? When you finish this section, you should be able to:

☐ **A.** Make a labeled diagram that shows a circuit that has more than one path for current.
☐ **B.** Compare two types of circuits.
☐ **C.** Describe two safety devices used in circuits.

Becky's lamp is not wired with a series circuit. If it were, all the light bulbs would be unlit. In a series circuit, the current can't pass through a burned-out bulb to reach the others. The light bulbs in Becky's lamp are connected in a **parallel circuit**. In a *parallel circuit*, there is more than one path for the current to take.

In a parallel circuit, each light bulb is on its own path. If one light bulb is turned off or burns out, the others stay lit. The current flowing through each light bulb is separate from the current flowing through the others. In this circuit, the brightness of one bulb is not changed if other bulbs are added to or taken away from the circuit.

Look at the circuit diagram of a parallel circuit. Is the switch open or closed in this circuit? How many paths can the charges flow through? If one bulb burns out, what happens to the others?

In the diagram, the switch is closed. Electrons can move through the circuit. There are three paths for charges to flow through. If one bulb burns out, it will not change the current flowing through the other two.

Parallel circuit: A circuit with more than one path through which charges can flow.

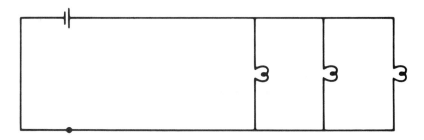

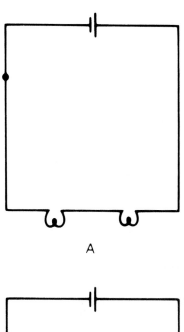

A

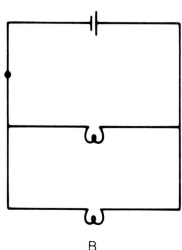

B

You should now be ready to compare a parallel circuit with a series circuit. Look at the two circuit diagrams in the margin.

Which of these circuits has one path for electrons? Which has two paths? Which circuit is a series circuit? Which is a parallel circuit? What would happen if one of the bulbs in circuit A burned out? What would happen if one of the bulbs in circuit B burned out?

In the diagram, circuit A is a series circuit. It has just one path for electrons. If one bulb burned out, the other bulb would also go out. Circuit B is a parallel circuit. Some charges go through one path, and some go through the other path. If one bulb burns out, the other will not be affected.

The lights and appliances in your home or school are wired in parallel circuits. When you shut off one appliance or light, the other appliances stay on. Think of the problems you might have if your home were wired with a series circuit. If just one small lamp burned out, no current would flow. All the appliances would then stop working.

Look at the two diagrams below. Which diagram is most like the circuit that your home uses? If you think that it is C, you are right. In C, if the TV is shut off, the refrigerator stays on. In D, if the TV is shut off, the refrigerator stops working.

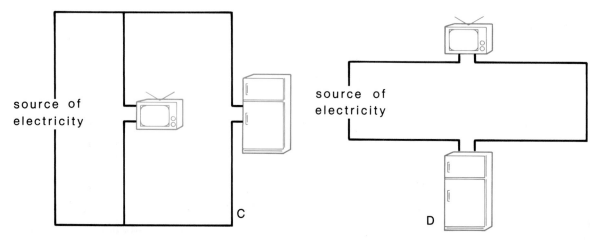

C

D

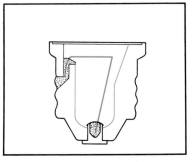

Have you ever noticed that the electrical wires in appliances sometimes get warm to the touch? All wires heat up a bit when current moves through them. Too much current passing through a wire can cause a big safety problem. Fires can start. The circuits in your home and school may have a safety device called a **fuse**. A *fuse* helps to keep wires from getting too hot. It contains a short length of wire that melts if too much current is passing through the circuit. When the special wire in the fuse melts, the circuit is no longer complete. The current stops flowing.

Fuse: A safety device for circuits with a piece of wire that melts to break the circuit.

What if fuses were not used in circuits? The wires might get so hot that they would set fire to the ceiling, floors, or walls that they passed through. The picture above shows a fuse. The diagram shows how it looks inside. Find the wire that melts if the circuit has too much current.

Some appliances have their own fuses. If too much current is passing through the appliance, the fuse burns out. For example, a stereo might have a fuse.

Circuit breaker: A safety device for circuits that opens a switch to break a circuit.

In some circuits a different safety device is used to keep wires from getting too hot. This device is called a **circuit breaker**. The photograph shows the *circuit breakers* used in one home. A circuit breaker is a switch that opens the circuit if too much current is flowing.

What if a circuit breaker opens and stops the current? Someone has to find the part of the circuit that is causing the problem. After the problem is solved, the circuit breaker is closed. The current flows again.

ACTIVITY

Exploring a parallel circuit

A. Obtain these materials: 1.5-volt dry cell, 3 light bulbs in sockets, 7 pieces of wire 30 cm long, screwdriver, switch.

B. Connect a parallel circuit as shown at the left.
   1. Make a diagram of the circuit. Label it.
   2. Predict what will happen when you close and open the switch. Record your predictions.

C. Close and open the switch.
   3. Write down your observations.

D. Unscrew one of the light bulbs.
   4. Predict what will happen when you close and open the switch.

E. Close and open the switch.
   5. Write a paragraph comparing your predictions with the results.

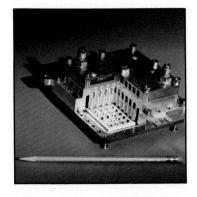

All of the circuits pictured in this chapter have shown wires connecting the source of electricity to the user. Can you imagine making a circuit without wires? How could the current travel from the source of electricity to the user?

Imagine you had some paint that contained metal. You could paint lines on a board. You could connect a battery and a bulb to the painted lines. They could carry the current. The metal in the paint would act like a conductor. This is how some kinds of circuits are made. They are stamped or printed on a board. These kinds of circuits are known as *printed circuits*. The photograph shows a printed circuit. Circuits can be printed on very tiny boards. This allows many circuits to take up a very small space. This is helpful in building machines such as computers. The printed circuits can provide many paths through which current can flow.

Section Review

Main Ideas: In a parallel circuit, there is more than one path through which current can flow. Electrical circuits sometimes contain safety devices, such as fuses or circuit breakers, to keep wires from getting too hot.

Questions: Answer in complete sentences.

1. In what type of circuit is there more than one path through which the charges can flow?
2. Compare a parallel circuit with a series circuit.
3. Why are the circuits in buildings usually parallel circuits?
4. Describe two safety devices that are sometimes used as parts of circuits. Explain how each works.
5. What is a printed circuit?

People in Science

Charles Proteus Steinmetz
(1865-1923)

Charles Steinmetz was a genius in mathematics, chemistry, and, most of all, electricity. He was born and educated in Germany. He became famous after coming to the United States in 1889.

Steinmetz was born with severe physical problems, including a deformed spine, which kept him from growing very tall. He had great difficulty walking. Steinmetz proved himself to be a true scientific thinker. One invention made it possible for people who lived far from a power plant to receive electrical power. Because of his ability, the company that Steinmetz worked for gave him all the equipment and money he wanted to do his research. Although he was so advanced in his thinking, he found time to promote the rights of all people. He also believed in good education.

CHAPTER REVIEW

Science Words
What word best fits each of the following definitions?

1. A type of electricity produced when objects gain or lose negative charges.
2. The path through which negative charges flow.
3. The smallest negative charge.
4. A circuit with only one path for electrons.
5. Part of a dry cell that has a shortage of electrons.

What word best fits each of the blanks?

6. The _____ are the parts of a dry cell to which wires are connected.
7. A _____ _____ has more than one path for charges.
8. _____ and _____ _____ are safety devices for circuits.
9. _____ are materials that allow current to flow through them easily.
10. _____ are materials that do not allow current to flow through them.

Questions: Answer in complete sentences.

1. What are the four parts of a complete circuit? Draw a labeled diagram of a series circuit.
2. Why are parallel, and not series, circuits used in buildings?
3. How could you pick up papers with a plastic comb?
4. What is the difference between static and current electricity?
5. Explain how a fuse works.
6. A student doing an experiment brings a positively charged and a negatively charged balloon near each other. What will happen? What would happen if the student brought two negatively charged balloons near each other?
7. Name the terminals of a dry cell.

CHAPTER 9

MAGNETISM

Kim is studying a stone that makes strange things happen. Paper clips, nails, and pins seem to be pulled toward the stone. The stone is called a *lodestone*. The lodestone behaves very much like something that you have probably seen before. What does it remind you of?

9-1.
Magnets

When you finish this section, you should be able to:

☐ **A.** Identify and describe an object that attracts iron, nickel, or cobalt.

☐ **B.** Describe the space around an object that attracts iron, nickel, or cobalt.

☐ **C.** Compare the results of bringing like and unlike ends of magnets near each other.

Magnets: Objects that pick up, or attract, iron, nickel, or cobalt.

The lodestone that Kim is looking at is an example of a **magnet.** *Magnets* are objects that pick up, or attract, iron, nickel, or cobalt. Objects that contain iron, nickel, or cobalt are metal. A magnet will not pick up or attract all objects. It won't attract paper, wood, plastic, tin, or rubber. Some magnets, such as lodestone, are found in nature. Others, like those shown below, are made out of steel and other metals.

Poles: The ends of a magnet.

The ends of a magnet are called the **poles.** Magnets are strongest at their *poles*. Magnets have two poles: a north pole and a south pole. The letters S and N show which is the north or south pole.

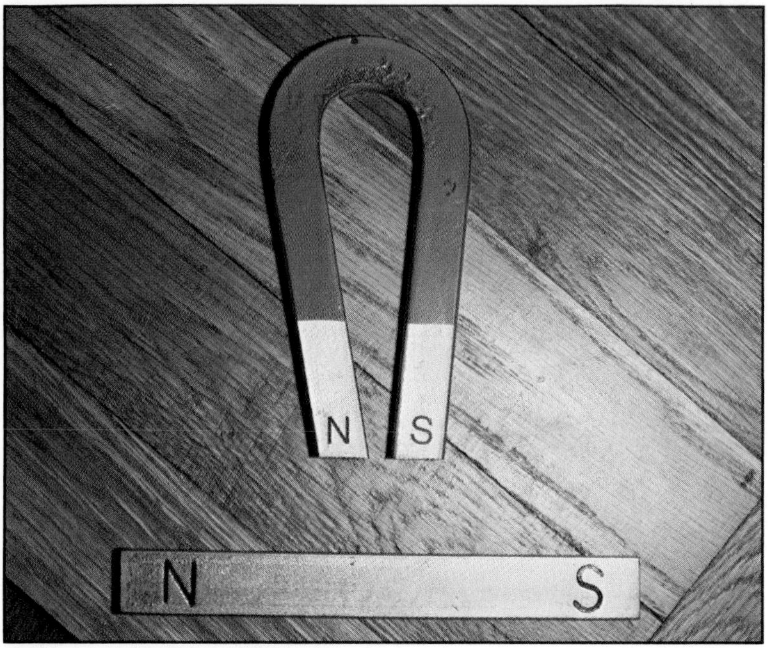

ACTIVITY

What is in the space around a magnet?

A. Obtain these materials: bar magnet, iron filings, plastic sheet 15 cm square.

   1. Predict what would happen if you sprinkled the iron filings onto the sheet covering the magnet.

B. Cover the bar magnet with the plastic sheet. Sprinkle the iron filings onto the plastic sheet, as shown.

C. Gently tap the edge of the plastic sheet.

   2. Write down what you observe. Draw a sketch of what you see.

   3. Write a summary for this activity that compares your prediction with your results.

If you sprinkle iron filings onto a sheet that covers a magnet, you will see patterns of lines like those in the pictures on page 186. These lines are called **lines of force.** *Lines of force* show that the space around a magnet has a magnetic force. The space around a magnet in which there is a magnetic force is called a **magnetic field.** The lines of force show where the *magnetic field* is located. Where are the lines of force closest together?

Lines of force: Lines around a magnet that show where the magnetic force is found.

Magnetic field: The space around a magnet in which there is a magnetic force.

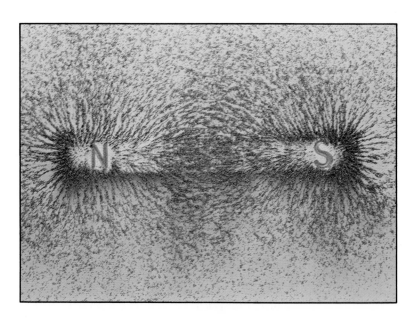

Look at the two pictures below. The picture on the left shows the lines of force around two magnets. The N pole of one magnet and the S pole of the other magnet have been brought close to each other. In the picture on the right, the N poles of both magnets have been brought close to each other. How are the lines of force shown in both pictures different from each other?

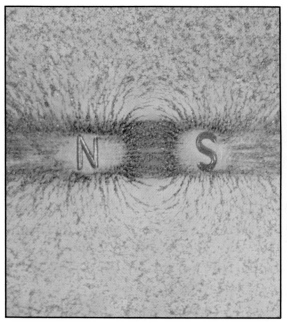

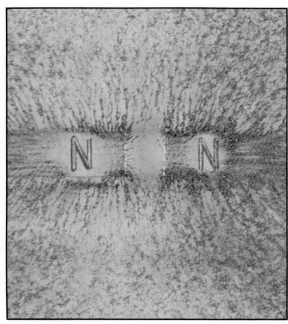

In the bottom left picture on page 186, the lines of force show a magnetic force from the N pole of one magnet to the S pole of the other magnet. This means that these poles of the magnets are attracting each other. N and S poles are opposite poles. Opposite magnetic poles attract each other.

In the bottom right picture, the lines of force do not show an attracting magnetic force between the two poles. The lines of force show that the magnetic force goes away from the poles. This means that the poles of the magnets are repelling each other. Two N poles are the same, or like, poles. Like magnetic poles repel each other. Do you think two S poles will attract or repel each other? If you think they will repel, you are right!

Section Review

Main Ideas: Magnets attract iron, nickel, or cobalt. Their magnetic forces are strongest at their poles. Opposite magnetic poles attract each other. Like poles repel each other.

Questions: Answer in complete sentences.

1. What is a magnet?
2. What parts of a magnet have the strongest magnetic forces?
3. How are the poles of a magnet named?
4. Compare what you observe in the lower left picture on page 186 with what is shown in the lower right picture.
5. Explain what would happen in each of the following:
   a. Bringing two north magnetic poles near each other.
   b. Bringing two south magnetic poles near each other. **c.** Bringing a north magnetic pole near a south magnetic pole.
6. What kinds of objects are attracted to magnets? What kinds are not?

9-2.

A Special Kind of Magnet

It is the 1780's. A young boy is carrying an armload of empty pill bottles across the room. He walks toward his father, a druggist. The boy drops a few on the floor. His father gives him a stern warning: "You'll never grow up and amount to anything if you remain so clumsy!" Little did the father realize that young Hans Christian Oersted was to become a very important scientist.

This young Danish boy soon studied at the University of Copenhagen in Denmark. He then became a famous scientist, known throughout Europe. Oersted was the first person to prove that electricity and magnetism had something to do with each other. When you finish this section, you should be able to:

☐ **A.** Explain how current electricity can be used to make a kind of magnet.
☐ **B.** Describe three ways in which the strength of this kind of magnet can be increased.

For hundreds of years before Oersted's discovery, scientists suspected that electricity and magnetism had something in common. No one was able to prove it. But Hans Christian Oersted performed an experiment that showed that magnetism could be produced by electricity. Oersted made his discovery by accident.

One day, Oersted left a compass needle near a wire through which current was flowing. A compass needle is a small magnet. The needle usually points in a north–south direction. It helps people find their direction.

Whenever Oersted brought the compass needle near the wire, the needle moved in the opposite direction. This surprised Oersted, but he realized he had made an important discovery.

Oersted believed that there must be a magnetic force around a wire through which current flows. Look at the picture below. A card was placed near the wire in the circuit shown. Iron filings were sprinkled on the card. The iron filings formed lines of force around the wire. The lines of force formed a pattern of circles.

The lines of force show that there is a magnetic force in the space around the flowing current. Therefore, current electricity is surrounded by a magnetic field. How can we put this discovery to use?

189

Scientists used Oersted's discovery to make magnets that could be turned on and off. They wrapped wire around a piece of steel and connected it to a source of current. That made a magnet. When they stopped the current, the magnet stopped working. A magnet that is made with current electricity is called an **electromagnet** (ih-lek-troh-**mag**-net). *Electromagnets* are found inside many devices. Tape recorders and large computers have them.

The picture below shows a large electromagnet. It is made of a huge piece of iron. It becomes an electromagnet when the person using it connects the circuit. This electromagnet is very strong. It can pick up heavy objects, such as scraps of metal.

There are three ways to increase the strength of an electromagnet. Look at the pictures above. The picture at the upper left shows a simple electromagnet. It has one dry cell and one iron nail with wire wrapped around it 15 times. How many paper clips does the electromagnet attract? Look at the next three pictures. How does each picture show how the electromagnet has been changed?

An electromagnet can be made stronger by adding more current to the circuit. How is this done in the circuit shown in the picture at the upper right? Look at the picture at the lower left. Adding another iron nail increases the strength of the electromagnet. Look at the last picture. Wrapping the wire around the iron nail many more times also makes an electromagnet stronger.

ACTIVITY

Experimenting with an electromagnet

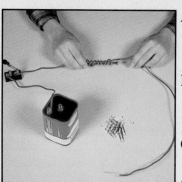

A. Obtain these materials: dry cell (1.5 volt), iron nail, paper clips, screwdriver, switch, 1 piece of wire 30 cm long, 1 piece of wire 60 cm long.

B. Attach the short wire from the dry cell to one side of the switch. Make sure the switch is open. Attach the long wire to the other side of the switch.

C. Wrap the long wire around the iron nail at least 20 times. Attach the end of the long wire to the dry cell.

D. Close the switch. Move the nail near the clips.
   1. Write down the results you observed.
   2. What will happen when you open the switch?

E. Open the switch.
   3. Write down the results you observed.
   4. Write a summary for this activity.

Section Review

Main Ideas: Current electricity can be used to make an electromagnet. The strength of an electromagnet can be increased by adding more current, more turns of wire, or more nails at the center of the electromagnet.

Questions: Answer in complete sentences.

1. What important relationship did Oersted discover?

2. Look at the photograph of the electromagnet on page 190. Why couldn't a very strong bar magnet or horseshoe magnet be used for this kind of job?

3. Why do iron filings form lines of force around a wire that is carrying current?

4. How would the strength of an electromagnet containing 20 turns of wire compare with the same kind of electromagnet with 10 turns of wire?

You have learned that electricity produces magnetism. Do you think the opposite is also true? Can magnetism be used to produce electricity? This question was on the mind of a 14-year-old boy who lived in London in 1805. His name was Michael Faraday. When you finish this section, you should be able to:

☐ **A.** Explain how magnetism can be used to produce electricity.
☐ **B.** Identify the parts of a modern machine that can be used to produce electricity from magnetism.

As a teenager, Michael Faraday had a job in a bookstore. In his spare time, he read all the science books on the shelves. As he read, he became more and more curious about electricity. Sometimes the books didn't have answers to the questions that came to his active mind. One day, he heard that a well-known scientist, Sir Humphry Davy, was going to give a speech nearby. Young Faraday went to hear the speech. He took notes on what Davy said. To show off a bit he sent Davy a copy of his notes. He hoped that the famous scientist would give him a job. Davy was very impressed with Faraday's notes. He told Faraday he could work as a helper.

Years later, Michael Faraday became more famous than Sir Humphry Davy. As a matter of fact, some scientists think that Davy's greatest discovery was Michael Faraday. In 1831, Faraday discovered that there was a way to produce electricity from magnetism.

In his experiment, Faraday used a coil of wire to make a **galvanometer** (gal-vuh-**nahm**-uh-ter). A *galvanometer* is an instrument that measures weak electric current. If current is present, the needle on the galvanometer moves. Faraday moved a magnet back and forth inside the coil of wire. When he did this, the needle on the galvanometer moved. That showed that current was present in the wire.

Galvanometer: An instrument that can measure a weak electric current.

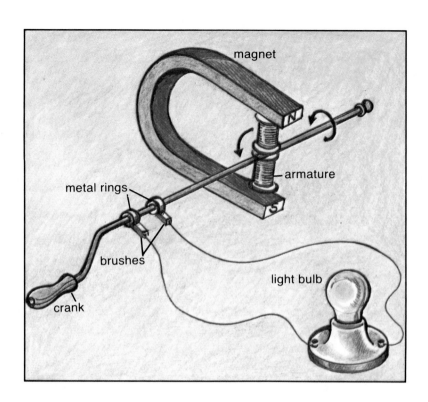

magnet

armature

metal rings

brushes

light bulb

crank

How is Faraday's discovery useful to us? Look at the drawing above. The drawing shows a **generator** (**jen**-uh-ray-ter). In a *generator*, current is produced with magnetism. A generator has four different parts. The first part is a coil of wire called an **armature** (**ahr**-muh-cher). It also has one or more horseshoe magnets, two metal rings, and metal brushes. The *armature* is found between the poles of the magnets. Find the crank in the drawing above. When the crank is turned, the armature moves between the poles of the magnet. In large generators, the magnet moves in and out of the armature. The metal rings are connected to the end of the coil. They collect the current produced in the armature. The brushes lead the current out of the generator. The generator shown in the drawing is a small one. It is cranked by hand. It produces enough current to light one bulb.

The large generators in power plants produce the current needed to light the thousands of lights that brighten

ACTIVITY

Making a galvanometer

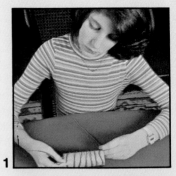

A. Obtain these materials: bar magnet, compass, cardboard roll, 2 pieces of wire 90 cm long.

B. Wrap 1 piece of wire around the cardboard roll, as shown in picture 1. Wrap the other piece of wire around the compass, as shown in picture 2. Make sure you can still see the compass needle. Leave about 30 cm of wire at each end.

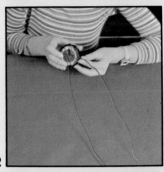

C. Attach the ends of the wires, as shown in picture 3. Then slide the cardboard roll out of the wrapped wire.

D. Move the bar magnet back and forth inside the coil of wire. As you move the magnet, look at the compass needle.

1. What did you observe?
2. What caused the effect you observed?

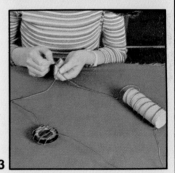

E. Hold the magnet still inside the coil of wire. Look at the compass needle.

3. What did you observe?
4. What explanation can you give for your observation?
5. Write a summary of the results of this activity.

cities like the one shown in the photograph. In these large generators, current is produced by huge magnets that whirl through thick coils of copper wire. In some generators the magnets stay still. The coils of wire are the moving parts.

Not all generators produce electricity for buildings. Some cars have their own generators. Some bicycles have a generator to turn on the headlight.

All generators need energy to turn their moving parts. You can't get current from a generator unless you use some other form of energy to make it move. For example, the generator on a bicycle gets its energy from the rider. The generator in a car gets its energy from the gasoline that powers the engine. The engine turns the moving parts of the generator.

Section Review

Main Ideas: Magnetism can produce current electricity. A generator is a device that uses magnetism to produce electricity.

Questions: Answer in complete sentences.

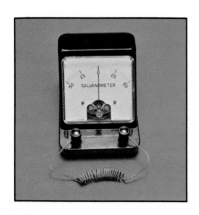

1. How can you produce current electricity in the wire shown in the picture at the left? How will you know if an electric current is present in the wire?
2. What are the four basic parts of a generator?
3. Describe the sequence of events that occur when a generator is producing electricity.
4. What is the source of energy for the generator that is shown on page 194?
5. What part of a generator is made of a coil of wire?

CHAPTER REVIEW

Science Words: Unscramble each of these words. Then write its definition.

1. SELOP
2. STENGAM
3. CETNAGMI LEIDF
4. MONTEERLAAGV
5. NAGMETCOTRELE

What word fits each of the blanks in the following sentences?

6. A _____ is a machine in which electricity is produced with magnetism.

7. An object that picks up or attracts iron, nickel, or cobalt is a _____.

8. A magnet has both _____ and _____ poles.

9. The _____ of _____ are lines around a magnet that show where the magnetic force is found.

10. The coil of wire in a generator is called the _____.

Questions: Answer in complete sentences.

1. Two students are experimenting with magnets. Each has a bar magnet with labeled north and south poles. They observe that there are two ways in which they can hold their magnets, so that the magnets repel. What are these ways? Explain your answer.

2. In question 1, how can you place the poles so they will attract each other? Explain your answer.

3. What is the difference between a bar magnet and an electro-magnet?

4. A student wishes to build an electromagnet. What equipment will the student need?

5. Make a labeled diagram of the electromagnet that could be built with the equipment you listed in question 4. List three ways to increase the strength of the electromagnet.

6. What is a galvanometer? What is it used for?

CHAPTER 10

USING ELECTRICITY

10-1.

Measuring Electricity

Have you boiled water lately? You know that you need plenty of heat to get the water to boil. This girl is boiling water. Do you see a flame? What kind of energy is making the water boil? When you finish this section, you should be able to:

☐ **A.** Identify four forms of energy into which electricity may be changed.

☐ **B.** Describe how the use of electricity is measured.

You have learned that electricity makes bulbs light. You have also learned that electricity can cause magnetism. The girl in the picture is using something that changes electric energy into heat energy. This oven is only one of many things that changes electricity into a more useful form of energy. Can you think of other things in your home that change electricity into other forms of energy?

Televisions, electric blankets, electric guitars, and even electric corn poppers are all energy changers. Are there any electrical energy changers in your classroom? What are they?

Your classroom contains light bulbs, which change electricity into light. Some classrooms have tape recorders, which change electricity into sound.

The picture below on the left shows an example of electrical energy changing into heat energy. Sometimes electricity produces so much heat that light is given off, too. This happens in a toaster. Current flowing through the wires in a toaster causes the wires to get hot. The hot wires glow. This shows that electrical energy can also change into light energy.

Mechanical energy: The energy of motion.

Electricity can produce motion. The energy of motion is called **mechanical** (muh-kan-ih-kul) **energy**. Electrical energy is changed to *mechanical energy* by motors. For example, the motor in an electric fan causes the blades of the fan to move. The motor changes electrical energy into the mechanical energy of the moving blades.

Sometimes electrical energy can change into several forms of energy at the same time. For example, when

ACTIVITY

Measuring kilowatt-hours

A. Obtain these materials: paper, pencil.

B. On your paper draw 2 groups of 4 boxes next to one another.

C. Look at the number on the electric meter in the first picture. Write the number in the first group of boxes.

D. The second picture was taken one month later. Write this number in the second group of boxes.

E. Subtract the number in the first group of boxes from the number in the second group of boxes.

　1. What is the remainder?

　2. How many kilowatt-hours were used in one month?

　3. If the cost for each kilowatt-hour is 10 cents, how much money will be owed?

your television set is on, what do you see? What do you hear? If you touch the back of the television set, what do you feel? In a television set, electrical energy changes into light, sound, and heat energy.

How much electricity does it take to use a toaster or run a fan? Electricity is measured in **watts**. Have you ever read the numbers on a light bulb? They tell you how many *watts* the bulb needs in order to light up. A bulb might use 100 watts. Other things in your home use much more. A larger unit is needed to measure that much electrical power. A **kilowatt** is equal to 1,000 watts. If something that uses a *kilowatt* of electricity is on for an hour, it uses a **kilowatt-hour** of electricity.

When electric current enters a building, it flows through an electric meter. The meter counts the number of *kilowatt-hours* used. The meter is usually read every month to find out how much electricity was used.

Watt: A unit that measures how much electricity is needed to run an electrical appliance.

Kilowatt-hour: A unit used to measure electricity use.

Account number: 432127128500013

For information call your representative: ANNA MATTHEWS at 212-473-6262

DEC 9

Previous balance

Service period From Month Day	To Month Day Year	Number of days	Service class	Meter readings Previous	Code	Present	Code	Meter multiplier	Usage Kwh. or 100 Cu. ft.	Current charges
10 7	11 983	33	EL1	3821	ACT	4170	ACT	1	349	5515
10 7	11 983	33	GS1	310	ACT	312	ACT	1	2	856

Service address: 82 WASHINGTON PLAC 3B

Demand in kilowatts

Sales tax included in bill: 245

Fuel and gas adjustments

	factor	amount
Electric	1.0790	377
Gas	1.4962	03

Payments received through this date have been credited to your account. NOV 08 1983

6371

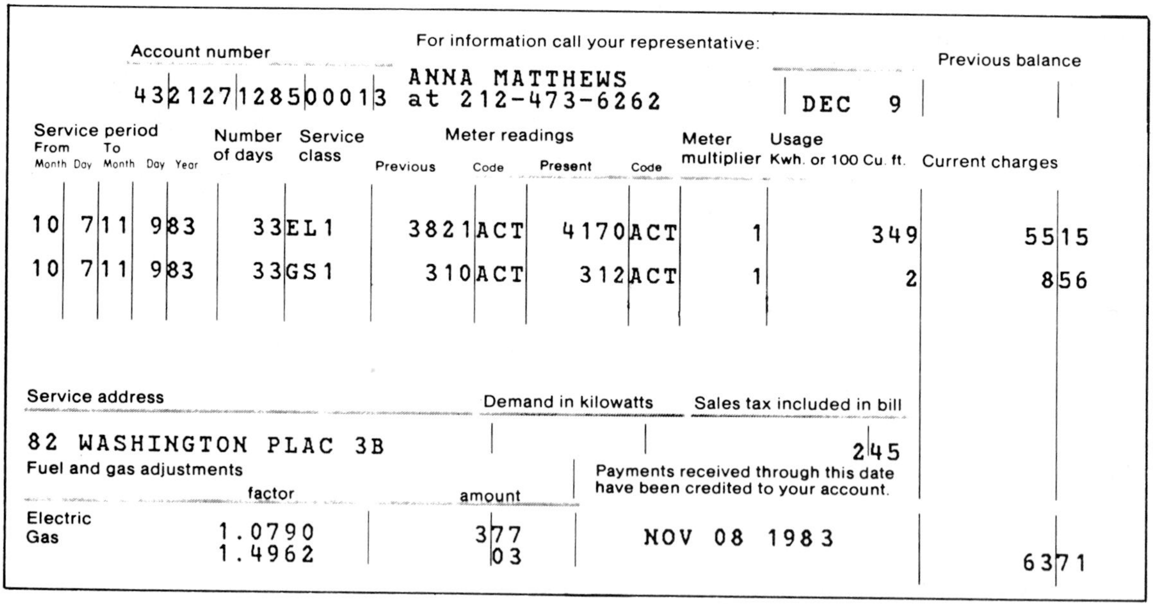

The picture shows a monthly bill for the use of electricity. The bill shows how many kilowatt-hours were used and the amount owed.

Section Review

Main Ideas: Electrical energy can be changed into many other forms of energy. The amount of electricity used depends on how much and how long we use it. Use of electricity is measured in kilowatt-hours.

Questions: Answer in complete sentences.

1. Electrical energy can be used to produce at least four other forms of energy. What are they?
2. Give an example of a device that will cause each energy change you listed in question 1.
3. Name three units that are used to measure how much electricity is being used. Explain what each unit measures.
4. How is the amount of electricity used by a building measured?

Producing Electricity

The students in the photograph below are visiting an energy fair. They are learning about the many ways in which energy can be produced. Do you know where the electricity in your home comes from? When you finish this section, you should be able to:

☐ **A.** Describe the events that take place when water power is used to produce electricity.

☐ **B.** Describe the events that take place when fuel is burned to produce electricity.

☐ **C.** Explain how nuclear energy is used to produce electricity.

For thousands of years people have used falling water as a source of energy. Falling water was used to turn large water wheels. The first water wheels made were used at grain mills. Their power turned the millstones that ground the wheat into flour. Today, falling water is used to turn water wheels called **turbines** (**ter**-bynz). *Turbines* are used to turn parts of large generators in power plants.

Turbines: Wheels that are used at electrical power plants.

This simplified schematic diagram shows the major steps required to produce oil from coal. First, coal is crushed and mixed with a solvent. Hydrogen is added to this slurry which is heated. Then the solid coal dissolves. Liquid fuels and gases produced are separated from the mixture.

When the Apollo astronauts raced to the moon, a new kind of small electrical generator provided the energy for li... and power inside their sp... craft. Fuel cells produced electricity from hydrogen... oxygen. Water, created as... ...oduct, was drunk by... ...uts.

...on Edison is installing... ...scale version of those... ...uel cells to help pro-... ...gy for New Yorkers... ...River Generating... ...anhattan, a 4.8... ...el cell power... ...generating... ...w York on... If this t... ...cell plar... ...useful w... ...ity for Ne... ...st is spon... ...overnmer... ...acturer an... ...s and resea... ...at organizat...

In operation, fuel cells are ...er and quieter than con-... ...al coal or oil-fired ge... plants. And they are ...even in smaller sizes. ...an be located near the ...ers they are intended to ...possibly deferring the ...for new transmission

...plants are now about ...t as the best steam-... ...erating plants. ...his efficient oper-... ...lls will allow us ...e use of precious ...rrived fuels. In the ...alls can be sup-... ...an fuels from coal.

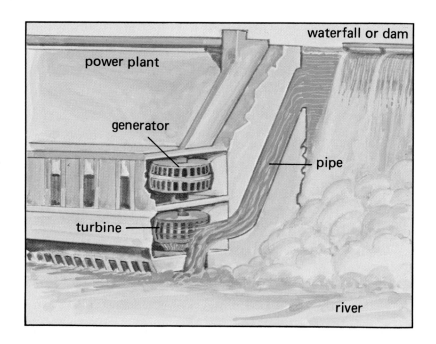

Many power plants are built near waterfalls or dams. Some of the water goes over the waterfall and down the river. Some of the water is directed into large pipes. The water moves down through the pipes to turbines in the power plant. The falling water makes the turbines spin.

A rod connected to the turbine turns. The other end of the rod connects to the magnets or coils of wire in the generator. The turning rod makes the coils or magnets turn. As a result, current electricity is produced in the generator.

A power plant that uses falling water for an energy source is called a **hydroelectric** (hy-droh-ih-**lek**-trik) plant. *Hydro* means *water*. The photograph on page 204 shows a *hydroelectric* plant at Niagara Falls, Canada.

Energy to turn turbines can also come from burning **fuel** (**fyoo**-el). *Fuel* is anything that can be burned to produce heat. Oil, gas, and coal are fuels. The heat from the burning fuel is used to change water into steam. The steam provides the energy needed to turn parts of the generator. Look at the drawing below. The water heated in the boiler changes into steam. The steam causes blades on the steam turbine to spin. The spinning blades

Hydroelectric plant: A power plant at which falling water is the energy source.

Fuel: Anything that can be burned to produce heat.

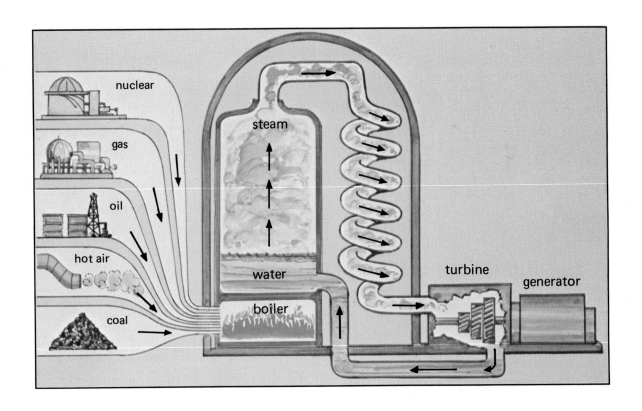

Nuclear reaction: A reaction that occurs when tiny particles of matter are split apart.

Transmission lines: Power lines that carry electricity from its source to where it is used.

turn a rod that connects to the generator. As a result, current is produced.

Scientists have found that a great amount of heat is produced in a **nuclear reaction** (**nyoo**-klee-er ree-ak-shun). A *nuclear reaction* takes place when tiny particles of matter are split apart. The heat from the reaction can be used to change water into steam. The steam can then turn turbines to produce electricity. Only a small amount of fuel is needed to produce a lot of energy in a nuclear plant. But nuclear power has problems, as we will see in the next section.

After electricity is produced in a power plant, what happens? The electricity is sent to places where people can use it. The electricity travels through powerful **transmission lines**. Through *transmission lines*, electricity moves from its source to cities and towns. It finally reaches homes.

Section Review

Main Ideas: Turbines are used at power plants to turn parts of large electromagnets. Falling water, fuels, and a nuclear reaction can supply the energy needed to turn turbines.

Questions: Answer in complete sentences.

1. Explain the steps that take place when water power is changed into electricity. Use the diagram on page 204.
2. What are the steps that occur when a fuel is burned to produce electricity?
3. In a nuclear power plant, what provides the heat energy needed to change water into steam?
4. Is this statement true or false? Turbines push water through electric generators. Explain your answer.
5. How does electricity get to your home or school?

Both students are mixing batter for pancakes. Compare the two methods. Which student will be finished first? Which pancakes will have a higher electricity cost? How might that electricity use be harming the environment? When you finish this section, you should be able to:

☐ **A.** Identify some of our *natural resources* and explain how they can be *conserved*.

☐ **B.** Identify some of the harmful effects that power plants have on our environment.

☐ **C.** Describe a way in which electrical energy can come directly from the sun.

The student using the electric mixer will probably be done first. That electric mixer is using electric energy that was produced at a power plant. Do power plants cause harm to the environment?

Fuels are burned for energy in many power plants. Oil, gas, and coal are often the fuels used. Oil, gas and coal are **natural resources**. A *natural resource* is something found in nature that is useful. The supplies of these natural resources are limited. We must make these supplies last. Being careful about our use of natural resources is called **conservation** (kahn-ser-**vay**-shun). A way to practice *conservation* is by using less electricity.

Natural resource: Something useful found in nature.

Conservation: Careful use of a natural resource.

Do you turn off the lights when you are the last person to leave a room? Does a television remain on when no one in the house is watching? When everyone uses just a little less electricity, a great amount of energy is saved. Using less electricity conserves the supplies of natural resources.

People concerned with conservation are also concerned about the environment. Burning fuels to produce electricity can cause **pollution** (poh-**loo**-shun). *Pollution* is the adding of harmful materials to the environment. For example, burning coal or oil releases materials such as **sulfur oxides** (**sul**-fer **ahk**-sides) into the air. *Sulfur oxides* can cause respiratory diseases in humans.

Nuclear energy does not pollute the air with sulfur oxides and smoke. However, it can harm the environment in other ways. Nuclear reactions produce harmful wastes. These wastes are stored at power plants. Many

Pollution: The adding of harmful materials to the environment.

Sulfur oxides: Materials released when coal or oil are burned.

ACTIVITY

What are some other sources of energy?

A. Obtain these materials: poster paper, marking pens, newspaper articles.

B. Use your imagination to invent a source of energy that could power electric generators. Make sure it does not depend on burning fuel, water power, or nuclear power as an energy source. Make a labeled drawing of your invention.

1. What is your energy source?
2. What are its advantages? What are its disadvantages?

C. Collect local newspaper articles on the topic of energy.

3. What energy sources are used in your area now?
4. What energy sources might be used in the future?

people are concerned that these wastes could enter the air or water if something happened at the power plant. Nuclear wastes can harm and even kill plants and animals. The effects of these wastes lasts for many years.

Sometimes nuclear plants pollute rivers by heating them. Such plants need a large water supply to cool off the reactors that produce the power. Cool water is removed from the river. It is pumped over the hot equipment to cool it down. The water is allowed to cool down a little. Then it is pumped back into the river.

The temperature of the river goes up. Just a small increase in the water's temperature may affect the growth of the plants and animals that live there.

Is there a way to produce electricity that does not harm the environment? There are several ways that are being developed by scientists. One is to use **solar cells**. *Solar cells* produce electricity directly from sunlight. *Solar* means coming from the sun. Solar cells are made of a material called **silicon** (**sil**-ih-kahn). *Silicon* is found in many places.

Silicon is mixed with small amounts of metals. Then it is cut into thin slices. These slices are the solar cells. When sunlight hits the solar cells, electricity is produced. One solar cell, shown on the right, produces the energy needed to move a small cart. When hundreds of solar cells are hooked up together, large amounts of electricity can be made. But solar cells are more expensive than other forms of electricity.

Solar cell: A piece of silicon that can produce energy from sunlight.

Silicon: A common material found in the earth.

209

Each year people find ways to produce solar cells more cheaply. It may not be long before many homes and schools will have rows of solar cells on their roofs like the ones shown. Each building would produce its own electricity. Best of all, the source of the energy would be free, and it would not cause any pollution.

Section Review

Main Ideas: By limiting our use of electricity, we can conserve our natural resources. The burning of some natural resources to produce electricity can cause pollution. Nuclear energy can produce harmful wastes. Other sources of energy such as solar cells do not pollute.

Questions: Answer in complete sentences.

1. What is a natural resource? Name two.
2. How can you conserve electrical energy?
3. How does burning fuel for electricity harm the environment?
4. What is an advantage of using nuclear energy? What are two problems it causes?
5. Name something that can be used to change sunlight to electricity. What are its benefits?

What's small enough to go through a needle's eye, but large enough to remember your name, birthday, and lots of other things? The answer is simple. A *chip* can do these things and more. Chips are found in all sorts of things. They are in watches, computers, and calculators. When you finish this section, you should be able to:

Electricity in the Computer Age

☐ **A.** Describe what a *chip* is.
☐ **B.** List the main parts of a *computer*.
☐ **C.** Describe several ways in which computers are used.

Chips are very small electric circuits. Chips are made of silicon. That's the same material solar cells are made of. If you looked at a chip under a microscope it would look like the picture on the right. The chip would look like a street map of a large city scratched onto a tiny square. The lines on a chip show different paths that electricity can take. Because chips are small, electricity can take many paths in a small space. This also means that chips can do many jobs.

There are chips that have special jobs. Certain chips have the ability to store information. These are called memory chips. Memory chips remember a certain pattern of electricity that passes through them. The pattern

Chip: A small electric circuit.

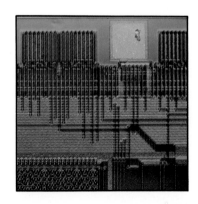

211

is like a language to the chip. Other chips act like calculators. They can do arithmetic problems in seconds. Electricity flows through their circuits to come up with the right answer.

Computer: A device that stores and handles information.

Chips are very important in **computers**. *Computers* are devices that store and handle information. They do this very quickly. Computers take only as much time to work as it takes for electricity to go through the circuits.

Computers can be big or small. Size depends on how much information they store. All kinds of things can be stored in a computer. A computer might store all the names and birthdays of the students in your school. Another computer might store the names of bicycle parts made at a plant. It would also store how many of each type were made each day.

212

Computers store large amounts of information on **disks.** *Disks* are made of either metal or plastic and coated with a material that has magnetic properties. The pattern of magnetism stores the information.

How can people get information from a computer? They must ask the computer for it. But they must ask in the computer's language. Sometimes this means typing a message on the computer's keyboard. The keyboard looks like a typewriter.

The keyboard is used to **input** information. You must put something into the computer to get results. If the right question is typed in, the question goes to the computer's "brain." The "brain" is its **central processing unit,** or **CPU.** The *CPU* then sends an electric message to the correct memory circuit and receives an answer.

The answer from a computer is often on a display screen. The screen is like a TV screen. A computer's answers are called **output.** The diagram shows the steps it takes to get an answer from a computer. Trace each step.

Disk: Magnetic device that stores information in a computer.

Input: The information that goes into a computer.

Central processing unit (CPU): The "brain" of a computer.

Output: The information that comes out of a computer.

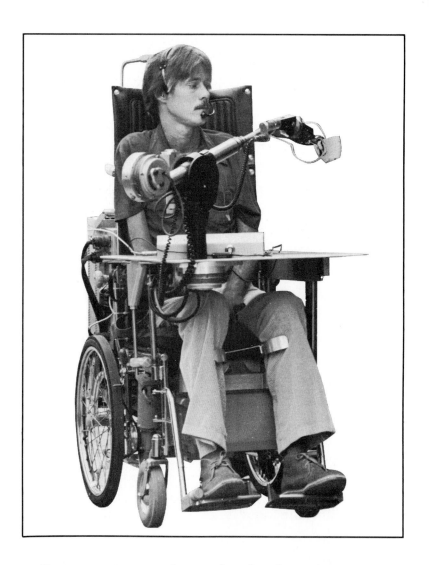

Every computer is directed to do jobs a certain way. A
computer program is a series of directions for the computer to follow. A computer can be programed to send a
rocket into space. Another computer may be programed to warm a house. A computer was built into the
wheelchair shown above. It has a program that listens to
this man's voice. When it "hears" words such as "up" or
"down," it moves the wheelchair or the cup.

The ways to use computers are almost endless. In
schools they can help students learn on their own. Special language computers can "hear" whether or not a student says a word correctly.

Doctors can use computers to find out why a person is ill. Newspapers and books are written and printed with the help of computers. Computers often print their results on a *printout*. This is another kind of computer output, as shown below.

At home, people store important information in personal computers. Personal computers can help people plan ways to use their money and time wisely.

Section Review

Main Ideas: Silicon chips are very small electric circuits used in computers to store information and do calculations. The main parts of a computer are the input, central processing unit, memory, and output. Different computers are programed for many different jobs.

Questions: Answer in complete sentences.

1. What is a silicon chip? What is its greatest advantage?
2. What is a computer?
3. Describe how you can get information from a computer. Use these terms in your answer: input, CPU, memory circuit, output.
4. Give three examples of how people can use computers at school or at home.

CHAPTER REVIEW

Science Words: Select the definition in column B that best fits each word in column A.

Column A	Column B
1. Fuel	**A.** Useful thing found in nature.
2. Nuclear reaction	**B.** Produces heat when burned.
3. Computer	**C.** Power plant in which falling water is the energy source.
4. Turbines	
5. Kilowatt-hour	**D.** Changes sunlight to electricity.
6. Mechanical energy	**E.** Reaction that occurs when particles of matter are split.
7. Chip	
8. Hydroelectric plant	**F.** A device that stores and handles information.
9. Natural resource	
10. Solar cell	**G.** Wheels used at power plants.
	H. Unit of electricity use.
	I. The energy of motion.
	J. A small electric circuit.

Questions: Answer in complete sentences.

1. Is it possible for something to change electrical energy into other forms of energy? Explain your answer with examples.
2. All these events occur in an electrical plant that burns fuel: **a.** Turbines spin. **b.** Fuel is burned. **c.** Electricity is produced. Use these events in their correct order to explain how a power plant produces electricity.
3. What is the main problem with the electrical plants described in question 2?
4. Compare a nuclear power plant with a hydroelectric plant. How are they alike? How are they different? What are the benefits and problems of each?
5. What are solar cells? What is their source of energy?
6. What are chips? How are they useful in our lives?

Making circuit puzzles

A. Obtain these materials: 1 rubber band, 2 D batteries, 3 pieces of bell wire (bare at each end) 20 cm long, 2 flashlight bulbs, 2 sockets.

B. Think of a way to light 1 bulb, using only the following: 1 battery, 2 wires, 1 bulb.

  1. Draw a labeled diagram of your hypothesis. What path will the electrons follow?

C. Check your hypothesis. Make the circuit.

  2. What were your results?

D. Think of a way to light 1 bulb, using only the following: 1 battery, 1 bulb, 1 wire.

  3. Draw a labeled diagram of your hypothesis. What path will the electrons follow?

E. Check your hypothesis. Make the circuit.

  4. What were your results?

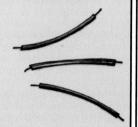

F. Light 2 bulbs, using 2 batteries, 2 bulbs, 2 sockets, 3 pieces of wire, 1 rubber band.

  5. Draw a labeled diagram of the circuit.

G. Predict which of the 5 circuits shown will work. Make the circuits as shown.

  6. Compare your predictions and results.

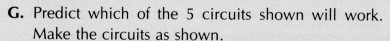

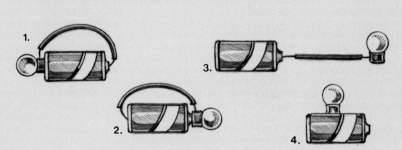

Electrical Engineer ▶

Designing circuits no larger than your fingernail is one of the jobs of an **electrical engineer.** The *engineer* decides what kinds of circuits are needed to perform tasks and run machines. Circuits are used in computers, calculators, digital watches, and video games. Electrical engineers attend a college or university. There they study electricity, magnetism, and mathematics.

◀ Electrician

People want to be able to use their toasters without having to shut off their lights. It is **electricians** who carefully design circuits for buildings. They also install wiring, fuses or circuit breakers, and electrical sockets. *Electricians* must know about building houses so that they install wires in their proper places. Electricians usually learn their trade by working with other electricians or by going to a trade school.

219

LIVING ORGANISMS

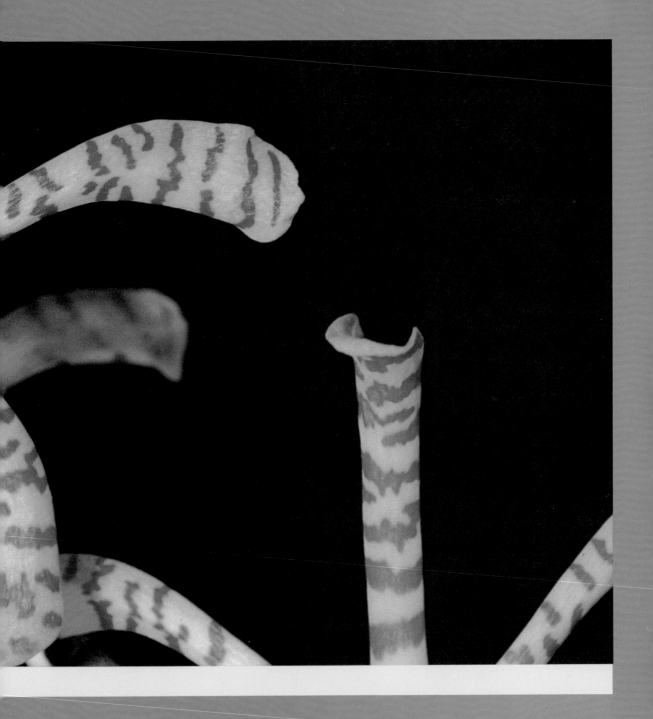

UNIT 5

CHAPTER 11

CELLS AND SIMPLE ORGANISMS

11-1.

Classifying Living Things

A frog jumps into the pond. The children listen. Insects buzz in the tall weeds. The dogs run through the grass. Frogs, children, weeds, and dogs are all alive. How else are some of these living things alike? When you finish this section, you should be able to:

- [ ] **A.** Describe three ways in which all living things are alike.
- [ ] **B.** Describe how scientists *classify* living things into groups.
- [ ] **C.** Explain why *classifying* things into different groups is useful.

Living things come in many sizes and shapes. They are almost everywhere on earth. Some fly high in the air; some live on the ground. Some even make their homes under the ground.

Living things also swim in the sea, crawl on the sea floor, and burrow beneath it. The smallest living things can only be seen with powerful microscopes. The largest living animal is the blue whale. It is about 35 meters (115 feet) long. In fact, the blue whale is larger than any other animal that ever lived, including the dinosaur. But the blue whale is not the largest living thing. That record belongs to the giant redwood tree. Redwoods grow as tall as 100 meters (330 feet).

All living things, from the smallest to the largest, share three **characteristics** (kar-ik-ter-**is**-tiks). A *characteristic* helps set things apart from others. These three characteristics set living things apart from things that are not alive. All living things need food. All grow and change. All come from the same kind of living things. Think of any living thing. Does a dog have each of these characteristics? Do you have them?

Living things show many differences, too. A kitten has fur and four legs. A snake has scales. A bird has feathers and wings. A grasshopper has a hard outer covering. We can use these different **structures** (**struk**-cherz) to help us sort out other kinds of living things. For example, pine trees and oak trees have thick, woody trunks and many branches. These *structures* are characteristics of trees. Pines and oaks belong to a group of living things called trees.

Characteristic: Something that helps set one thing apart from another.

Structure: Part of a living thing, such as a wing, leg, or leaf.

223

ACTIVITY

Classifying living things

A. Obtain these materials: paper and pencil.

B. Look at all the living things in the picture. List the ones that have wings. Make another list of the things that do not have wings.

    1. Is this a good way to group things? Why or why not?

C. Group just the animals in the picture according to their structures. Copy the chart below and use it to help you organize the animals. One animal has been done for you.

Wings	Covering	Number of Legs	Kind of Animal
yes	feathers	2	gull

    2. Which animals on your chart would scientists probably group together?

D. Compare your chart with your lists of the living things in the picture that fly and that do not fly.

    3. What living things in the picture do not show up on your chart?

    4. Are they part of another group of living things? Can you name the group?

    5. How are these living things alike?

    6. How are the living things from question 4 different from the ones on your chart? Write a short paragraph describing these differences.

But pines and oaks are also different in some ways. The leaves of the oak are broad and flat. The leaves of the pine are long and needle-shaped. Pines keep their leaves all year round. Oaks lose theirs in the fall. So pines belong to a different group of trees than oaks. Which of the photographs on the right shows an oak?

We sort things into groups according to ways they are alike and ways they are different. Sorting things into groups is called **classification** (klas-ih-fih-**kay**-shun). We use *classification* every day to make looking for things easier for us. The books in a library are classified by likes and differences. But you have to be careful to pick useful likes and differences. Suppose books were classified according to the colors of their covers. Would that be helpful if you were looking for a book on a certain subject?

There are many kinds of living things, or **organisms**. It would be impossible to study all these *organisms* without classifying them. It would be like trying to find a certain book in a pile of millions of books. With classifications, we can study one group at a time. We can also compare different groups.

Classification: A way of sorting things into groups according to ways they are alike and ways they are different.

Organism: A living thing.

Section Review

Main Ideas: All living things share three characteristics. These set them apart from things that are not alive. Living things with similar structures are classified into groups. Classification helps us compare living things.

Questions: Answer in complete sentences.

1. Name three characteristics that all living things have.
2. In what ways are pine trees and oak trees alike? In what ways are they different?
3. Which of the following are grouped with gulls? **a.** robins **b.** grasshoppers **c.** catfish **d.** eagles **e.** chickadees **f.** wasps. Give a reason for each answer.
4. Why do you think scientists classify living things?

11-2.

Building Blocks of Life

What are living things made of? A house may be built of bricks, stone, or wood. Living things are built of tiny "building blocks." Your body is made up of trillions of these building blocks. What are they? When you finish this section, you should be able to:

☐ **A.** Describe four parts of a living *cell* and the job each part does.
☐ **B.** Identify what a *cell* does by its shape.
☐ **C.** Compare and contrast plant and animal *cells*.

The building blocks of living things were discovered by an English scientist, Robert Hooke, over 300 years ago. He was looking at thin slices of cork under a microscope. Cork is made from the outer bark of an oak tree that grows in the Mediterranean area. Under Hooke's microscope, the cork showed a regular pattern of tiny, boxlike, open spaces. The pattern reminded him of tiny rooms. The Latin word for room is *cella*. He named the boxlike structures **cells** (**selz**).

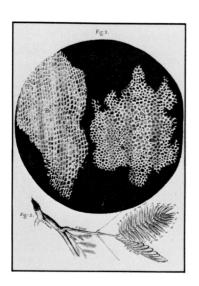

Cells: Tiny living parts, of which all organisms are made.

All the activities of life take place in each *cell*. Every cell in your body is a living building block. Each cell takes in food and gets rid of wastes. Each cell needs oxygen. This is true of all plant and animal cells.

Food, water, and oxygen pass into the cell through the cell **membrane** (**mem**-brain). Wastes pass out of the cell through the cell *membrane*.

Membrane: The thin skinlike covering of a cell.

226

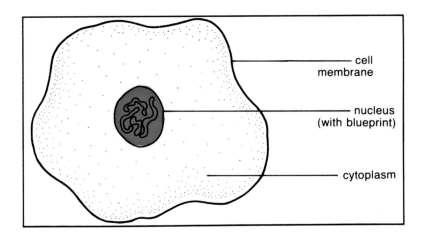

cell membrane

nucleus (with blueprint)

cytoplasm

Near the center of each cell is the **nucleus** (**noo**-klee-us). Packed tightly within the *nucleus* is a kind of chemical blueprint. A blueprint is a printed plan that people follow when they build something. Under a microscope, a nucleus looks like a tangled mass of string.

This blueprint controls most of the cell's activities. It controls what material the cell makes. It controls how the cell grows and what it does. When a cell splits into two new cells, the nucleus splits, too. A new copy of the blueprint forms. Now each new cell has a nucleus and an exact copy of the original blueprint.

A jellylike liquid surrounds the nucleus. This liquid fills up the rest of the cell. This is the **cytoplasm** (**sy**-toh-plaz-um). The *cytoplasm* is where the food, water, and oxygen taken in by the cell are used.

There are many kinds of cells in the human body. Think of all the cells in a girl's body that are working when she is running. Heart muscle cells are working to pump blood faster to her leg muscles. Red blood cells are bringing extra oxygen to the cells in her leg muscles. Messages from her brain are traveling through her nerve cells. These messages are going to her muscles to help control muscle movements.

Running smoothly and keeping your balance is a harder job than it looks. To do these things, it takes trillions of body cells working together as a team.

Nucleus: The part of the cell that controls its activities.

Cytoplasm: The liquid inside the cell where the cell's activities take place.

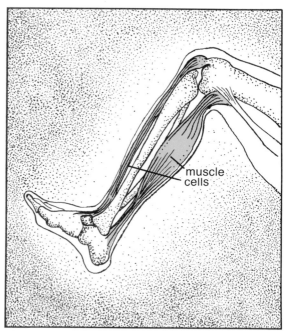

muscle cells

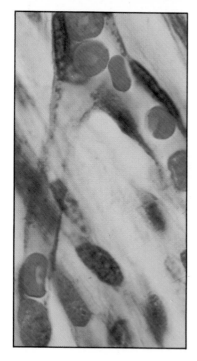

Chlorophyll: Green material in plants' cells that helps them make their own food.

Look at the drawing of the muscle cells that move the girl's leg. Muscle cells are long. When a muscle cell is doing its work, it pulls together and gets shorter. It is much like what happens when you stretch a rubber band and then let it snap back again. Why do you think muscle cells are long? Does it help them work better?

Red blood cells are smaller than most body cells. They are shaped like tiny round coins. Red blood cells carry oxygen all over the body. They must pass through very small blood vessels, not much bigger than the red blood cells themselves. Does their shape fit their job?

Plant cells have special shapes and special jobs, too. Root cells at the tip of a plant's roots are long and slender. Root cells grow rapidly, spreading through the ground.

Cells inside the trunk of a tree form long tubes. Through these tubes, food and water travel up from the roots to the branches and leaves.

Green leaves have special cells that contain **chlorophyll (klor-uh-fil)**. *Chlorophyll* is a green material that takes energy from sunlight. Leaf cells use that energy to make their own food.

228

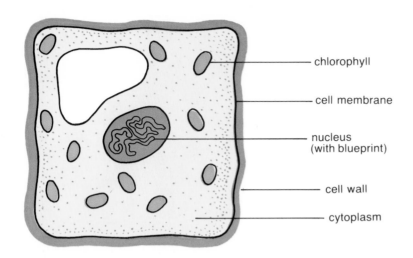

chlorophyll

cell membrane

nucleus
(with blueprint)

cell wall

cytoplasm

Chlorophyll is one thing that makes plant cells different from animal cells. Another is the **cell wall**. The *cell wall* is a sturdy, woody layer around the cell membrane of plant cells. What Robert Hooke actually saw through his microscope were the cell walls of the cork, or bark, of an oak tree. The insides of the cells had dried out.

Cell wall: A stiff protective layer around plant cells.

Section Review

Main Ideas: Cells are the building blocks of all animals and plants. Cells do many different jobs and have different shapes. All plant and animal cells need food, water, and oxygen. Plant cells have chlorophyll and cell walls, which animal cells do not have.

Questions: Answer in complete sentences.

1. Name three parts that every cell has. Explain what each part does.
2. Name two different kinds of cells in your body. Describe how each is shaped. How does its shape help it do its job?
3. Trees are tall and heavy. What structures in their cells might be useful for carrying this weight?
4. Name two things found in plant cells, but not in animal cells.

11-3.

The Simplest Organisms

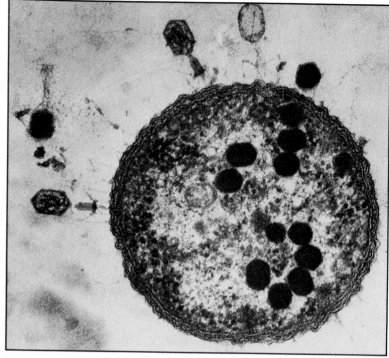

What does the picture show? Are these strange crystals or creatures from another world? Look out. Creatures like these may already be in your town. When you finish this section, you should be able to:

- ☐ **A.** Describe how *viruses* are like both living and nonliving things.
- ☐ **B.** Explain how *protists* are like both plants and animals.
- ☐ **C.** Explain how *bacteria* are classified.

The picture shows tiny structures that are shaped like crystals. They are attacking a living organism made of only one cell.

Each crystal is a **virus** (vy-ris). *Viruses* are real scientific puzzles. Viruses are very small. The period at the end of this sentence could hold about 50,000 viruses. Many hundreds of viruses could fit inside a single cell.

You have learned that the nucleus holds a kind of blueprint for running a cell. Most viruses are nothing more than a similar blueprint wrapped in a protective layer.

Viruses: Particles much simpler than cells. Viruses can only reproduce inside living cells.

Virus blueprints are very different from the blueprints inside living cells. They are a master plan for just one thing: making more viruses. The new viruses will be like the ones from which the blueprints came.

This can only happen inside a living cell that a virus attacks. The virus injects its own blueprint into the living cell. The virus blueprint blocks the cell's own blueprint from working. Instead, the virus blueprint runs the cell. The cell begins making new viruses.

The cell keeps making viruses until its store of food and energy is used up. Then the cell dies. Its membrane bursts. Hundreds of viruses spill out. They can attack other cells. The diagram below shows this process.

Viruses cause many diseases in humans. Some diseases caused by viruses are smallpox, colds, polio, and flu. Smallpox and polio are very rare these days. Special medicines help the body fight these viruses.

Are viruses alive? Scientists don't agree on that. *Sometimes* might be a good answer. Viruses show signs of life only when they are inside cells. A virus is not a cell. It does not feed, grow, or breathe. It has none of the parts of a cell, except a blueprint.

Most scientists think viruses are on the borderline between living and nonliving things. By studying them, scientists are sharpening their ideas about what life is.

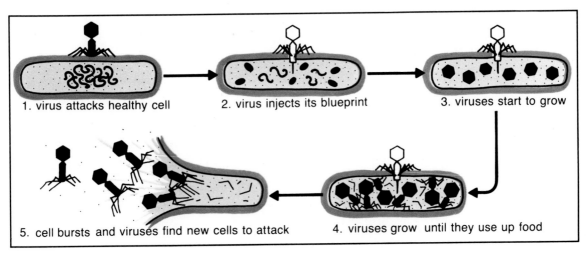

1. virus attacks healthy cell   2. virus injects its blueprint   3. viruses start to grow

5. cell bursts and viruses find new cells to attack   4. viruses grow until they use up food

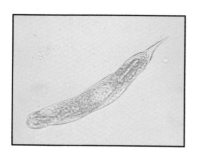

Euglena: A one-celled organism that is like both an animal and a plant.

Protists: A group of living things that are not animals or plants, but have some characteristics of each.

Ameba: A one-celled animal-like protist with no regular shape.

Paramecium: An animal-like protist shaped like a slipper.

This picture shows another scientific puzzle. It's a **euglena** (yoo-**glee**-nuh). The *euglena* is a one-celled organism. Until recently, scientists classified all living things as plants or animals. What is a euglena?

The euglena swims through the water. So it could be an animal. But the euglena also has chlorophyll. Only plants have chlorophyll. So the euglena could be a plant.

Scientists argued about this. Then they realized that the old animal-plant classification system did not work for living things such as the euglena. Scientists made a new classification of living things called **protists** (**pro**-tists). So scientists now classify living things into several groups. The three main groups are animals, plants, and *protists*.

Protists are usually very small. They may look like animals or like plants. One example of an animal-like protist is the **ameba** (uh-**mee**-buh). *Ameba* comes from the Greek word that means *change*. As the picture on the left shows, amebas can be almost any shape!

The **paramecium** (par-uh-**mee**-see-um) is another animallike protist. *Paramecium* comes from the Greek word for *oblong*. A paramecium is shaped like a slipper. Both the ameba and paramecium live in water.

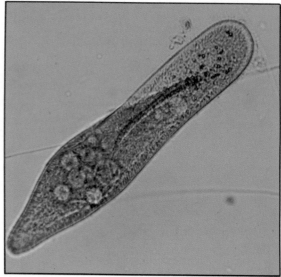

ACTIVITY

Observing protists

A. Obtain these materials: large jar of freshly collected pond water, cover slips, glass slides, eyedropper, lamp, microscope, pencil, drawing paper.

B. Put a drop of water on a slide. Cover the slide with a cover slip.

C. Put the jar aside for a couple of hours in a cool, dark place. Set a high-intensity lamp next to it so that the strongest light hits the water near the top.

D. Put the slide on the microscope. Turn the microscope barrel down until it nearly touches the slide. Look through the microscope. Raise the knob slowly until you can see the water clearly. You may have to focus up and down slightly to see different organisms.

1. How many kinds of protists can you see? Look carefully. Paramecia dart quickly in a spiral path. Amebas are harder to see because they are nearly colorless. Changing the light will help you see some organisms better.

2. Draw the protists that you can see. Don't try to make the drawing look like a drawing in a book. Label any parts of cells that you can see.

E. Use an eyedropper to take one drop of water from the brightly lit part of the jar and one from the dimly lit part. Put one drop on each of the two slides. Label one D for dim, and the other L for light.

F. Look at the dark slide under the microscope.

3. Do you see any organisms?

G. Repeat the observation with the light slide.

4. Did you see more or fewer organisms on the light slide?

5. Write down what you have learned from this activity.

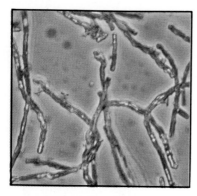
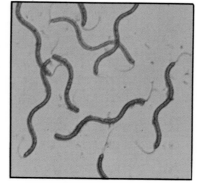
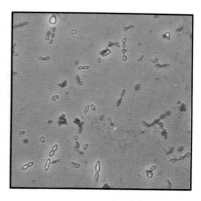

Bacteria: The smallest one-celled organisms that are clearly alive.

Another group of very small protists are the **bacteria** (bak-**teer**-ee-uh). *Bacteria* have a simple cell structure. It takes over 100 million bacteria to cover a penny. Bacteria are classified according to their shapes. Some are shaped like **rods**. Some are **spiral**. Some are **round**.

Some bacteria cause disease. Most do not. Many are necessary to life on earth. They help break down the remains of dead plants and animals. This returns materials that are needed for plant growth to the soil.

Section Review

Main Ideas: Viruses are on the borderline between living and nonliving things. Protists are a group of living things that are not considered plants or animals. Bacteria are classified by their shapes.

Questions: Answer in complete sentences.

1. What are the three main groups of living things?
2. In what way are viruses like living things? In what way are viruses different from living things?
3. How is euglena like a plant? How is it like an animal?
4. How are bacteria classified?
5. Scientists have changed the classifications of some organisms. Do you think they might change them again in the future? Why or why not?
6. Name three protists you could find in pond water.

Have you ever picked up seaweed from an ocean beach? It feels tough and rubbery. Seaweed contains a jellylike material. This material is often added to candies and jellies to keep them from being too watery. When you finish this section you should be able to:

☐ **A.** Compare and contrast *algae* and *fungi*.
☐ **B.** List two ways that *algae* are important.
☐ **C.** Give examples of both useful and harmful *fungi*.

Seaweeds are called the "grasses of the sea." But seaweeds are simpler plants than grasses. Seaweeds do not have stems, roots, or leaves. They are **algae** (al-jee). *Algae* are plantlike protists that have chlorophyll. Most algae grow in water. Seaweed grows in the ocean and supplies food for many organisms in the sea. Some people eat seaweed for food. Other people use material from seaweed to thicken foods like jellies. The largest kind of seaweed is **kelp** shown on the lower right. *Kelp* grows about 35 m (115 ft) long.

Other kinds of algae grow in fresh water such as ponds. One kind is **spirogyra** (spy-roh-**jy**-ruh), shown below. Each strand of *spirogyra* is one cell thick. The chlorophyll you see inside each strand gives spirogyra its name which means a "turning spiral."

Algae: Plantlike protists that have chlorophyll and grow in water.

Kelp: The largest kind of seaweed.

Spirogyra: A freshwater alga one cell wide and many cells long.

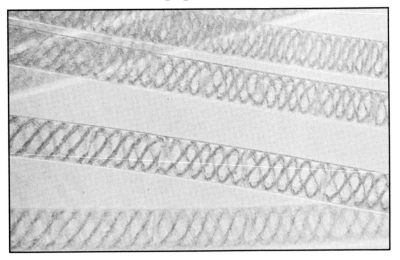

Fungi: Plantlike protists that cannot make their own food.

Other plantlike protists are the **fungi** (**fun**-jy). Like algae, *fungi* do not have roots, stems, or leaves. Unlike algae, fungi do not have chlorophyll. Without chlorophyll they cannot make their own food.

Fungi live in or on other organisms. Some fungi grow on living organisms. Others grow on dead ones. The photographs show some different kinds of fungi.

Like some bacteria, fungi break down animal and plant matter. This helps return useful chemicals to the soil.

Molds are fungi. Some molds are harmful. Have you ever had athlete's foot? It is caused by a fungus growing on the skin of the feet. Do you think that fungus is more likely to grow on dry skin or on wet skin? Another kind of mold spoils bread. Common bread mold is shown in the photograph above.

Some molds are useful. Certain molds are used to make some kinds of cheeses like the one shown. A similar mold that grows on fruits is used to make the medicine we know as penicillin. The penicillin mold makes penicillin to protect itself from bacteria. We use it as a medicine to cure diseases caused by bacteria.

Section Review

Main Ideas: Algae are plantlike protists with chlorophyll. Most of them live in water. Fungi are plantlike protists without chlorophyll. Fungi usually live on dead or living organisms.

Questions: Answer in complete sentences.

1. How are algae like other green plants?
2. What common features of green plants do algae lack?
3. How are algae useful to us?
4. Are fungi helpful or harmful? Explain.

CHAPTER REVIEW

Science Words
Unscramble the letters to find the terms that fit the definitions.

1. Cell liquid: CLAPSMTYO
2. Organisms that are not plants or animals: TIPORTSS
3. Particles that only show signs of life inside a live cell: UVRIESS
4. Thin layer covering a cell: MBMRANEE
5. Plantlike protists with chlorophyll: GAAEL
6. Control center of a cell: CUSENUL
7. A type of protist: ANUGLEE
8. Helps green plants to make food: YLLCHPHLROO
9. Smallest living one-celled organisms: TERIABAC
10. Plantlike protists without chlorophyll: GINUF

Questions: Answer in complete sentences.

1. List four ways that a cat and a euglena are alike.
2. Could classification be useful to other people besides scientists? Explain.
3. Are words in a dictionary classified? Tell how they are classified. Why do you think that words in a dictionary should be classified?
4. Are plant cells and animal cells exactly alike? Explain.
5. Plant cells that have chlorophyll are often flat and thin. Can you explain how this might help these cells do their job?
6. How does a virus make new viruses? Is this way different from the way other organisms make new organisms?
7. Why did scientists decide to classify some living things as protists?
8. Why are ameba and paramecium grouped together?
9. When might you eat seaweed? When might you eat mold?
10. How are algae and fungi alike? In what ways are they different?

CHAPTER 12

PLANTS

Does your state have a flag? What colors are in it? If plants had a flag, it would be green. Trees are green. So is grass. In damp places, still smaller plants cover the ground and rocks with a green carpet. Why do you think that most of the plants you see are green? What do all

12-1.

Classifying Plants

plants have that makes them green? When you finish this section, you should be able to:

- ☐ **A.** Explain what green plants need to make their own food.
- ☐ **B.** Explain why all living things depend on plants.
- ☐ **C.** Describe the steps in the carbon dioxide-oxygen cycle.

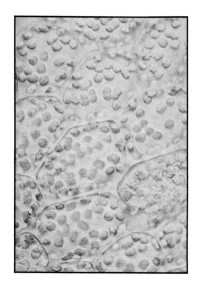

Photosynthesis: The process by which plants use light energy to make food.

There are many different kinds of plants. Most of the plants you know best have roots, stems, and leaves. The tiny plants that cover soil and cling to rocks do not.

Some plants, such as rosebushes, have flowers. Other plants, such as pine trees, have cones. Scientists use structures like flowers and cones to divide plants into groups. However, all plants have something in common. They are green. In plant cells, the green comes from a material known as chlorophyll. Plants use chlorophyll to make their own food. *Chloro* means "green" and *phyll* means "leaf." Chlorophyll is usually found in leaf cells. Often it is in stem cells, too. Chlorophyll makes these cells look green. The photograph on the left shows how chlorophyll looks in a leaf cell.

Plants use chlorophyll to make their own food during **photosynthesis** (foh-toh-sin-thuh-sis). *Photo* means "light." *Synthesis* means "putting together." That's just what *photosynthesis* is: "putting together with light."

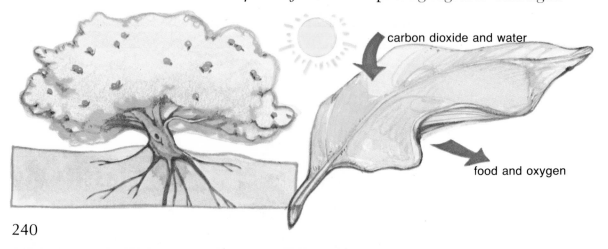

carbon dioxide and water

food and oxygen

240

ACTIVITY

Do plants need light to make chlorophyll?

A. Obtain these materials: 2 pots with soil, 2 lima beans, watering can.

B. Place 1 lima bean on soil in each pot. Cover with about 1 cm of soil. Place both pots in a sunny window. Keep the soil moist.

C. After both plants have formed green leaves, put 1 pot in a dark place. Keep both plants watered.

    1. Predict how the 2 plants will look in a week.

D. Examine the 2 plants a week later.

    2. How do your observations compare with your prediction?

    3. Which plant looks healthier? Can you explain why?

    4. What color are the leaves of the plant that has been in the dark? What is missing from these leaves?

E. Place the "dark" plant in the sun for a week.

    5. What color are the leaves of the "dark" plant after a week in the sun? Why do you think this happened?

    6. Write a conclusion about this activity. Use the terms *chlorophyll* and *sunlight*.

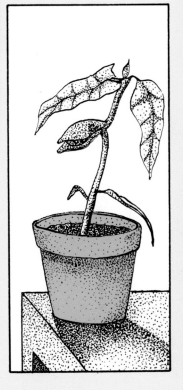

Chlorophyll traps energy from sunlight. Leaf cells use this energy to make food from water and carbon dioxide. Carbon dioxide is a gas found in the air. After making food, the plant releases oxygen into the air. For food to be made, light is needed. Light is also needed for the cells to make chlorophyll.

Plants use sunlight, carbon dioxide, and water to make oxygen and simple foods. These foods are sugars and

starches, such as those found in apples and potatoes. All animals depend on plants for food. They either eat plants or they eat other animals that eat plants.

All animals also depend on plants for oxygen. Animals take in food and oxygen for energy. Their cells combine oxygen and food to make energy. Animals also produce carbon dioxide and water. The plants use the carbon dioxide and water to make oxygen and food again.

What you have just read about is the carbon dioxide-oxygen cycle. The arrows show the cycle. It is called a cycle because the steps are repeated over and over.

Section Review

Main Ideas: Plants need chlorophyll, sunlight, carbon dioxide, and water to make their food. All animals depend upon plants for food and oxygen.

Questions: Answer in complete sentences.

1. What is photosynthesis? What do plants need for photosynthesis?
2. Would a houseplant stay healthy in a dark room? Explain your answer.
3. Do meat-eating animals need green plants? Why or why not?
4. What are the steps in the carbon dioxide-oxygen cycle?

Do you eat roots? Do you eat stems and leaves? When you eat a salad, you probably eat all three. Which parts of the plant are the vegetables that are shown in the photograph below? What jobs do roots, stems, and leaves do in a living plant? When you finish this section, you should be able to:

☐ **A.** Describe the basic jobs of *roots*, *stems*, and *leaves*.
☐ **B.** Compare two types of root systems.
☐ **C.** Compare the stem of a woody plant with the stem of a nonwoody plant.

Roots, such as those of the radish and carrot, are storehouses of food for the plant. That's why they are good for us to eat. After plants make food, they store it in the *roots*. Roots also keep the plant in the ground. They take up water and minerals from the soil.

The water and minerals flow upward through the roots to the **stem** of the plant. Usually the *stem* is above ground. The stem supports the part of a plant that is above ground. It is a plant's transportation system. There are two systems of tubes in the stem. One carries the minerals and water from the roots to the **leaves**. Inside the *leaves* food is made. The other tube system in the stem carries food from the leaves to the stem and the roots.

Root: The plant structure that takes in water and keeps the plant in the ground.

Stem: The plant structure that carries food and water through the plant and that also gives it support.

Leaf: The plant structure that usually makes food.

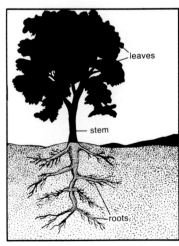

leaves

stem

roots

243

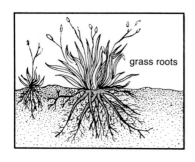

grass roots

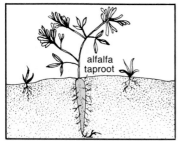

alfalfa taproot

Taproot: The main root of a root system.

There are two kinds of root systems. One is shallow, with many small branches. The other has one main root. Grass has the first kind of root system. Grasses often grow on wide, flat plains. In summer, hot, strong winds blow over the plains. They dry out the ground fast after rain. The shallow roots of the grass take in water before it dries up.

The grass roots also help to hold the soil in place. Have you ever tried to pull grassy weeds out of the ground? The soil clings to the roots in a large clump. Without a cover of grass, soil may wash away in floods or blow away in dust storms.

Another plant that grows on hot, dry plains is alfalfa, shown on page 245. It has the other kind of root system. Alfalfa has one big main root, the **taproot**. Like a drill looking for water, the *taproot* digs into the ground. It may grow down 4.5 meters (15 ft) in a single season!

ACTIVITY

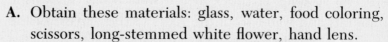

How do materials move up the stems of plants?

A. Obtain these materials: glass, water, food coloring, scissors, long-stemmed white flower, hand lens.

B. Fill a glass one-quarter full of water. Add a few drops of food coloring.

C. Trim the end of the stem of a fresh long-stemmed white flower. Put it in the glass and leave overnight.

   1. What does the flower look like the next day? Why?

D. Use the scissors to cut the stem above the water line. Look at the cut top of the stem in the glass. Use a hand lens.

   2. What do you see?

      3. What was it that transported water up through the stem?

244

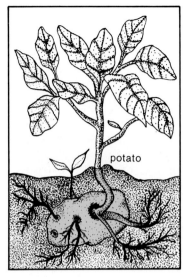

The soil dries out from the top downward. There is still water deep in the ground long after the soil near the surface is dry. In hot, dry summers, the taproot of the alfalfa grows straight down fast. It grows down faster than the ground dries out!

Roots usually grow in the ground. But did you know some stems grow in the ground, too? In some plants the parts that are above ground die out each winter. If these plants grow from year to year they have underground stems. The white potato is an example of an underground stem. Food is stored in the underground stem. It is protected from the wind and cold. When spring comes, a new stem and new leaves grow up from the underground stem of the potato.

The potato is also an example of an **herb**. An *herb* is a plant that does not have a woody system to support it. The tubes that conduct water and food in herb stems are in little bundles. The bundles are scattered through the stem. Find the bundles in the diagram on the right.

In plants such as bushes and trees, the stem must survive the winter above ground. These stems have a tough, woody outside. It protects and supports the plant. The diagram on the right shows a woody stem. What is the outside layer of a tree called? A woody stem also has tubes that conduct food and water. Bundles of tubes form a circle in the stem.

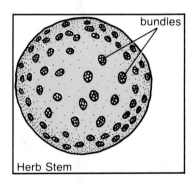

Herb: A plant without a woody stem.

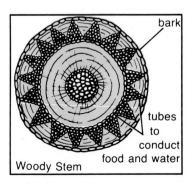

245

Plants have different kinds of roots and stems. Let's examine leaves. Leaves are usually thin and wide. Thin leaves allow lots of light through to the chlorophyll. Wide leaves let each leaf catch as much sunlight as possible. Have you ever noticed how the leaves of houseplants turn toward the sun? Why do they do that?

The leaves of **cactus** plants look very different from the leaves of other plants. *Cactus* plants grow in deserts, where there is very little rain. Their leaves are small and thick, and covered with a waxy coating. The smaller and thicker the leaf, the more slowly it loses water. Desert plants must hold in as much water as they can. The waxy coat slows down water loss, too.

Some cactus plants have leaves that are just long, sharp thorns. They have barrel-like stems that hold lots of water. The thorns protect the stems against thirsty desert animals. The stems are green. They do the work of photosynthesis.

Cactus: A desert plant.

Section Review

Main Ideas: Most plants have roots, stems, and leaves. Some roots are shallow and others, such as taproots, are deep. Stems may be woody or nonwoody. Leaves are usually thin and wide, but desert plants have thick, waxy, or thorny leaves that slow down water loss.

Questions: Answer in complete sentences.

1. Describe two types of roots. Give an example of a plant with each type.
2. What is the usual shape of plant leaves? Are there any exceptions?
3. Name a plant with a woody stem.
4. What is an example of a plant with an underground stem? How does this kind of stem help a plant?
5. Does photosynthesis always take place in a plant's leaves? Explain.

It is over 400,000,000 years ago. There are no animals on the land. But in wet places, tiny green plants cover the cracks in bare rocks. Do you know what they are? When you finish this section, you should be able to:

☐ **A.** Name four types of plants.
☐ **B.** Describe some examples of each type of plant.
☐ **C.** Describe how each type of plant produces more of its own kind.

Most of the plants below are **mosses**. *Mosses* are small plants that have no real roots, stems, or leaves. Mosses are often only as big as your fingernail. They grow mostly in damp, shady places.

Mosses: Small plants without real roots, stems, or leaves.

Mosses can grow on bare rock and tree trunks. Nearly all other plants need soil to grow on. Mosses grow into the cracks in the rocks. They help break the rock down into smaller and smaller bits. Remains of the mosses mix with the bits of rock. This is one way soil is formed.

You have learned that roots and stems carry water and food to all parts of a plant. Because mosses have no real roots and stems, food and water just spread slowly from cell to cell. Without stems, mosses cannot support the weight of a heavy plant. Mosses can never be very large. They have no real roots to keep them in soil, or to dig for water. The bigger a plant is, the more water it needs.

Spores: Special cells made by some living things that develop into new organisms like the organisms that made them.

Reproduction: The process by which living things make more of their own kind.

Ferns: Plants with roots, stems, and leaves, and that reproduce by spores.

Mosses do have tiny leaflike parts where food is made. They are only one cell thick. The leaflike parts are on small stalks. Rootlike structures help the stalks cling to the rocks and the ground.

New mosses grow from **spores.** *Spores* are special cells that some living things make. These cells can grow into new organisms like the organisms that made the cells. This process is the way mosses **reproduce.** When a moss plant is fully grown, it *reproduces* by spores. The little caps in the photograph show where spores are formed.

Some mosses that grow in wet places are called peat mosses. Many people use peat mosses to enrich the soil in their gardens.

Ferns are another type of plant. *Ferns*, like mosses, grow best in moist, shady places. But ferns have roots, stems, and leaves. Some ferns are tree-sized. About

300,000,000 years ago, ferns were the most common type of land plant. There were great forests of ferns.

The ferns you usually see are around 1 meter (3 feet) high at the most. Only the leafy part of the plant is above ground. The roots and stem grow underground. The photograph on the bottom left of page 248 shows a common fern, the cinnamon fern. The photograph next to it shows small dark spots that form underneath the fern leaves. Each dot holds hundreds of spores. The dots break open when the spores are ripe. The spores drift in the wind. The spores are the way the ferns reproduce.

About 280,000,000 years ago, a new group of plants appeared. They were the **cycads** (sy-kadz). *Cycads* are like ferns in many ways. Some have underground stems and a crown of fernlike leaves just above the ground. Others have trunks up to 18 meters (60 feet) high, with a crown of fernlike leaves.

Cycads do not produce spores like ferns. Instead they produce **seeds**. Each *seed* contains a tiny plant and stored food. Seeds can survive for many years, sometimes centuries. When conditions are right, the seed grows into a new plant. That is how plants with seeds reproduce.

About 100,000,000 years ago, cycads replaced ferns as the most common kind of plant. Dinosaurs lived in forests of giant cycad trees like the one shown.

Cycads: The earliest plants that reproduced by seeds.

Seeds: The structure by which most plants reproduce. Each seed contains a complete tiny plant and stored food.

Gymnosperms:
Seed-bearing plants that form seeds on cones exposed directly to the air.

Today, most cycads are found in hot rain forests. They belong to a group of seed-bearing plants called **gymnosperms** (**jim**-nuh-spermz). *Gymnosperm* means "bare seed." Gymnosperms produce their seeds on structures called cones. The place where the seeds form on the cones is exposed to the air. That is why this group is called the "bare seed" group. The photograph on the left shows a cone. Some of its seeds have been removed.

You have probably seen some common gymnosperms. They include evergreen trees, such as spruce, fir, cedar, pine, and redwood. They are among the biggest, tallest, and oldest living trees. Bristlecone pine trees are thought to live the longest. One tree of this kind is about 4,900 years old!

Many parts of the world are covered by huge forests of evergreens. Evergreens often live in cold places. The fir forest shown below is in Alaska.

Most of the plants you see around you do not belong to any of the groups mentioned so far. Common plants are not mosses, ferns, or gymnosperms. They are **angiosperms** (an-jee-uh-spermz). *Angiosperm* means "covered seed." Angiosperms are also called flowering plants. Their seeds are produced inside their flowers. Most familiar plants are angiosperms.

Grass is an angiosperm. Dandelions, rosebushes, apple trees, and daisies are all angiosperms. All flowering plants and trees are angiosperms. They produce seeds like the ones you see in the photograph. Every seed contains a tiny plant and stored food.

Angiosperms:
Seed-bearing plants that form their seeds inside a flower.

Section Review

Main Ideas: Classifying Plant Groups

Group	Structures	Reproduce by	Examples
Mosses	No true plant organs	Spores	Peat moss
Ferns	Roots, stems, leaves	Spores	Cinnamon fern
Gymnosperms	Roots, stems, leaves	Bare seeds	Firs, pines, spruce
Angiosperms	Roots, stems, leaves	Covered seeds	Grasses, flowers

Questions: Answer in complete sentences.

1. Name four types of plants.
2. Could a moss plant grow very tall? Explain.
3. How do ferns reproduce?
4. What is the difference between gymnosperms and angiosperms? Give two examples of each.

People in Science

Barbara McClintock

Dr. Barbara McClintock has been planting corn for the last 40 years. But she is not a farmer. She is a scientist who studies how characteristics of corn plants are passed along from one year's crop to the next. At a laboratory in New York, Dr. McClintock observed that corn plants produce kernels of different colors. Sometimes they are yellow. Other times the kernels have spots of purple and pink. Dr. McClintock is discovering why the colors change. She is studying an area of science called **genetics** (juh-**neh**-tiks). *Genetics* is the study of how characteristics are passed along from one generation to the next. Dr. McClintock carefully "crosses" plants of certain colors. She examines the plants that result. In 1983, she won the Nobel Prize for her work on how plants pass on characteristics to their young.

CHAPTER REVIEW

Science Words

Think of a word for each blank. List the letters **a** through **l** on paper. Write the word next to each letter.

Green plants make their own food during the process of __**a**__. Food making usually takes place in the __**b**__ of plants. Food is often stored in the __**c**__ of plants which also take in water. The part of the plant above the ground is usually supported by its __**d**__. Some plants, known as __**e**__, have no real roots, stems, or leaves. They reproduce by __**f**__. Another group of plants that reproduce in this way are the __**g**__, which grew as tall as trees millions of years ago. Trees such as spruce, fir, and pine belong to a plant group called the __**h**__, which means "bare seed." These plants produce their seeds in structures called __**i**__. All the flowering plants reproduce by forming __**j**__. They are known as the __**k**__. That name means "__**l**__ seed."

Questions: Answer in complete sentences.

1. How are sunlight and chlorophyll important to a plant?
2. Is this statement true or false: All animals depend on plants for food. Explain.
3. What does a root do? What does a stem do?
4. What is one important difference between an herb and a tree?
5. Copy the names of each of the plants listed below. Beside each name, write the plant group to which it belongs: cedar, peat moss, rose, cinnamon fern, corn, white pine, grass.
6. Explain one way mosses helped pave the way for later land plants.
7. What are spores? What are seeds?

CHAPTER 13

ANIMALS WITHOUT BACKBONES

13-1.

Simple Animals

Is this organism an animal or a plant? It may be a surprise to you that it is an animal. Some animals look like plants. They stay in one place all their lives. How can you tell it is an animal? When you finish this section, you should be able to:

☐ **A.** Explain how *sponges*, *corals*, and *jellyfish* get their food.

☐ **B.** Compare and contrast three types of worms.

There are more than 1,200,000 different kinds of animals known today. New kinds are found every year. Scientists classify these animals into two groups. One group includes all animals with backbones. These animals are called **vertebrates** (**ver**-tuh-brayts). *Vertebrates* include frogs, snakes, birds, cats, dogs, and humans. The other group is called the **invertebrates** (in-**ver**-tuh-brayts). *Invertebrates* are animals without backbones.

Sponges are a group of simple invertebrates. Most of them live in the ocean attached to rocks. Many *sponges* are shaped like vases. The body of a sponge is made up of two cell layers. They form the sides and bottom of the "vase." The top has an opening.

Sponges have small holes all over their bodies. The holes are lined with special cells. Each cell has a whiplike structure. It beats back and forth causing water to flow through the holes into the sponge. Other cells take tiny organisms out of the water for food.

Bath sponges are often made of plastic. Natural bath sponges are made from the dried bodies of sea sponges.

Vertebrates: Animals with backbones.

Invertebrates: Animals without backbones.

Sponge: A simple invertebrate that has one body opening and small holes all over its body.

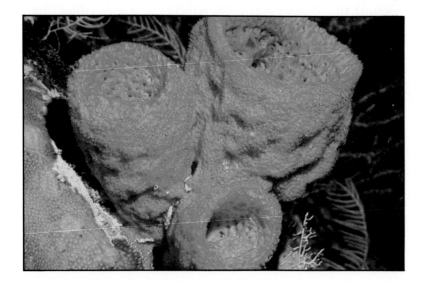

Hollow-bodied animal: A simple invertebrate with one body opening that is surrounded by tentacles.

Hollow-bodied animals are another group of simple invertebrates. They include jellyfish, corals, and sea anemones (uh-**neh**-muh-neez). Like the sponges, these animals have only one body opening. Their bodies are made up of two cell layers. Sea anemones and corals stay attached to one place. The picture on the upper left shows a sea anemone. The picture on page 254 shows a coral.

Hollow-bodied animals have fingerlike structures around the open end of their bodies. These structures are called *tentacles*. When one tentacle touches a small animal, other tentacles close around the animal, too. Stinging cells in the tentacles inject a poison into the animal. The tentacles pull the animal inside, where it is eaten. Find the tentacles in the jellyfish shown above.

Worms are also invertebrates. They are more complicated than sponges and corals. Their bodies are three cell layers thick. Worms grow new parts of their bodies when they are cut apart. There are three major groups of worms. **Flatworms** have long, flattened bodies. *Flatworms*, such as the tapeworm, live inside other animals and cause disease.

Flatworm: A worm with one body opening and a long, flattened body.

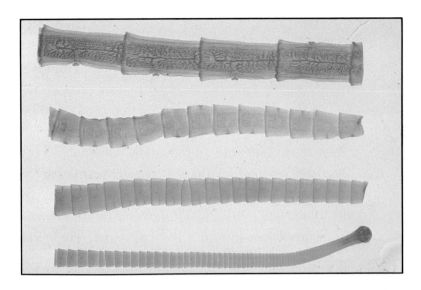

Sometimes flatworms are found in fish or meat that is bought for food. If the fish or meat is cooked well, the worms will be killed. But if it is not cooked long enough, the living worms will be eaten with the food. They will infect the person who has eaten the food. The picture shows parts of a tapeworm seen through a microscope.

Roundworms have round bodies that are pointed at both ends. They have two body openings. Food enters through one opening. Wastes go out through the other.

Many *roundworms* live inside plants and animals. Hookworms are roundworms that infect humans. They live mostly in the warmer parts of the world. Hookworms on the ground enter the body of a person through the skin of the feet. That's why it's important not to walk barefoot in areas where there may be hookworms.

Segmented worms are worms whose bodies are divided into many similar parts or sections. These sections are called segments. *Segmented worms* are more complicated than flatworms or roundworms. They have a heart and blood vessels, for example. They also have a nervous system. This allows them to sense what is around them.

Earthworms are segmented worms. Their nervous system gives them good control of their bodies as they dig through the ground.

Roundworm: A worm with a round body pointed at both ends.

Segmented worm: A worm with a body that is divided into many similar parts.

Each earthworm's segments—except the first and last—has four pairs of stiff bristles. The earthworm burrows by pushing its front end into the ground. Then the front bristles move to pull the earthworm further in. Now the bristles further back are in the ground. The front bristles relax. The back bristles go to work and push the earthworm deeper into the ground.

Earthworms are good for the soil. Their wastes enrich it. Their burrows let more air and water into the soil. In very good, moist soil, there may be over a million earthworms in an area the size of a big backyard! They can bring tons of soil up from under the surface. Because they move the soil at night, earthworms are commonly called "night crawlers."

Section Review

Main Ideas: Classifying Simple Invertebrates

Main Group	Structures	Features	Examples
Sponges	One body opening. Two cell layers.	Attached to one place.	Freshwater or saltwater sponges
Hollow-bodied animals	One body opening. Two cell layers. Tentacles.	Attached to one place.	Jellyfish, coral
Worms	One or two body openings. Three cell layers. Segmented worms have a heart, blood vessels, and a nervous system.	Move about.	Flatworm (tapeworm) Roundworm (hookworm) Segmented worm (earthworm)

Questions: Answer in complete sentences.

1. Name the only way sponges are like plants.
2. How do sponges get food?
3. How are hollow-bodied animals different from sponges?
4. What are the three groups of worms?
5. What does "invertebrate" mean?

What kind of animal has its stomach on its foot? What kind of an animal can push its stomach into its food to eat? What kinds of animals have arms around their mouths? The animal you see below has its eyes around its foot. It is called a blue-eyed scallop. When you finish this section, you should be able to:

☐ **A.** Describe what structures *mollusks* have in common.

☐ **B.** Compare and contrast three different kinds of *mollusks.*

☐ **C.** Describe what structures spiny-skinned invertebrates have in common.

☐ **D.** Explain how a starfish gets its food.

Mollusks (**mahl**-usks) are another large group of invertebrates. Most *mollusks* live in fresh or salt water. Some, like slugs and certain kinds of snails, live on land.

Mollusks are like segmented worms in some ways. They have soft bodies, two body openings, a heart, blood vessels, and a digestive system. However, they are not segmented. They have a thick, muscular "foot" that moves them from place to place. Many mollusks have hard shells that protect their soft bodies. There are three kinds of mollusks. They are grouped according to the differences in their shells and feet.

Mollusk: An invertebrate with a soft body, usually protected by a shell.

Hatchet-footed mollusks make up one group. Clams, oysters, mussels, and scallops have a hatchet foot. They also have two parts to their shells. The two parts are hinged. A muscle attached to their shells can open or close the shell.

When the shell is open, the hatchet-shaped foot can stretch out. Then the muscle in the foot makes it draw together. That pulls the mollusk along the sandy bottom of the lake or ocean. These mollusks feed on tiny protists that live in the water.

Stomach-footed mollusks have one-part shells. Snails and slugs belong to this group. Most snails live in water, although some giant ones live on land. You may have seen pond snails moving on the walls of an aquarium. The foot lays down a trail of slime. The snail glides along the trail. The snail's foot is actually a part of its digestive system, too. That's where the name "stomach-footed" comes from.

ACTIVITY

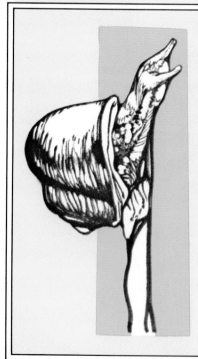

Observing snails

A. Obtain these materials: aquarium with pond snails, hand lens, pencil.

B. Observe snails crawling up the glass sides of the aquarium. Use a hand lens to see how the snail's "foot" moves.

   1. Describe how the foot moves.

C. The front part of the "foot" is the snail's head. Look at it with a hand lens while the snail is moving.

   2. What can you see on the snail's head?

   3. What do you think these structures do?

D. Tap the aquarium glass sharply near a snail.

   4. What happens?

   5. Does the snail react quickly? Do you think this is a useful reaction? Why?

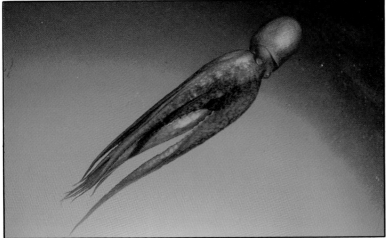

Head-footed mollusks make up the third group. In these mollusks, the "foot" is divided into eight or more tentacles. The tentacles are arranged around the mouth of the animal. The octopus has eight tentacles that have suckers for holding on to food. The octopus has no shell. It feeds mostly on crabs. An octopus is shown above.

The squid has ten tentacles with suckers. It has a shell inside its body. The squid has sharp jaws. It feeds largely on fish. The squid and the octopus can swim rapidly by squirting a jet of water out of their bodies. Which way is the octopus moving? Each animal can change color quickly to match its surroundings. Both can release a cloud of ink into the water to escape from enemies.

Among the oddest of the invertebrates are the *spiny-skinned invertebrates*. Like mollusks, spiny-skinned invertebrates have two body openings, a digestive system, and a heart and blood vessels. They have firm bodies. Spiny-skinned invertebrates get their name from the spines that cover their bodies. Some are long and sharp as needles. Others are short. This group includes starfish, sea urchins, sand dollars, sea cucumbers, and sea lilies. They all live in salt water.

Starfish are the best known of the spiny-skinned invertebrates. Most have five arms spread out from the center of their bodies. The undersides of the arms are covered with many tiny, hollow tubes called tube feet. They work like suction cups.

The feet are used for walking and feeding. A starfish may wrap its arms around a mussel, as shown in the picture on the bottom left. The tube feet hold tightly to the two parts of the mussel's shell. The starfish's arms pull steadily on the shell, trying to make it open. This may go on for hours. Sooner or later, the mussel's shell muscle gets tired. It can no longer hold the shell closed. The shell opens.

Then the starfish pushes its stomach out through its mouth and into the open shell of the mussel. The soft

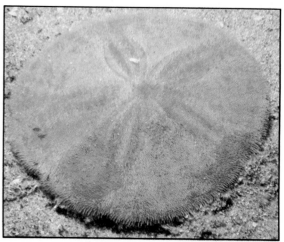

body of the mussel is digested. The starfish pulls its stomach and the digested mussel back inside itself.

Because of their long, needlelike spines, sea urchins look like living pincushions. When a sea urchin dies, its spines fall off. The picture on the right shows a sea urchin. Sand dollars look like round, flattened pieces of dough. That's because their spines are very short. You can see the star-shaped pattern on a sand dollar's body in the picture on page 262. Both sea urchins and sand dollars can be found washed up on beaches.

Section Review

Main Ideas: Invertebrates that have shells and spines are classified as shown in the following chart.

MOLLUSKS			SPINY-SKINNED INVERTEBRATES	
Structures	**Groups**	**Examples**	**Structures**	**Examples**
Soft bodies. Two body openings. Heart and blood vessels. Digestive system. Most have a shell.	Hatchet-footed. Two-shelled.	Clam, oyster, mussel, scallop.	Firm body. Two body openings. Heart, blood vessels. Digestive system. Spines.	Starfish, sea urchin, sand dollar, sea lily, sea cucumber.
	Stomach-footed. One-shelled.	Snail, slug.		
	Head-footed. Many legs or tentacles.	Octopus, squid.		

Questions: Answer in complete sentences.

1. Mollusks are divided into three groups according to two of their structures. What are these structures?
2. In what ways are mollusks like segmented worms?
3. A starfish eats in an unusual way. How?
4. Name five structures that many mollusks have in common.
5. In what two ways does a starfish use its feet?

13-3.

Arthropods

**Arthropods:
Invertebrates with
jointed legs and an
outer skeleton.**

**Exoskeleton: The hard
outer covering of
arthropods.**

One of the animals shown below can fly. Do you think it is a bird? Why not? One animal lives on land and spins webs. The other lives in the sea. All three are related to each other. When you finish this section, you should be able to:

☐ **A.** Name three ways in which all *arthropods* are alike.

☐ **B.** Name one difference used to separate *arthropods* into five groups.

☐ **C.** Explain how a caterpillar and a butterfly can be the same animal.

There are over a million different kinds of **arthropods** (**ahr**-thruh-pahdz). Yet all *arthropods* have some things in common. They all have a hard **exoskeleton** (ek-so-skel-uh-tun). *Exoskeleton* means an outer skeleton.

The human skeleton is inside the body. It supports the weight of the body. Muscles are attached to the bones.

The exoskeleton of an arthropod has the same purpose. It supports the animal's weight. Muscles are attached to the inside of the exoskeleton. The exoskeleton is not made of bone. The material it is made of is like the material that makes up our fingernails. This material can be very hard. If you have ever tried to crack a lobster shell, you know that. Lobsters are arthropods.

Once formed, an exoskeleton cannot get larger. But the arthropod inside it is growing. When it gets too large for the exoskeleton, the exoskeleton splits. The arthropod sheds the old exoskeleton. It grows a new one as you can see in the top left picture. It takes time for the new exoskeleton to harden. During that time, the arthropod stays in one place and hides from enemies.

Arthropod means "joint-footed." That is another way that all arthropods are alike. All have several pairs of jointed feet and bodies made of several segments.

Arthropods are divided into five main groups. Each group has a different number of legs. The first group is made up mostly of animals that live in water. Their scientific name is *crustaceans*, which means "hard-covered." These animals have an especially tough exoskeleton. This group includes lobsters, crabs, crayfish, and shrimp. Have you ever eaten any of these animals?

The hard-covered arthropods have five pairs of legs. They also have two body sections and two pairs of **antennas** (an-**ten**-uz). *Antennas* are many-jointed structures on the heads of most arthropods. The everyday word for them is "feelers." But they are used for much more than feeling. They are used for smelling and sometimes for hearing. Can you find the lobster's antennas in the top right picture?

Antennas: Jointed structures on the heads of many arthropods that are used for feeling, smelling, and hearing.

The second group of arthropods is the *arachnids*, made up of spiders and spiderlike animals. These animals all have two body sections. They have four pairs of legs and no antennas. Nearly all of these animals live on land.

Many spiders are useful to humans. They catch and kill huge numbers of pests such as houseflies and mosquitoes. All spiders have poison fangs. They use them to kill or stun their prey. Very few spiders are poisonous to humans.

Most spiders catch their prey in sticky webs. A jumping spider, such as the one shown below, can catch prey by leaping on it. It has several pairs of eyes to help it see its prey from a distance. Spitting spiders squirt long, sticky threads at nearby prey. The spiders are so fast that they can catch a resting fly before it takes off.

Ticks and mites belong to the same group of arthropods as spiders. Many are harmful to humans. Some destroy plants that we grow for food. The tick shown on the left sucks the plant's juices. Other ticks and mites burrow into the skin of humans or animals and often spread disease. Have you ever had a tick or removed one from a pet? Ticks must be carefully removed.

The third group of arthropods is the insect group. All insects have three pairs of legs. All have three body sections and one pair of antennas.

Insects are the most numerous of all animals. There are more kinds of insects than there are animals in all the other groups put together. Can you name the ones shown? Some you have certainly seen.

Why are there so many insects? One important reason is that each female insect can lay many thousands of eggs at a time. Even if only a few eggs from each batch develop into adult insects, there will still be lots of new insects!

Another reason for the large number of different insects is that they eat almost anything that can be eaten. Everything we think of as food, some insect will also eat. And some insects eat things that few other animals will touch. Termites eat wood. Tobacco beetles eat tobacco leaves. The young of some moths eat cloth.

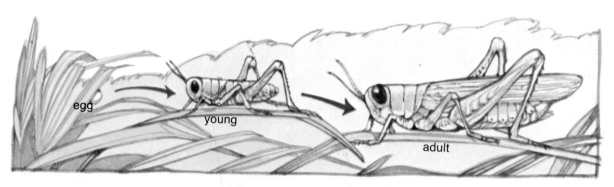

egg → young → adult

Most insects go through a series of changes as they develop from egg to adult. These changes are called **metamorphosis** (met-uh-**mor**-fuh-sis).

Some insects go through incomplete *metamorphosis*. A grasshopper egg, for instance, hatches into a very tiny grasshopper. It looks like a full-grown grasshopper, but without wings. The young grasshopper grows and sheds its exoskeleton several times. By the third or fourth time, the young grasshopper has wings. It is an adult.

Insects with complete metamorphosis change a great deal more. They go through four stages. The egg hatches into a wormlike animal. For example, the eggs of moths and butterflies hatch into caterpillars. The eggs of grain beetles hatch into mealworms. The insects are now at the feeding stage. Caterpillars feed constantly on leaves. Mealworms feed on almost any kind of grain. After eating during the summer, the insect goes into a resting stage. Many caterpillars spin a cocoon. After a while, the caterpillar changes into an adult butterfly or moth. The mealworm changes into a small beetle. Adult insects are very different from what they were at younger stages.

Metamorphosis: A series of major changes in the structure of an animal as it develops from its early stages to become an adult.

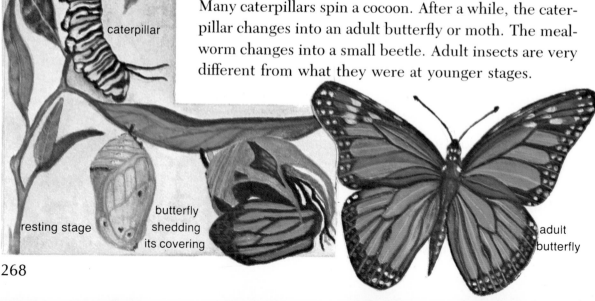

egg stage

caterpillar

resting stage

butterfly shedding its covering

adult butterfly

268

ACTIVITY

Observing Mealworms

A. Obtain the following materials: hand lens, mealworm culture, pencil, drawing paper.

B. Take a mealworm from the class culture. Use the lens to observe the mealworm carefully. Draw what you see. Label head, segments, antennas, legs.

   1. How many segments are there?

   2. How many pairs of legs are there? How many pairs of antennas?

   3. What group of arthropods do mealworms belong to? Explain your answer.

C. Look at the class culture. Use the lens. Try to find eggs, resting stage, and adult beetles.

   4. What kind of metamorphosis does the mealworm go through?

Many insects are serious pests. Some spread disease in animals and in humans.

Other insects, such as bees, are very useful. Bees visit flowers for food. As they do, the bees pick up a fine dust from the male structures of the flower. This dust is called pollen. Pollen must be carried to the female structures of the flower before a flower can make seeds. The bees carry the pollen as they go from flower to flower.

Fruit trees will not produce fruit unless their flowers produce seeds. And their flowers will not produce seeds unless they are pollinated. When their fruit trees are in flower, some farmers pay beekeepers to bring their hives into the orchards.

The fourth group of arthropods is made up of **centipedes** (**sen**-tuh-peedz). The name means "a hundred legs." *Centipedes* have bodies made of many segments.

Centipede: An arthropod with many body segments and one pair of legs on most segments.

Millipede: An arthropod with many body segments and two pairs of legs on most segments.

Most segments have one pair of legs. Centipedes can have from 30 to 340 legs. They feed on many insect pests, including horseflies and cockroaches. The picture shows a centipede that is commonly found in the United States.

Millipedes (mil-uh-peedz) are the fifth group of arthropods. Their name means "a thousand legs." *Millipedes*, like centipedes, have many body segments. Each segment has two pairs of legs. So millipedes look more "leggy" than centipedes. But actually, millipedes never have more than 115 pairs of legs, or 230 legs in all. Millipedes usually eat plants. Although many millipedes are small, some grow as long as 28 cm (11 in.). Both centipedes and millipedes have one pair of antennas.

Section Review

Main Ideas: Classifying Arthropods

Structures in common	Group	Special structures	Example
Exoskeleton Joint-footed Segmented body	Hard-covered	Five pairs of legs. Two pairs of antennas. Two body sections.	Lobster, shrimp
	Spiders, spiderlike animals	Four pairs of legs. Two body sections.	Spiders, mites, ticks
	Insects	Three pairs of legs. Three body sections.	Butterflies, bees, beetles
	Centipedes	Many segments. One pair of legs per segment.	Centipedes
	Millipedes	Many segments. Two pairs of legs per segment.	Millipedes

Questions: Answer in complete sentences.

1. In what three ways are all arthropods alike?
2. What one structure do scientists use to separate the five main groups of arthropods? Name the groups.
3. Draw a picture of the metamorphosis of a caterpillar.

CHAPTER REVIEW

Science Words: Match the terms in Column A with the definitions in Column B.

Column A

1. Hollow-bodied invertebrates
2. Arthropods
3. Invertebrates
4. Sponges
5. Metamorphosis
6. Antennas
7. Spiny-skinned invertebrates
8. Flatworms
9. Mollusks
10. Exoskeleton

Column B

a. Changes some insects go through
b. Feelers
c. Invertebrates with exoskeletons and jointed legs
d. Supports an animal's weight on the outside of the body
e. Animals without backbones
f. Invertebrates with one body opening
g. May cause disease if eaten in undercooked meat
h. Starfish
i. Octopus, squid, clam
j. Jellyfish, corals, and sea anemones

Questions: Answer in complete sentences.

1. What is different in the ways sponges and jellyfish feed themselves?
2. In what important ways are segmented worms different from flatworms or roundworms?
3. Companies that sell seeds to gardeners sometimes sell earthworms, too. Why do you think this is so?
4. Name the three main groups of mollusks.
5. What structures do mollusks have in common?
6. Is there anything strange about the stomach of a starfish? If so, explain.
7. Do arthropods need bones? Why or why not?
8. What are the five main groups of arthropods?

CHAPTER 14

ANIMALS WITH BACKBONES

14-1.

Fish and Amphibians

This shark is not too interested in eating the fish that are swimming around it. It is sleeping! The shark and the other fish have many things in common. Can you see some of them in the picture? When you finish this section, you should be able to:

☐ **A.** Compare the body systems of *vertebrates* and *invertebrates*.

☐ **B.** Describe the body plan of a fish.

☐ **C.** Describe the life cycle of an *amphibian*.

Fish are the largest group of vertebrates, the animals with backbones. You have learned that most animals without backbones do not have an inside skeleton. Some have an exoskeleton, or a skeleton on the outside of the body. But all vertebrates have an **endoskeleton** (**en**-doh-**skel**-uh-tun). This is a hard framework inside the body that supports muscles and softer body parts.

Vertebrates have complex body systems. They have a nervous system with a well-developed brain. They have a closed system of blood circulation. This means that the blood stays in the blood vessels all the time.

Invertebrates have a simple blood system. An insect has a heart that acts like the rubber bulb on an eyedropper. It squeezes and opens, sending blood sloshing through the insect's body and bringing food to all cells. That is fine for an insect with a small body. But for vertebrates, blood must bring food and oxygen to trillions of cells. Blood must carry carbon dioxide and other wastes away from the cells. Red blood cells do this.

In a fish, the heart has two parts or *chambers*. Blood from all over the body comes into the first chamber. This blood carries carbon dioxide from the cells of the fish.

Endoskeleton: A hard support structure inside the body of some vertebrates, made of cartilage and bone.

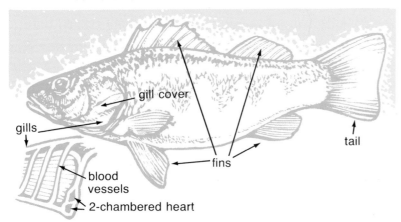

gill cover

gills

tail

fins

blood vessels

2-chambered heart

Gills: Structures in some water-dwelling animals that pick up oxygen from the water.

Cold-blooded animals: Vertebrates whose body temperature stays about the same as the temperature of their surroundings.

Cartilage: A firm but bendable material that forms the skeleton of some fish, and is found in many animals.

The first chamber squeezes the blood into the second chamber. The second chamber pumps the blood through blood vessels to the **gills**. Since fish live in water, they use *gills* instead of lungs to breathe. The gills pick up carbon dioxide from the blood as it passes through them. Then they pass the carbon dioxide out into the water that bathes the gills.

At the same time, the gills pick up oxygen from the water. The oxygen passes to the blood around the gills. The blood travels to the body cells, carrying oxygen and food. It picks up carbon dioxide from the cells and returns to the first chamber of the heart.

Fish are **cold-blooded** animals. This means that their body temperature stays about the same as the temperature of the water around them.

Some fish have skeletons made of **cartilage** (kar-tuh-lij). *Cartilage* is a firm material, but it is not as hard as bone. Cartilage bends, while bones are stiff. The firm ridges in your ears and nose are made of cartilage.

Fish with skeletons made of cartilage include sharks, skates, and rays. Most sharks have jaws lined with several rows of sharp teeth. The shark's skin is made up of sharply pointed scales of tooth-like material. In fact, sharkskin is used to make a kind of sandpaper. Only nine of the 250 kinds of sharks are dangerous to humans.

Skates and rays have broad, flat bodies. As they swim through the water, they look like living kites. This is especially true of skates. They have long, sharp tails.

Fish with bony skeletons are found in almost every natural body of water. They live in oceans, lakes, rivers, and ponds. There are 25,000 different kinds of bony fish. Salmon, haddock, and trout are some of them.

Most fish have the same body plan. The body is streamlined. It is narrow at the head end, wider in the middle, and then narrower again toward the tail end. This is the best shape for moving easily through the water. Even boats have a similar shape.

Fish have two sets of paired fins. They are like the four legs of land-living vertebrates. The paired fins of the fish are used for swimming. In addition to the paired fins, many fish have other, unpaired fins. There may be one or two on a fish's back, one on its bottom, and one on its tail. Can you find the fins on this fish?

Fish have a good sense of balance and of taste. They can hear noises and vibrations in the water. Sound travels very well through water. You may have noticed this if you have ever swum underwater.

The next group of vertebrates is the **amphibians** (am-fib-ee-unz). *Amphibian* means "two lives." Most amphibians do live two lives. They spend the early part of their lives in the water. They get their oxygen from the water through gills. As adults, they have lungs and live on land. Amphibians include frogs, toads, and salamanders. Like fish, they are cold-blooded.

Amphibians: Cold-blooded vertebrates that must live in or near water. Amphibians lay their eggs in water.

ACTIVITY

Observing fish

A. Obtain these materials: aquarium with several fish, paper, pencil.

B. Watch the fish as they swim through the water. Look at how their tails and fins move.
  1. How does a fish push itself through the water?
  2. Can a fish turn? How?
  3. Can a fish stop? How?

C. With a pencil, gently tap one side of the aquarium below the water level.
  4. How do the fish respond?

D. Hold a sheet of paper against one side of the aquarium. Tap gently on the paper with a pencil.
  5. How do the fish respond? What sense are they using? Explain your answer.

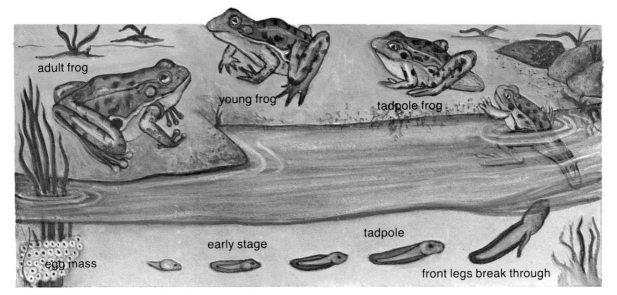

adult frog

young frog

tadpole frog

egg mass

early stage

tadpole

front legs break through

Living "two lives" means amphibians go through a big change. Like insects, they undergo a metamorphosis.

The eggs of frogs and toads hatch into young called *tadpoles*. Tadpoles live in the water. They have gills and tails. After a while, the tadpoles begin to change. Their tails disappear. Bumps develop on the sides of their bodies. These become front and hind legs. The animals lose their gills and develop lungs.

Now the tadpoles must come up to the surface for air. Soon they move onto land as adults. This life cycle takes over two years for a bullfrog. Leopard frogs go through it in about three months.

Even though adult amphibians can live on land, they must stay near water. They have thin skins. They take in water through their skins from damp air. In a sense, amphibians use their skins to "breathe in" water. Only near a pond or in swampy places is the air moist enough for this. In dry air, amphibians would lose water rapidly through their skins. Then they would die.

Amphibians have a more complex heart than fish do. It has three chambers. As in all vertebrates, the blood carries food and oxygen to the body cells. The three-chambered heart does a somewhat better job of this than the two-chambered heart of fish.

Land-living animals need a better working heart and blood system than fish do. They use more energy as they move about. That's because their bodies are not supported by water. An animal weighs more on land than in the water. Think of how much lighter you feel in a bathtub full of water. You can feel your weight return as the water goes out of the tub.

Land-living animals also have a well-developed nervous system. A frog has a larger brain than a fish.

Section Review

Main Idea: Classifying Some Cold-blooded Vertebrates

Main Groups	Structures	Subgroups	Examples
Fish (water)	Endoskeleton. Well-developed brain, nervous system. Closed circulation. Gills. Fins. Two-chambered heart.	Bony Cartilage	Salmon Shark
Amphibians (water/land)	Endoskeleton. Well-developed brain, nervous system. Closed circulation. Gills/lungs. Fins/legs. Three-chambered heart.		Frog, toad

Questions: Answer in complete sentences.

1. What is the main difference between a vertebrate and an invertebrate animal?
2. Explain what a closed system of circulation is.
3. Describe the shape of a fish. How does this shape help a fish swim?
4. What does the word "amphibian" mean? Why are some vertebrates called amphibians?
5. Describe the life cycle of a frog.

14-2.

Reptiles and Birds

Reptiles: Cold-blooded vertebrates that lay their eggs on land and have thick skins made of scales or plates.

The animal shown in this rock lived 150 million years ago. What is it? It had feathers and wings like a bird. But it also had a long, bony tail, and teeth in its jaws. Scientists think it was the first bird. When you finish this section, you should be able to:

☐ **A.** Explain why *reptiles* are true land animals.
☐ **B.** Name the structures that allow *birds* to fly.
☐ **C.** Compare and contrast *reptiles* and *birds*.

Reptiles (**rep**-tylz) are true land animals. Like amphibians, they are cold-blooded and lay eggs. Like amphibians, most *reptiles* have a three-chambered heart. Many reptiles spend all of their entire lives on land. They lay their eggs on land.

Reptiles, unlike amphibians, have a skin of hard plates or scales. They do not lose water from their skins. So they can live in dry places—even in deserts.

Amphibian eggs are soft and jelly-like. They dry out easily. They must be hatched in water. The eggs of reptiles have a tough shell and do not dry out easily.

Millions of years ago, most land animals were reptiles. Dinosaurs of all shapes and sizes roamed the land. Reptiles with wings soared through the air and dove for fish. Unlike modern birds, these flying reptiles had beaks with teeth. Their wings were covered with leathery skin, not feathers. Other reptiles swam in the seas. They had

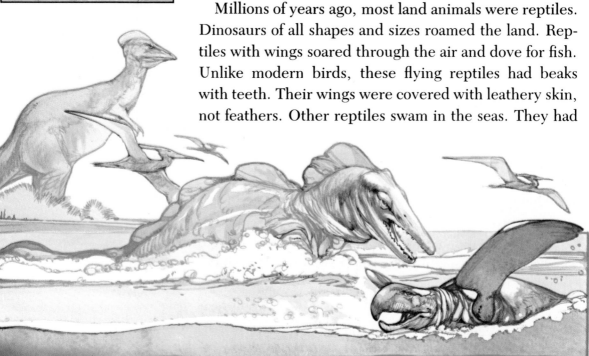

fish-shaped bodies with tails and fins. Their scientific name means "fish-lizard." But they were not fish. They had lungs and breathed air.

Today, these animals no longer exist. Only three main groups of reptiles are still living: the turtles, the alligators and crocodiles, and the lizards and snakes.

Turtles are easily recognized by their hard, protective shells. A few kinds live on land, but most live in water.

The most famous is the green turtle. Adult green turtles weigh up to 400 kilograms (880 pounds). Many feed on plants along the Atlantic Ocean shore of Brazil, in South America. Every few years, the turtles head out to sea. They swim across the Atlantic to a small island only 10 kilometers (6 miles) wide. Somehow the turtles find it. There, they mate and lay their eggs on the shore.

After hatching, the young turtles head straight for the sea, even when it is hidden by sand dunes. Eventually, the young turtles cross the ocean to the same beaches in Brazil that their parents came from.

How do they do it? The turtles may get clues from the position of the sun. They may use chemical clues like changes in the taste of the water they swim in. How they travel is a fascinating scientific puzzle.

Crocodiles and alligators are reptiles. They also spend a lot of time in the water. Their strong jaws and razor-sharp teeth make them fierce and dangerous hunters. Crocodiles and alligators are the only reptiles that have a four-chambered heart.

The four-chambered heart is more complex than the three-chambered heart. It works better. Animals with a four-chambered heart have a richer supply of oxygen in their blood. They can be more active and use more energy. That's important for animals that must run on land or fly through the air.

Snakes and lizards make up the third group of reptiles. Scientists classify them together because they are alike in so many ways.

You might think that there is one big difference between them—that lizards have legs and snakes do not. But in fact, that's not true. Some lizards have no legs. One that has no legs is the worm lizard. Another is the glass snake, shown above. In spite of its name, the glass snake is really a lizard. Why? Because its eyelids can move. True snakes cannot move their eyelids. This is one of the few real differences between lizards and snakes.

Snakes kill their prey in three different ways. Some snakes swallow an animal whole, while the animal is still alive. Their jaws "unhinge" so that their mouths can open very wide. The smooth green snake kills in this way. Some snakes kill by coiling around an animal until the animal can no longer breathe. The boa constrictor kills in this way. The middle photograph shows a boa. These snakes also swallow their prey whole. Some snakes, such as the rattlesnake, kill by injecting poison from their fangs into their prey.

The largest snakes in the world are constrictor (squeezing) snakes. Pythons and anacondas reach a length of 9 meters (30 feet).

Most lizards are less than half a meter (20 inches) long. They eat insects and small animals. One lizard, the Komodo dragon of southeastern Asia, is much bigger. It grows to a length of about 3 meters (10 feet). It can outrun and catch small pigs and even deer. Watching a Komodo dragon run is like looking back into the past. Perhaps small dinosaurs ran like them to catch their prey.

Another group of vertebrates is the **birds.** *Birds* lay eggs, but in almost every other way, they are different from the vertebrates we have seen so far.

All birds have feathers and wings. Even those birds that do not fly have feathers and wings. An ostrich, for example, may be 2.5 m (8 ft) tall and weigh about 160 kg (350 lb), so its small wings are useless for flying. But ostriches can run almost 50 km (30 mi) an hour. They use their powerful legs to protect themselves against enemies.

Even penguins have wings and feathers. Their wings act like flippers. They can swim as fast as seals.

Flying birds have light, hollow bones. Their wing feathers are made to "catch" the greatest possible amount of air. Powerful wing muscles move the wings up and down in a twisting motion.

Birds are **warm-blooded** animals. A bird's body temperature stays the same no matter how cold or hot the air or water is. Unlike cold-blooded animals, birds can be active even in very cold weather. A bird's feathers help it keep warm.

Warm-blooded animals: Vertebrates whose body temperature does not change.

ACTIVITY

Where do some birds migrate?

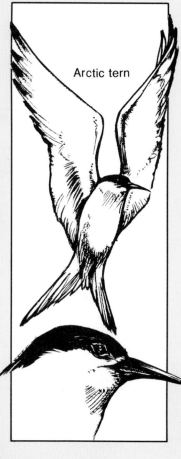

Arctic tern

A. Obtain these materials: tracing paper, pencil.

B. The map below shows the summer and winter homes of the arctic terns. They are the champions of bird migration. Trace the map onto tracing paper.

    1. The terns leave their northern home in late summer and head across North America to the Atlantic Ocean. With an arrow, show this.

    2. The terns fly across the ocean to Europe. Show this part of their trip.

    3. Then the terns head south across Europe to Africa. Draw an arrow to show this.

    4. The terns fly over Africa to their winter home. Draw this as well.

    5. Where is their winter home?

C. The arctic tern's fall migration is 17,700 kilometers long. The birds fly north again in the spring.

    6. What is their round trip each year?

D. These birds are adapted to their long trip. Look at the picture on the left.

    7. What do you notice about the bird's tail?

    8. From the bird's bill, what do you think it eats?

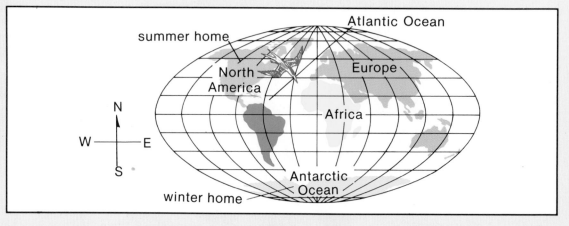

There are about 8,500 different kinds of birds. The ostrich is the largest bird. The fairy hummingbird is the smallest. It is only 5½ centimeters (2¼ inches) from head to tail. All hummingbirds are small. Their wings can beat as many as 75 times per second. This makes the humming noise that gives these birds their name. Because of the fast wingbeat, hummingbirds can hang almost motionless in the air as they use their long beaks to suck nectar, a sweet liquid, from flowers.

Birds are good navigators. Some birds fly at night using the stars to guide them. But how birds make long migrations is still puzzling.

Section Review

Main Idea: Classifying Reptiles and Birds

REPTILES			
Group	**Structures**	**Features**	**Example**
Turtles	Scales. Shell. Three-chambered heart. Legs. Teeth.	Cold-blooded. Lay eggs. Navigate.	Green turtle
Crocodiles, alligators	Scales. Four-chambered heart. Legs. Teeth.	Cold-blooded. Lay eggs.	Crocodile, alligator
Snakes, lizards	Scales. Three-chambered heart. May be legless.	Cold-blooded. Lay eggs.	Komodo dragon, rattlesnake

Questions: Answer in complete sentences.

1. What does "warm-blooded" mean? How is it different from "cold-blooded"?

2. What three structures do birds have that reptiles do not have?

3. What are two reasons that make it possible for reptiles to live entirely on land, something that amphibians cannot do?

BIRDS
Structures
Feathers. Wings. Hollow bones. Four-chambered heart.
Features
Warm-blooded. Lay eggs. Navigate.

14-3.

Mammals

Here's a living puzzle. What animal has a bill and webbed feet like a duck, but no feathers or wings? What lays eggs with tough, leathery shells that are similar to reptile eggs? What animal is covered with thick hair and feeds milk to its young? One animal has all these characteristics. When you finish this section, you should be able to:

☐ **A.** Compare and contrast *mammals* with birds.
☐ **B.** Compare and contrast *mammals* with reptiles.
☐ **C.** Explain why *mammals* can live in so many different places.

The animal shown is a duck-billed platypus. It lives in Australia and on Tasmania, a nearby island.

In some ways, the platypus is like a reptile. In some ways, it is like a bird. But the platypus is different from both of these groups. Scientists classify the platypus as a **mammal**. The platypus has hair. All *mammals* have hair or fur. In winter, some mammals grow thick coats of hair for warmth.

Unlike reptiles, the platypus is warm-blooded. Mammals are warm-blooded. The platypus feeds milk to its young. This is a characteristic of all mammals.

Mammals: Vertebrates that have hair and feed milk from their bodies to their young.

The young of mammals live and grow in the mother's body until they are ready to be born. But the platypus is different from other mammals. The platypus lays eggs and the young hatch from them. The platypus is probably a very early mammal. That is why it looks like a kind of "halfway" animal.

The next group of mammals is the pouched mammals. Kangaroos and opossums are pouched mammals. The young of pouched mammals begin life in the mother's body. But they are born before they are ready to live in the outside world. They are tiny and very weak. They crawl to the mother's pouch and settle down inside it. There, they get milk. They are protected until they are big enough to move on their own.

In all the rest of the mammals, the young get food from the mother's blood stream before they are born. They are not born until they are completely developed. This allows mammals to live in places all over the earth.

Bats are the only mammals that fly. The structure of their front limbs has changed to support their wings. The wings are made of skin. Four very long fingers hold the skin outstretched. The thumbs are hooked. Some bats, like the ones shown, eat fruit. Some eat insects.

Meat-eating mammals have sharp teeth for cutting and tearing. Claws are used for catching and holding prey, and for digging and climbing.

Rodents: Mammals with chisel-like teeth.

Many mammals live in the sea. The front limbs of walruses and seals are flippers. These animals have a fish-like tail. Dolphins and whales have fish-like bodies and fins. Some of these mammals are also meat-eaters.

Mammals like mice and squirrels are **rodents.** *Rodents* have sharp teeth shaped like chisels. They are used for cutting and gnawing. Rodents reproduce very quickly, and they live almost everywhere. They dig, run, leap, hop, climb, and swim. There are even squirrels that glide. The picture shows a gray squirrel.

Hoofed mammals, such as cows, eat plants. They have flat, sturdy teeth for chewing and crushing tough plants. Their hoofs help them to run fast to escape enemies.

Elephants are also plant-eaters. They are the largest living land mammals. Like other plant-eaters, they have broad teeth for grinding food. The tusks are actually a pair of upper teeth that have grown very long. The elephant's trunk is an extension of its nose and upper lip. It can pick up huge logs, and gently move tiny twigs without breaking them.

Primates are the most intelligent of the mammals. *Primates* have hands with movable fingers and flat nails instead of claws. They can pick up small objects and handle them with skill. This is a great advantage in looking for food and for making and using tools. Both eyes of the primates look forward. This makes it easier for them to judge how far away things are. Monkeys, chimpanzees, and humans are primates.

Primates: The most intelligent mammals.

As you have seen, mammals live almost everywhere on earth where life is possible. They live in the cold of the Arctic and in the world's highest mountains. They live in the heat of jungles and deserts. Some live in the water and have bodies like fish. Mammals have hair or fur at some time in their lives. Even the young of whales and dolphins have fur before they are born. Some mammals can even fly. But they all breathe air, are warm-blooded, and feed milk to their young.

Section Review

Main Ideas: Mammals are warm-blooded vertebrates with fur or hair that feed milk to their young.

MAMMALS			
Group	**Structures**	**Features**	**Examples**
Pouched mammals	Pouch.	Born undeveloped. Develop in pouch.	Opossum, kangaroo
Flying mammals	Fingers form "wings."	Can fly.	Bats
Meat-eating mammals	Sharp teeth. Claws.	Catch prey for food.	Cheetah, cat
Sea-living mammals	Flippers. Fins.	Swim in ocean. Most eat meat.	Walrus, seal
Rodents	Sharp teeth shaped like chisels.	Can gnaw. Reproduce quickly.	Squirrel, mouse
Hoofed mammals	Hoofed feet. Flat teeth.	Eat plants.	Cow, horse
Elephants	Tusks. Trunk.	Largest mammal. Eat plants.	African elephant
Primates	Developed hands, eyes.	Most intelligent mammal.	Chimpanzee, human

Questions: Answer in complete sentences.

1. Does the platypus seem like a bird in any way? Why do scientists classify it as a mammal?
2. Name three ways in which reptiles and mammals are different.
3. Do any mammals live in the sea? Why don't scientists classify whales and dolphins as fish?
4. Name two advantages that primates have over other mammals.

CHAPTER REVIEW

Science Words: Think of a word for each blank. List the letters **a** through **v** on paper. Write the word next to each letter.

Animals with backbones are called ___a___. All of them have a hard framework within the body. This is called the ___b___. Some fish are bony and some are supported by a substance known as ___c___. All fish breathe through ___d___. Their body temperature changes with the temperature around them. That means that fish are ___e___. Animals that live "two lives" are ___f___. They undergo a big change known as ___g___. Instead of a two-chambered heart like the fish have, the amphibians have a ___h___ heart. Snakes, alligators, and turtles are three kinds of ___i___. ___j___ have a hard, protective shell. Although all ___k___ are legless, there are some ___l___ that do not have legs either. ___m___ and ___n___ are the only reptiles with a four-chambered heart. A bird is considered ___o___ because its body temperature always stays the same. Birds are covered with ___p___. Most of them fly with their ___q___. Many birds have ___r___ bones that also help them to fly. Animals that are covered with fur and that feed their young milk are called ___s___. These animals live in many places, even in the ___t___, where the walruses and seals live. Mammals with sharp teeth shaped like chisels are the ___u___. Monkeys belong to the group known as the ___v___.

Questions: Answer in complete sentences.

1. How do scientists use the backbone to help them classify different kinds of animals?
2. Describe how fish get oxygen.
3. Why do we say that frogs live "two lives"? Give details.
4. Which is a true land animal, a toad or a snake? Explain.
5. What is one way that all reptiles and all birds are alike?
6. How do wings help birds to fly? How do feathers and hollow bones help them?
7. Most birds can fly, but only one kind of mammal can. Name two other ways mammals are different from birds.

Classifying plants and animals

A. Obtain these materials: paper, pencil, reference book.

B. Using the clues below, match each organism pictured with its correct group. Then unscramble the letters for its name.

Clues:

1. Hunts for food on the forest floor at night. Thin, moist skin. Lays eggs in water.

2. Hunts in the desert at night. Scaly skin. Lays hard, leathery eggs.

3. Has fins and fish-like tail. Mother pushes newborn to surface of water to breathe, and nurses young.

4. Warm-blooded. Triangle-shaped scales made of hair. Mothers nurse young.

5. Has hinged leaves and small white flowers. Leaves snap shut when insects walk on them.

6. Grows on trunks of dead trees. Uses wood for food.

Groups:

Angiosperms: USNEV TRYFLAP
Fungi: EFBEATESK ROUSMMOH
Amphibians: RITGE DESLAAMARN

Reptiles: NADDEB COGEK
Mammals: INPHOLD
GANPLINO

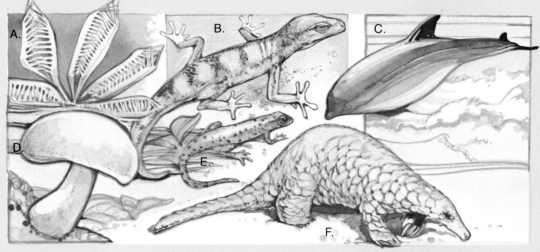

CAREERS

Beekeeper ▶

A **beekeeper** cares for colonies of honeybees. The best time to start beekeeping is in the spring when fruit trees and dandelions begin to bloom. In the early fall, the *beekeeper* checks each bee colony to see that it has at least 23 kilograms (50 pounds) of honey and several frames of pollen. A person who wants to become a beekeeper should work with a skilled beekeeper and read books about the subject.

◀ Wildlife Manager

A **wildlife manager** works to preserve and manage animals in public forests, wildlife refuges, and privately owned land. *Wildlife managers* plan conservation programs and organize surveys to find out the number of animals in given areas. They work to provide environments where animals will reproduce. An interest in animals and a background in science is needed for this work.

EXPLORING THE
UNIVERSE

UNIT 6

CHAPTER 15

THE EARTH, MOON, AND SUN

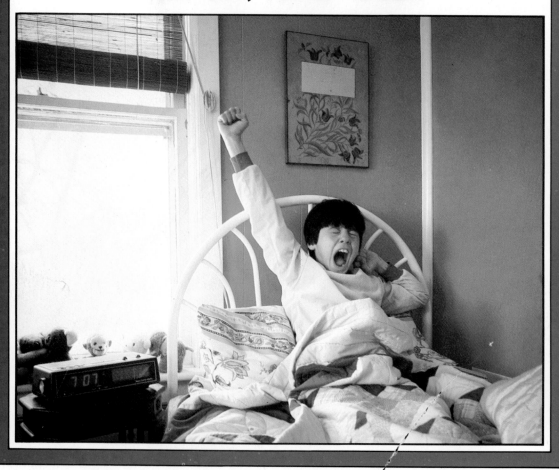

15-1.

Day, Night, and the Seasons

Morning already? It always happens, doesn't it? Night and day are two things we can depend on. Bob slept soundly through the night. But he was actually moving! He and all the things around him were speeding along on the earth through space. It is the movement of the earth that causes day and night. When you finish this section, you should be able to:

- ☐ **A.** Explain what causes night and day.
- ☐ **B.** Describe how the earth moves around the sun.
- ☐ **C.** Explain what causes the seasons.

Look at the two photos in the margin. What can you tell about the time of day? The change from day to night happens during every 24-hour period. During the day the sun brightens the sky. At night the sky is dark. But in another part of the world it is light. Ancient people did not know this. They believed the sun moved across the sky each day. But it is really the earth that moves.

The sun is many times larger than the earth and very far away. Great amounts of light from the sun reach the earth. The side of the earth facing the sun receives the light. It is daytime for that part of the earth.

The earth is spinning. At the equator, it moves at about 1,600 kilometers per hour (1,000 miles per hour). As the earth moves, new parts of it come into the sun's light. This spinning motion of the earth is called **rotation.** It takes 24 hours to complete one *rotation*. During that time, there is one day and one night.

Rotation: The spinning of an object.

night | day

sun

spin of the earth

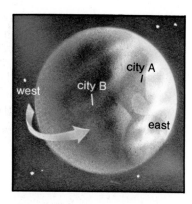

Axis: An imaginary line around which the earth spins.

In what direction do you look to see the rising sun? The sun appears to rise in the east. What is really happening is that the earth rotates from west to east. Look at the diagram at left. If you are in city A, it is already morning. But in city B you might still be sleeping.

The earth rotates around its **axis**. The *axis* is an imaginary line. It goes from the top of the earth, through the center, to the bottom of the earth. Use a pencil to get an idea of the earth's axis. Place a pencil point on a piece of paper. The pencil should stand straight up. Now slowly rotate the pencil. Imagine a round earth spinning with the pencil at its center. Now tip the pencil slightly so it is no longer straight up and down. Rotate again. This is more like the way the earth spins. Its axis is tilted slightly. This tilt of the earth is what causes the seasons.

Revolution: The movement of one object around another.

Do you dress differently in January than you do in June? The months of the year bring different weather. The earth rotates on its axis and moves through space at the same time. The earth makes a trip around the sun. This trip takes one year. Every 365¼ days the earth completes its **revolution** around the sun. During one *revolution* most places on earth have four seasons. What are the names of the seasons?

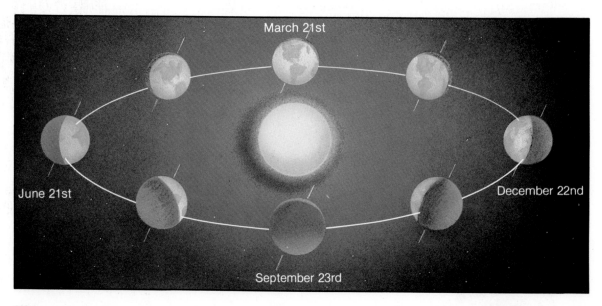

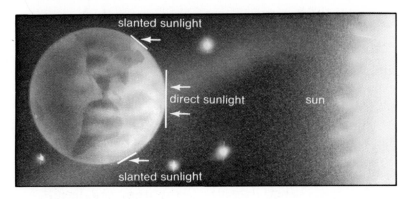

slanted sunlight

direct sunlight

sun

slanted sunlight

The first day of summer in the Northern Hemisphere is June 21. The diagram shows that on this day the axis of the earth is pointed toward the sun. This means that the Northern Hemisphere receives a great deal of the sun's energy. Sunlight hits the Northern Hemisphere directly. It gives the light and heat we think of when we think of summer. June 21 is known as the **summer solstice**.

The diagram on page 296 also shows the earth on December 22. It is on the opposite side of the sun. Notice that the earth's tilt is still the same. But the earth has moved. Now the Southern Hemisphere is facing directly into the sun. The Northern Hemisphere is pointed away from the sun. The Northern Hemisphere is receiving sunlight that is weaker. The sun's rays hit the Northern Hemisphere on a slant, not directly. December 22 is the first day of winter. It is also known as the **winter solstice**.

Look at the two other positions of earth. March 21 is the first day of spring. It is also called the **vernal equinox**. September 23 is the first day of autumn. It is the **autumnal equinox**. In these seasons, the earth has moved to positions that are halfway between winter and summer. The tilt of the earth has not changed. In these seasons, neither the Northern Hemisphere nor the Southern Hemisphere receives sunlight that is direct.

The diagram above shows the difference between the slanted and direct light. You can imitate how sunlight strikes the earth by using a flashlight.

Summer solstice: The first day of summer in the Northern Hemisphere.

Winter solstice: The first day of winter in the Northern Hemisphere.

Vernal equinox: The first day of spring in the Northern Hemisphere.

Autumnal equinox: The first day of fall in the Northern Hemisphere.

ACTIVITY

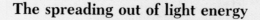

The spreading out of light energy

A. With a partner, obtain these materials: chalk, flashlight, 1 sheet of construction paper.

    B. Hold the flashlight about 10 cm from the paper. Have your partner draw a circle around the lit area.

      1. What does the light from the flashlight represent?

      2. What does the paper represent?

      3. Predict how the lit area will look when the paper is tilted away from the light.

      C. Tilt the paper away from the light. Draw a line around the lit area.

      4. What do you observe?

      5. Compare your predictions and results.

Section Review

Main Ideas: The earth rotates around its axis every 24 hours, causing day and night. The earth makes one revolution around the sun in 365¼ days. The tilt of the earth's axis and its movement around the sun cause the seasons: summer, autumn, winter and spring.

Questions: Answer in complete sentences.

1. How long does it take for earth to complete one rotation? How long for one revolution?
2. How can it be light in one city and dark in another?
3. Draw a simple diagram that shows the earth's axis.
4. What is the direction of the earth's tilt on June 21? What is this date called?
5. Weak, slanted rays describe the light that hits the Northern Hemisphere during which season?

The Moon

On July 20, 1969, these words were sent to earth: "Houston . . . the *Eagle* has landed." Those words were spoken by astronaut Neil Armstrong. He was speaking to the Mission Control Center in Houston. The *Eagle* he mentioned was not a bird. It was the first spacecraft with passengers to land on the moon's surface. Neil Armstrong and Edwin Aldrin were in the *Eagle*. Neil Armstrong was the first human to step on the moon's surface. When you finish this section, you should be able to:

☐ **A.** Describe the surface of the moon.
☐ **B.** Explain why the moon seems to change in shape.
☐ **C.** Describe what happens when the moon or earth blocks the sun's light.

The moon is the earth's closest neighbor in space. It is only 400,000 kilometers (250,000 miles) away! But the moon and earth are quite different. The earth is a **planet.** The *planets* are the main bodies in space that revolve around the sun.

Planets: The main bodies in space that revolve around the sun.

Satellite: An object in space that revolves around a planet.

The moon is a **satellite** (sat-uh-lite) of the earth. A *satellite* is an object in space that revolves around another object. The moon makes one complete trip around earth in 27⅓ days, or about once a month.

You can observe the moon's motion in the sky. But some people have observed the moon up close. In three years, 12 brave Americans landed on the moon. They took pictures and made maps. They brought back moon rocks. They gathered 2,000 rocks, weighing over 380 kilograms (840 pounds). Most of the rocks, like the one shown at left, were given to scientists for study.

The scientists learned that the moon once had lots of volcanoes. They sent out huge amounts of melted rock material. This material flowed outward and formed the flat parts of the moon. Between the flat parts are bowl-shaped holes. These are called **craters** (**kray**-terz). The picture on the left below shows a *crater*.

Craters: Bowl-shaped holes.

Scientists think the moon's craters were formed when objects traveling in space hit and dented the moon's surface. The flat, smooth places on the moon's surface are called **maria** (sing. **mare**). This means "seas" in Latin. But these seas are dry. The picture on the right shows two *maria*, named the Sea of Serenity (suh-**ren**-ih-tee)

Maria: Smooth places on the moon's surface.

and the Sea of Tranquility (tran-**kwil**-ih-tee). Some of the craters have also been given names. One is named Copernicus (kuh-**per**-nih-kus) and another is named Tycho (**ty**-koh) after the famous scientists. There are also mountains on the moon's surface. Some are as high as the highest mountains on the earth.

Even though the moon has mountains and "seas," it is not at all like earth. It has only its barren, rocky surface. The moon has no air around it like earth has. That is why the astronauts brought their own air supply to the moon.

Probably you have seen the moon many times. Does it always look the same to you? How does the moon change? The moon appears to change its shape. The moon, of course, does not change shape. The moon, like earth, does not produce any light of its own. That may be a little hard to believe, since the moon seems so bright on some nights. Actually, the light we see from the moon is reflected sunlight. Sunlight strikes the moon, bounces off, and comes to earth. But remember—at any one time, only half of the moon is lit by the sun. So when the moon moves around the earth, we can't always see the entire lighted side of the moon. We only see part of that side. As a result, the moon seems to change shape.

The pictures on the right show some of the shapes the moon seems to have. Sometimes we see only a tiny part of the lighted side of the moon. This is called a crescent moon. As the moon moves in its path around the earth, more of its lighted side can be seen. The second picture shows a first quarter moon. The moon is one quarter through its trip around the earth. When the whole lighted surface is seen, the moon is full. Then the moon seems to shrink again. It goes through its last quarter and then a crescent shape again. Then the moon disappears altogether. When the moon's entire lighted surface faces away from the earth, it is known as a new moon. These shapes of the moon are its **phases**. Have you seen each of the moon's *phases*?

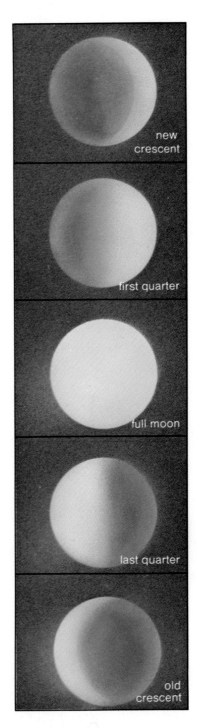

Phases: The shapes the moon appears to be as seen from the earth.

ACTIVITY

The phases of the moon

A. Obtain these materials: lamp, orange.

B. Imagine that the lamp is the sun, the orange is the moon, and you are earth. Place the lamp on a table so that it is level with your eyes. You may need to place books under the lamp. Turn on the lamp. Stand about 60 cm from the lamp, facing it.

C. Hold up the orange, halfway between the lamp and your eyes.

    1. How much of its lit surface can you see?

D. Turn so that your side faces the lamp. Hold up the orange about 25 cm from your eyes.

    2. How much of its lit surface can you see?

E. Turn so that your back is facing the lamp. Hold up the orange about 25 cm from your eyes, but slightly to the left of your head.

    3. How much of its lit surface can you see?

    4. Write a summary of your results. Explain why the shape of the moon seems to change.

The moon goes through all the phases each time it makes a complete trip around the earth. Do you know what phase the moon is in right now? Check a calendar to see. Better still, look at the moon tonight.

The moon revolves around earth at the same time that earth revolves around the sun. Sometimes the moon passes between earth and the sun. The moon slowly blocks the sun's light. When this happens, a shadow of the moon is cast on earth. Even though it's daytime, the sky gets dark. The moon has caused a **solar eclipse** (soh-ler ee-**klips**). It is a *solar eclipse* because the sun is blocked out as you can see in the photograph. The total solar eclipse can only be seen from the small area on earth where the moon's shadow falls. Find that area in the diagram below. From other parts of the earth, the sun looks partially blocked out. Total solar eclipses do not happen often. A total solar eclipse won't be seen from North America until after the year 2000.

Solar eclipse: Occurs when the moon passes between the earth and the sun.

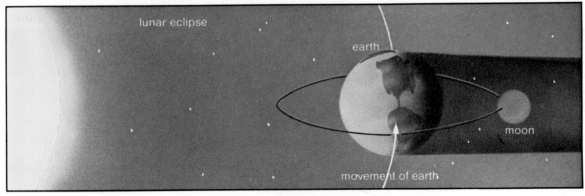

Sometimes earth passes between the moon and the sun. Earth blocks the sun's light that would light up the moon. A shadow of earth is cast on the moon. The moon loses its light. It may appear to have a red color. This is a **lunar eclipse** (**loo**-ner ee-**klips**), shown above. The bottom diagram on page 303 shows the positions of the moon, earth, and sun during a *lunar eclipse*.

Lunar eclipse: Occurs when the earth passes between the moon and the sun.

Section Review

Main Ideas: The moon is earth's satellite. Its surface has craters, mountains, and maria. The moon seems to change in shape. At certain times, solar and lunar eclipses can occur.

Questions: Answer in complete sentences.

1. What is a satellite? What is the earth's satellite called?
2. Name and describe two features that are found on the moon's surface.
3. Why does the moon seem to change shape?
4. Name six phases of the moon. In which phase is the moon invisible?
5. What is the difference between a solar eclipse and a lunar eclipse?

How would you like to fly the plane shown below? This was the first plane to fly using the energy of the sun. When you finish this section, you should be able to:

☐ **A.** Describe some characteristics of the sun.
☐ **B.** Explain one way in which the sun's energy can be used.

The sun is a **star**. *Stars* are objects in space made of hot gases. The gases are so hot that they glow, giving off light. Unlike planets, stars give off their own light. Our sun is a star that is about 150 million kilometers (93 million miles) away. The sun is spinning through space, as are the earth and the other planets.

The sun is made of the gases hydrogen (**hy**-druh-jen) and helium (**heel**-ee-um). The sun has a central **core** with layers around it. At the *core*, hydrogen takes part in a nuclear reaction. The hydrogen changes to helium. This

Core: The central part of the sun.

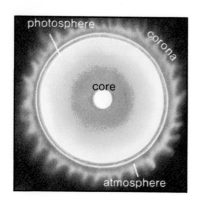

photosphere

corona

core

atmosphere

Photosphere: The surface of the sun.

Sunspots: Dark spots on the sun.

Solar flares: Bright areas in the sun's atmosphere from which hot gases shoot out.

occurs at a temperature of about 15 million degrees centigrade. The process of changing hydrogen to helium releases huge amounts of energy. The energy is in the form of heat and light. The heat and light move outward from the core to the sun's surface.

The sun's surface is the **photosphere** (**foh**-toh-sfeer). Above the *photosphere* are layers of gases. They form the sun's atmosphere. The sun's energy leaves the photosphere and travels outward into space. Some of the sun's energy reaches the earth and the other planets.

Look at the picture below. Do you see dark spots on the sun's surface? These dark spots are **sunspots**. *Sunspots* are places on the sun where the gases have cooled. Cool gases do not give off as much light as hot gases.

Sometimes there are bright areas in the sun's atmosphere from which hot gases shoot out into space. These bright areas are called **solar flares**. *Solar flares* seem to affect things on earth. For example, they can interfere with radio messages.

You have already learned about a solar eclipse. Look back at the picture on page 303. It shows the sun during a

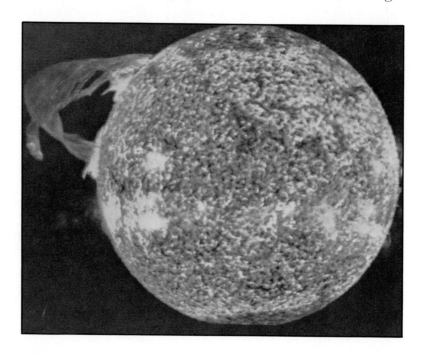

solar eclipse. The moon is blocking most of the sun's light. Notice the faint white light around the edges of the sun. This light is called the **corona** (kuh-**roh**-nuh). The word *corona* also means *crown*. Why do you think the light is called the corona?

Life on earth depends on the sun. Without the sun, earth would be an empty, cold place. There wouldn't be any plants or animals. The sun is earth's main source of heat and light.

Examine the photograph above. It shows a house that uses *solar energy*. The glass panels on the roof are solar panels. Inside the solar panels are pipes carrying water. The sun's light heats the water in the pipes. The pipes carry the hot water to a storage tank under the house. When hot water is needed for washing, it is carried through other pipes from the tank to the faucets. To heat the house, hot water in pipes passes by a fan that blows air on the pipes. The air is warmed by the hot water. The warm air is sent around the house through air vents.

The airplane pictured on page 305 also uses the sun's energy, but not for heat. The sun's energy is changed into electricity by solar cells like those on page 210.

Corona: The faint, white light seen around the sun during a solar eclipse.

ACTIVITY

pencil

tape

cardboard

Making a sundial

A. Obtain these materials: pencil, tape, cardboard 20 cm square, watch, compass, marking pen.

B. Draw a circle 15 cm across on the cardboard. Mark one place on the circle N for north.

C. Make a hole in the center of the circle big enough for the pencil. Tape the pencil to keep it upright.

D. Bring the sundial outdoors on a sunny day. Find north with the compass. Turn the cardboard so that the N faces north. Mark the place where the shadow of the pencil points. Write the time there. Do this several times during the day.

1. What direction is the sun when the shadow of the pencil is the shortest? the longest?

2. Can you tell the time by the shadow the next day?

Section Review

Main Ideas: The sun is a star 150 million kilometers (93 million miles) from earth. The sun produces great amounts of energy. Some of this energy travels to earth. The sun's sunspots, solar flares, and corona can be seen from earth. Solar energy is used to heat the air and water in some homes.

Questions: Answer in complete sentences.

1. From what does the sun get its energy?

2. Make a diagram of the sun's corona. When can you see the corona?

3. What is a solar flare?

4. Why do sunspots look dark?

5. What is one way in which people can use the sun's energy?

CHAPTER REVIEW

Science Words:

On a sheet of paper, write the word that fits each definition.

1. The movement of one object around another.
2. An object in space that revolves around another.
3. The first day of summer in the Northern Hemisphere.
4. The first day of autumn in the Northern Hemisphere.
5. Smooth places on the moon's surface.

Define each of these terms.

6. Crater
7. Winter solstice
8. Photosphere
9. Rotation
10. Phase

Questions: Answer in complete sentences.

1. What causes day and night?
2. In Washington, D.C., the sun has just come up. In a town that is 2,000 km to the west, has the sun come up yet? Explain your answer.
3. List the four seasons. Identify the direction in which the Northern Hemisphere is pointed for each.
4. True or false: The tilt of the earth changes with each season. Explain your answer.
5. You have just landed on the moon. Describe all the features that you see.
6. During which phase of the moon do you see the entire side of the moon that faces the sun? How often can you see this phase?
7. Sketch the sun, moon, and earth in the order they would be during a solar eclipse. What part of the sun can be seen then?
8. What are two different features that are visible on the surface of the sun?

CHAPTER 16

THE SOLAR SYSTEM

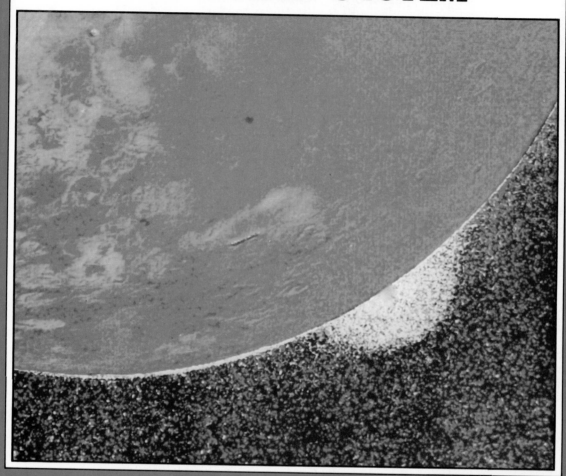

16-1.

The Inner Planets

310

Imagine a place with huge volcanoes that are constantly erupting. That's what it's like in the place that you see above. The photograph shows a moon of one of the planets in our *solar system*. When you finish this section, you should be able to:

□ **A.** Identify and describe the characteristics of the four inner planets.

□ **B.** Compare two ideas about the movements of the earth and the planets.

Earth is not the only planet that revolves around the sun. Eight other planets do, too. These nine planets, their moons, and the sun are called our **solar system**. For thousands of years, people have looked at the planets of our *solar system*. Ancient people noticed that some objects in the night sky did not twinkle. These objects also seemed to wander through the night sky. They appeared to change positions with respect to the stars. These objects were named "planets," after the Greek word for *wanderer*.

Most ancient people believed that the sun, stars, and planets traveled around the earth. Almost 2,000 years ago, a man named Ptolemy (**tul**-uh-mee) wrote a book that described these ideas in great detail. This book was studied by people for hundreds of years. People agreed

Solar system: The nine planets, their moons, and the sun.

with Ptolemy's ideas. They thought all the objects in the sky moved around the earth.

In 1543, a Polish scientist, Nicolaus Copernicus, wrote a book that announced a new idea. He said that the earth and the planets moved around the sun. People were shocked at that idea. They wanted to believe that the earth was the center of everything. Galileo, an Italian scientist, agreed with Copernicus. He wrote a book that used the same ideas. Galileo got into trouble for his book. It went against the beliefs of the time. As the years passed, other scientists observed that the earth moved around the sun. Today we have instruments and spacecraft that help us explore our solar system. We now know much more about the planets.

The planets revolve around the sun in paths called **orbits** (or-bits). Their *orbits* are shaped like stretched-out circles, or **ellipses**. The drawing shows the planets in their orbits around the sun. Look at the four planets closest to the sun. They are **Mercury** (mer-kyer-ee), **Venus** (vee-nus), **Earth**, and **Mars** (marz). They are called the inner planets.

Orbit: The path of one object in space around another.

Ellipses: The shapes of the orbits of the planets.

Mercury, Venus, Earth, Mars: The four planets closest to the sun. They are also called the inner planets.

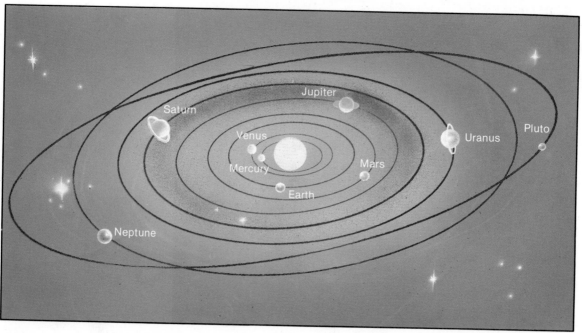

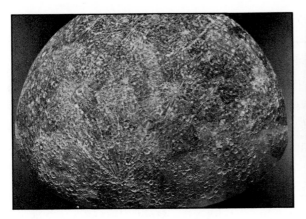
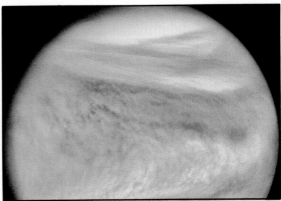

Mercury is the smallest planet. It is also the closest to the sun. The surface temperature on the side of Mercury facing the sun can be as high as 430°C (806°F). The surface temperature on the dark side can be −200°C (−330°F). Pictures taken by spacecraft sent to Mercury show a surface like that of the moon. Look at the top left picture. Mercury has craters. Scientists believe that there is no air, water, or life on Mercury. The planet has no moons.

Venus is the second planet from the sun. Venus has no moon. It is the closest planet to earth. Venus has often been called earth's twin. Both planets are about the same size. Both planets are covered with clouds. But the yellow clouds of Venus are so thick that only a gloomy light reaches the surface. The sun's light and heat are trapped in the clouds. That makes the temperature at the surface about 480°C (896°F). The air is almost all carbon dioxide. There is no water. There are erupting volcanoes. Winds roar. Lightning flashes.

The cloud cover kept scientists from knowing what Venus was like. We know more now because of the use of **space probes**. A *space probe* is a rocket in space that contains cameras and other devices. Space probes record what it's like on other planets. Some space probes fly past objects in space. The *Pioneer* space probe flew past Venus. It sent back information that helped scientists learn more about the surface of Venus.

Space probe: A rocket launched into space to send information back to earth.

313

ACTIVITY

Charting the inner planets

A. Obtain these materials: paper, pencil, ruler.

B. Study the chart below.

	Mercury	Venus	Earth	Mars
Distance from sun (millions of km)	58	103	155	228
Diameter (km)	4,840	12,200	12,756	6,760
Length of planet year (days)	88	225	365	687

C. Prepare three bar graphs. Each graph will compare the inner planets on a different characteristic. They are: distance from the sun, diameter, length of the year (one revolution around the sun). Prepare one graph for each characteristic.

    1. Which planet has the largest diameter? Which planet has the smallest diameter?

    2. Which planet is the farthest from the sun? Which planet is the closest?

    3. Which planet has the longest year? Which planet has the shortest?

    4. Write a summary for your graphs.

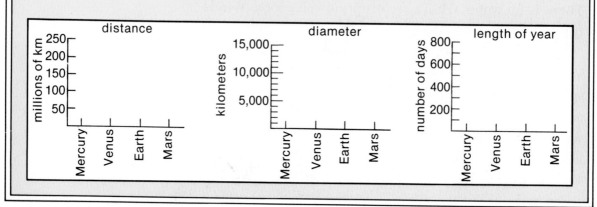

Earth is the third planet from the sun. Scientists believe earth is the only planet that has water and air that contains oxygen. Therefore, they think it is the only planet in our solar system that has life as we know it. Earth has one moon.

Mars is the fourth planet from the sun. It is about half the size of earth. Mars appears to be red, except for white spots at its poles which are ice caps. You can see one in the photo below. The ice caps are made of solid carbon dioxide. There is no water on Mars. Its air is mostly carbon dioxide. Its surface is covered with mountains, craters, and volcanoes. You can see a volcano below. During the day on Mars, the temperature can reach 27°C (80°F). At night, the temperature may drop to −123°C (−190°F). Why do you think it is colder on Mars than it is on earth? Mars has two moons.

The *Viking* space probe shown above landed on the cold, rocky surface of Mars. Samples of Martian soil were taken by the scooping arm of the space probe. From that soil, scientists think that there is no life on Mars.

Section Review

Main Ideas: The nine planets revolve in elliptical orbits around the sun. The four planets closest to the sun are called the inner planets.

Questions: Answer in complete sentences.

1. Compare Ptolemy's ideas about the solar system with those of Copernicus.
2. Which planet is described in each phrase below?
   a. red planet with ice caps
   b. closest planet to the sun
   c. about the same size as earth
   d. has one moon
   e. has surface temperatures of 430°C and −200°C
   f. has water and air that contains oxygen
   g. has constant cloud cover
3. What is an orbit? What shape are the orbits of the planets?
4. What help do scientists have in learning about the inner planets?

The Outer Planets

In October 1981, *Voyager 2* sped close to the planet *Saturn*. This spacecraft sent wonderful photographs of Saturn's famous rings back to earth. Saturn is one of the outer planets of our solar system. When you finish this section, you should be able to:

☐ **A.** Identify and describe the characteristics of the outer planets.

☐ **B.** Compare the orbits of the outer planets around the sun.

The outer planets are **Jupiter** (**joo**-pih-ter), **Saturn** (sa-tern), **Uranus** (yoo-**ray**-nus), **Neptune** (**nep**-toon), and **Pluto** (**ploo**-toh). For years, people have searched the sky for these outer planets. Two of them are bright and can be seen easily. *Jupiter* and *Saturn* are very large. They reflect a lot of light. The other planets are small. They are also very far away. To see them, scientists need powerful instruments. Scientists use **telescopes** to gather light from distant objects. *Telescopes* make distant objects appear closer and larger. Scientists who study objects in the sky are called **astronomers** (uh-**strah**-nuh-merz).

Jupiter, Saturn, Uranus, Neptune, Pluto: The outer planets.

Telescope: An instrument that makes distant objects appear closer and larger.

Astronomer: A scientist who studies objects in space.

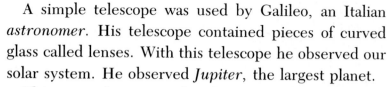A simple telescope was used by Galileo, an Italian *astronomer*. His telescope contained pieces of curved glass called lenses. With this telescope he observed our solar system. He observed *Jupiter*, the largest planet.

This giant planet is so big that 1,300 earths could fit into it. Jupiter is covered by bands of clouds. It also has a giant red spot. Find it in the photograph of Jupiter below. Scientists think this spot on Jupiter may be a large and long-lasting storm. The red spot is believed to be as wide as earth and four times as long. There is no water on Jupiter. It is made of frozen gases.

In 1610, when Galileo looked at Jupiter, he saw four objects near it. These were four of Jupiter's 16 moons. With modern telescopes we can see these moons. One of Jupiter's moons is **Io** (**eye**-oh). The picture in the margin below shows Io. This moon has many erupting volcanoes. One of Io's volcanoes is shown on page 310. That picture of Io was made by computers which can add bright colors to photographs that are taken in space.

Io: One of Jupiter's moons.

Voyager 2 sent many photographs of the planet *Saturn* back to earth. Saturn is the second largest planet in our solar system. It is the next planet from the sun after Jupiter. Saturn is covered with clouds. Its bright rings extend out into space around the planet. Saturn has about a thousand rings made of millions of frozen particles.

Saturn has at least 17 moons. The photograph below shows Saturn with some of its moons. The one in the front is Dione. This moon may look big, but it is really much smaller than Saturn. The picture in the margin shows Dione in orbit with Saturn in the background.

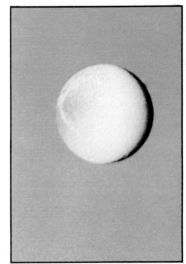

orbits in 1999

Neptune

Earth

Sun

Pluto

Neptune's orbit

Pluto's orbit

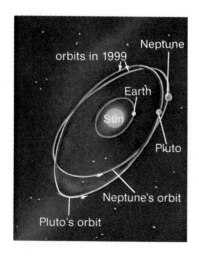

orbits in 1999
Neptune
Earth
Sun
Pluto
Neptune's orbit
Pluto's orbit

The next planet from the sun is *Uranus*. It is so far away that little is known about the planet. Uranus has rings like Saturn, but fewer. The planet has five moons. Unlike the other planets, Uranus lies on its side as it orbits the sun.

Beyond Uranus are the planets *Neptune* and *Pluto*. These two planets are far from the sun. Their orbits have different shapes. In 1979, Pluto moved inside Neptune's orbit. Now Pluto is the eigth planet from the sun. Neptune is the ninth. In 1999, Pluto will again move outside Neptune's orbit.

Neptune is about the same size as Uranus. Pluto is about the size of our moon. Neptune has two moons. Pluto has one rather large moon. Pluto's moon is about

Planet	Distance from sun in millions of km (mi)	Rotation	Revolution
Mercury	58 (36)	58 days, 18 hr	88 days
Venus	103 (62)	243 days	224.7 days
Earth	155 (93)	23 hr, 56 min	365.2 days
Mars	228 (141)	24 hr, 37 min	687 days
Jupiter	778 (482)	9 hr, 50 min	11.86 years
Saturn	1,427 (856)	10 hr, 14 min	29.46 years
Uranus	2,869 (1,721)	15 hr, 30 min	84.01 years
Neptune	4,427 (2,656)	15 hr, 48 min	164.8 years
Pluto	5,900 (3,660)	6 days, 9 hr	248.5 years

one half its own size. Both Neptune and Pluto are extremely cold.

When planets come close to each other, their orbits change a little. Scientists have noticed changes in the orbits of Uranus and Neptune. But Pluto is too small a planet to cause these changes. Some scientists feel a tenth planet may be beyond Neptune and Pluto.

The chart on page 320 compares the planets in different ways. The chart shows how far away from the sun each planet is. It shows how long it takes for each planet to rotate on its axis and to revolve around the sun.

Section Review

Main Ideas: Astronomers look at the planets through telescopes. Jupiter, Saturn, Uranus, Neptune, and Pluto are the outer planets. *Voyager 2* has sent back many photographs of Jupiter and Saturn and their moons.

Questions: Answer in complete sentences.

1. Which planet is described in each phrase below?
   a. will be the farthest away until 1999
   b. the largest planet
   c. has a thousand rings
   d. lies on its side in orbit
   e. has a giant red spot

Use the chart on page 320 to answer questions 2 through 4 below.

2. Which planet rotates in about the same amount of time as earth?
3. Which planet revolves around the sun in the shortest amount of time?
4. Which planet takes the longest time to make one revolution around the sun?
5. How has observing the planets changed since Galileo's time?

16-3.

Asteroids, Meteors, and Comets

Meteoroids: Chunks of iron, nickel, and other materials that move through space.

Meteor: A burning meteoroid.

Meteorite: A meteoroid that lands on a surface.

What caused the hole in the ceiling the man below is looking at? The chunk of metal on the right crashed through the roof of someone's home! Millions of tons of this material enter the earth's atmosphere each year. When you finish this section, you should be able to:

☐ **A.** Identify three types of objects other than planets that move through our solar system.
☐ **B.** Describe each type of object and where each is found.

Meteoroids (**mee**-tee-er-oydz) are chunks of iron, nickel, and other materials that move through space. Millions of tons of *meteoroids* enter the earth's atmosphere each year. Most burn up as they move through our atmosphere. The light they cause can be seen across the sky. People call them shooting stars. A shooting star is really a **meteor** (**mee**-tee-or). Some meteoroids actually hit the earth's surface. When the material lands, it is called a **meteorite**. Most *meteorites* that strike the surface are very small. The one shown below is about the size of a grapefruit. Now and then a large one hits the earth. Our moon is also hit by meteorites. Because the moon has no atmosphere, they do not burn up. Many more meteorites hit the surface. They form craters.

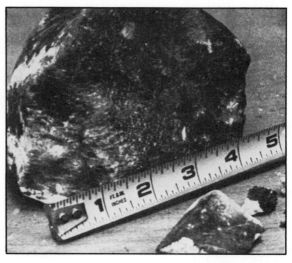

ACTIVITY

Making a model solar system

A. Obtain the following materials: basketball, clay, meter stick.

B. The chart lists the nine planets. It also lists scale numbers to use in making a solar system model. For each planet, make a ball of clay that measures across the number shown for the model scale.

C. When all the planet models are complete, go outside to the schoolyard with the models. Have a classmate stand at one end of the yard and hold the basketball. The basketball represents the sun. Have another classmate stand 12 m from the "sun" and hold up the Mercury model.

D. Measure the distances from the "sun" for each planet shown on the chart.

   1. What planets did not fit in your schoolyard?
   2. Where would you put the asteroids?
   3. What would the path of a comet be like?
   4. Based on your model, which planet do you think we probably know the least about? Explain your answer.

Planet	Model scale	Distance scale
Mercury	1 mm	12 m
Venus	2 mm	22 m
Earth	2 mm	30 m
Mars	1 mm	46 m
Jupiter	28 mm	155 m
Saturn	26 mm	285 m
Uranus	10 mm	574 m
Neptune	9 mm	899 m
Pluto	1 mm	1,191 m

Asteroids: Rocky objects that orbit the sun.

Comets: Objects that are made of ice and rock particles and orbit the sun.

If you traveled between Mars and Jupiter, you would see a strange sight. You would see thousands of rocky objects much smaller than planets. They are called **asteroids** (as-ter-oydz). About 1,600 *asteroids* have been observed and named. The largest asteroid is less than 1,000 kilometers (600 miles) long. Some scientists think that asteroids are pieces of a planet that broke apart. Others think asteroids are pieces of material that will someday form a planet. Each asteroid has its own orbit around the sun.

Comets are objects that are made of ice and rock particles and orbit the sun. *Comets* travel from beyond the outer planets toward the sun. As a comet comes close to the sun, some of the ice changes into gas. The gas is pushed away from the comet. It forms a tail. The tail of a comet always streams away from the sun. Each time a comet comes near the sun, more of its ice changes to gas. It gets smaller and smaller. Comets are named for the people who discover them. The most well-known comet is Halley's comet.

Section Review

Main Ideas: Meteoroids are objects that travel through the solar system. Some become meteors or meteorites. Comets made of ice and rock particles orbit around the sun. Asteroids located between Mars and Jupiter also orbit around the sun.

Questions: Answer in complete sentences.

1. What is a meteoroid? What is a meteorite?
2. Give two possible explanations for the asteroids.
3. Where are the asteroids found?
4. How can you tell where the sun is in a picture of a comet?
5. A comet goes around the sun three times. The third time it is smaller. Explain.

Does this photo of a *space shuttle* lift-off look familiar? Right now only people with special training can take trips in it. But in the future, people without special training will travel in it. They will be able to get on board, buckle up their safety belts, and blast off. Imagine yourself going on a journey that will be out of this world! When you finish this section, you should be able to:

☐ **A.** Describe what a rocket is.
☐ **B.** Describe the events that occur when a space shuttle is launched and returns to earth.

People have been interested in space travel for many years. The thought of breaking free of the earth's atmosphere and exploring the solar system is an exciting one. The dreams of space travel did not come true until this century.

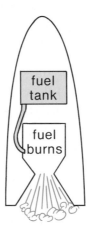

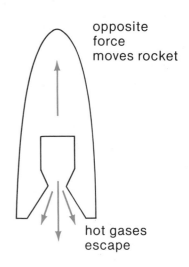

fuel tank

fuel burns

opposite force moves rocket

hot gases escape

Rocket: An engine that burns fuel and moves forward by pushing exhaust backward.

Travel in space presented a big problem. How could an object get away from the pull of the earth? What was needed was a special engine. It would have to produce enough force to lift a spacecraft weighing many tons. Airplane engines use oxygen. There is no oxygen in space. So a spacecraft needs an engine that works without oxygen. Finding the right kind of engine took many years. Modern scientists used a very old idea—the **rocket**.

A *rocket* is an engine that burns fuel and moves forward by pushing exhaust backward. Rockets operate by burning fuel in a tube. When the fuel burns, the hot gases produced are allowed to escape in one direction only. This causes a force to push in the opposite direction. Rockets do not need the presence of air. Any oxygen they need is in the fuel mixture that they burn.

Rockets can be used to place satellites, such as the one at left, in orbit. The rocket provides the power for the satellite to get into space. Once the satellite is far enough away from earth, the rocket falls off. The satellite then circles around earth on its own.

In 1957, the Soviet Union used a rocket to put the first spacecraft into orbit around earth. It was called *Sputnik I*. One year later, the United States sent a spacecraft named *Explorer I* into space. These events marked the start of the space age. Since then, powerful rockets have placed heavier satellites into orbit. They have carried astronauts to the moon. Rockets have launched space probes to fly near the other planets. Powerful computers help these spacecraft to stay on course.

Large spacecraft are very expensive to build. The United States has developed a spacecraft that is powerful and can be reused. It is the **space shuttle**. The *space shuttle* is different from other spacecraft. It can do three important things. It takes off like a rocket. It can fly in orbit around the earth like a rocket. Most important of all, it can land like an airplane. The shuttle is used to place satellites in orbit. It can also repair satellites that are in orbit. Someday the shuttle will carry people to orbiting space stations. Best of all, the same shuttle will fly to space and back more than 100 times.

The drawing shows the launching of a shuttle and its return to earth. Refer to it as you read. The shuttle is made of two parts: the **booster** and the **orbiter**. The *booster* contains large rockets. The *orbiter* looks like an airplane. The orbiter is attached to the top of the rockets.

Space shuttle: A reusable spacecraft that can orbit the earth and return like an airplane.

Booster: Powerful rockets that help spacecraft reach orbit.

Orbiter: The part of the shuttle that orbits and returns to the earth.

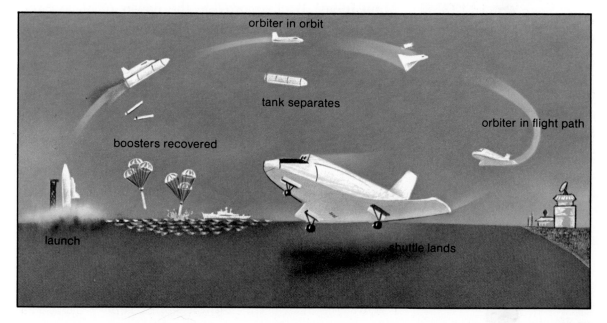

orbiter in orbit

tank separates

orbiter in flight path

boosters recovered

launch

shuttle lands

At lift-off the rockets push the orbiter about 40 kilometers (25 miles). There they separate from the orbiter. The rockets fall to the ocean by parachute. They are picked up, cleaned, and used again.

The orbiter keeps flying, using its own engines. The fuel for this part of the trip comes from large tanks. The fuel tanks drop off as the fuel is used up. Then the orbiter does what its name says it will do. It enters an orbit around earth.

When its mission is over, the shuttle flies back to earth like an airplane. The orbiter lands without any engine power. Small rockets get the orbiter on a path to the landing area. The pilot carefully aims for the runway. The pilot flies to the surface of earth without power. These pilots are experts. Can you imagine landing an object weighing 68,000 kilograms (150,000 pounds) going 335 kilometers per hour (210 miles per hour)? They only get one try. There is no way of getting back into the air once they have started down.

Section Review

Main Ideas: Rockets provide the power to place satellites in orbit. The space shuttle is placed into orbit by rockets and lands like an airplane.

Questions: Answer in complete sentences.

1. What causes a rocket to move forward?
2. What makes the space shuttle different from other spacecraft?
3. What is a booster?
4. What are some uses of the space shuttle?
5. Describe the lift-off, orbiting, and landing of the space shuttle. Then answer these questions.
   a. What drops from the shuttle as it goes into orbit?
   b. What part of the shuttle goes into orbit?

CHAPTER REVIEW

Science Words: Think of a word for each blank. List the letters **a** through **r** on paper. Write the word next to each letter.

The ___a___ _____ is made of the sun and the nine ___b___. The planets travel in ___c___ around the sun. ___d___ is the planet closest to the sun. The planet often called the earth's twin is ___e___. It is the ___f___ planet from the sun. Our own planet, earth, is the ___g___ planet from the sun. Just beyond us is ___h___ which appears red. The largest planet is ___i___ which has 16 ___j___. Beyond that planet is ___k___ with its thousand rings. The last three planets, ___l___, ___m___, and ___n___ are so far away from us that we do not know very much about them. Between the inner and outer planets are rocky objects called ___o___ that orbit around the sun. ___p___ are bright objects with tails that speed through space. We have learned much from the samples and photos sent back from the ___q___. People will get into space on the ___r___, a reusable spacecraft.

Questions: Answer in complete sentences.

1. Was Ptolemy's idea about the movement of the sun and planets correct? Explain.
2. List the names of the inner and outer planets in order, starting with the planet closest to the sun.
3. How has space travel helped astronomers learn about the solar system?
4. Compare the planets Venus and Jupiter in three ways: size, distance from sun, and number of moons.
5. What are the parts of a comet? What happens to a comet each time it goes around the sun?
6. You're at the controls of the space shuttle and are about to leave your orbit and head for home. What will you depend on to get you safely to earth?

CHAPTER 17

THE STARS AND BEYOND

17-1.

The Stars

Do you ever look up at the stars and wonder about them? On a clear night stars may seem very close. They are actually very, very far away. It takes years for the light from even the closest stars to reach us. When you finish this section, you should be able to:

□ **A.** Explain how the distance to a star from earth is measured.

□ **B.** Describe three ways in which stars differ from each other.

□ **C.** Describe the events that take place in the life of a star.

Imagine that you are traveling from one city to another. What units would you use to measure the distance? You would probably use kilometers or miles. However, the stars, except for the sun, are so far away that kilometers or miles are too small to use. Instead, a star's distance from earth is measured by the time it takes for the star's light to reach earth. Light travels at 300,000 kilometers per second (186,000 miles per second). The distance that light travels in one year is known as a **light-year**. This is how to figure out how many kilometers are in a *light-year*: Find the number of seconds that are in a year. Then multiply that number times 300,000 kilometers. You'll get a very large number. Do you see why light-years are used instead of kilometers?

The chart below lists the names of four stars. Next to each name is that star's distance from earth. The light leaving the star **Sirius** (**seer**-ee-us) will take 8.6 years to travel to earth. Which star listed is farthest from earth? How far away is it? Which star is closest? **Proxima Centauri** (**prox**-ih-muh sen-**tor**-ee) is the closest star to earth, other than the sun.

Light-year: The distance light travels in one year.

How many seconds are in one year?
1 minute has 60 seconds
x
1 hour has 60 minutes
x
1 day has 24 hours
x
1 year has 365 days
? seconds in 1 year

Star	Distance from Earth
Proxima Centauri	4.27 light-years
Sirius	8.6 light-years
Betelgeuse	520 light-years
Polaris	1,086 light-years

Stars differ from each other in three ways: color, brightness, and size.

331

Magnitude: The brightness of a star as seen from earth.

Dwarfs: Small stars.

Giants: Stars that swell and become large.

Supergiants: Very large stars.

What color are the stars you see at night? You probably said white. Stars may be blue, white, yellow, orange, or red. Stars differ in color because of their different temperatures. Look at the bar of iron being heated. First it turns red. As it gets hotter, it turns white. When it is hottest, it is bluish white.

Stars are balls of hot gases. Like the flame, stars with a high temperature are blue or blue-white in color. Red stars have lower temperatures. Yellow and orange stars have medium temperatures. The chart below lists the names of some stars, their colors, and their surface temperatures. What color star is our sun?

Star	Color	Temperature
Rigel	blue-white	12,000°C (21,600°F)
Sirius	white	10,500°C (18,900°F)
Sun	yellow	5,500°C (9,900°F)
Arcturus	orange	4,200°C (7,600°F)
Antares	red	3,000°C (5,400°F)

When you look at the stars at night, some stars look brighter than others. The brightness of a star is called its **magnitude** (mag-nih-tood). A star's *magnitude* depends on its size, temperature, and distance from earth. The brightest star in the night sky is Sirius, although Proxima Centauri is the closest star to earth. What star is the brightest in the daytime sky?

Stars are different sizes. The smallest stars are a little larger than earth. Small stars are called **dwarfs**. Stars that swell and become large are called **giants**. And of course very large stars are called **supergiants**.

By observing many stars, some scientists have made a very interesting hypothesis. They think that stars come into being, exist for a while, and then die. Stars begin as giant clouds of dust and gas. All the parts of the giant

ACTIVITY

Graphing star temperature data

A. Obtain these materials: sheet of graph paper, colored pencils or markers.

B. Prepare a bar graph that shows the temperature of stars and the colors of their light. Use the chart for the information.

Star color	Temperature
Red	4,000°C
Yellow	6,000°C
White	9,000°C
Blue	20,000°C

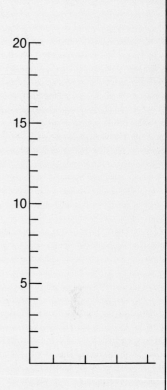

C. Along the left side of your graph, show the temperature. Along the bottom line, show the color of the light from the star. Use the graph shown as a guide. Color the bar so it is the color of the light from stars at that temperature.

D. Use the chart of stars shown on page 332 to answer the following.
   1. Where would each of the following stars be in your graph? Rigel, Sirius, Sun, Arcturus, Antares.
   2. Place a black dot to show them. Label each.

cloud pull on all the other parts. The particles of matter move closer and closer together. As this happens, the temperature of the cloud rises. For many stars, the temperature reaches about 10 million degrees. The cloud begins to glow. It keeps shrinking in size. Inside it, nuclear reactions take place. Energy is released into space. Some of the energy reaches us on earth. We see the light glowing from the star.

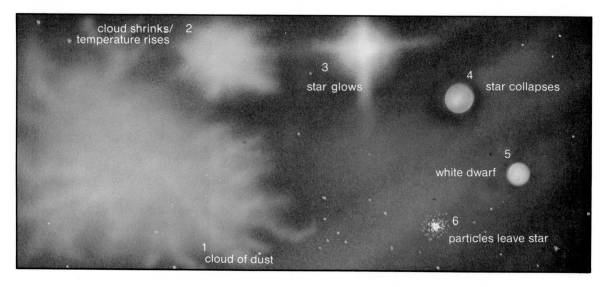

cloud shrinks/ 2 temperature rises

3 star glows

4 star collapses

5 white dwarf

6 particles leave star

1 cloud of dust

The energy of a star comes from the reactions that change hydrogen to helium. Our sun produces energy in the same way. As long as there are hydrogen and high temperatures, the star releases energy. When the hydrogen is all used up, great changes take place.

One thing that happens is that the inside of the star collapses. The star shrinks in size. It becomes a special kind of dwarf star called a **white dwarf**. A *white dwarf* is about the size of the earth. The white dwarf's energy moves outward into space. The magnitude of the dwarf star gets less and less. It gets dimmer and dimmer. The star is dying. As the star dies, gas and other materials leave it. It takes hundreds of millions of years for a star to be born and die as a white dwarf. The matter and energy that were part of the white dwarf go into space. Someday the matter from the old star may come into contact with matter from other stars. The particles will be drawn together slowly. The process will begin. The remains of old stars become the raw material for new stars.

Have you ever heard of **quasars** (**kway**-zarz)? They are objects about the size of stars that move very rapidly. They give out huge amounts of energy. One *quasar* may give out as much energy as hundreds of millions of stars. Quasars are billions of light-years away.

White dwarf: A star that has begun to shrink. It is about the size of the earth.

Quasar: An object about the size of a star that gives off huge amounts of energy.

334

Quasars were first discovered in 1961. Scientists noticed that large amounts of energy were coming from a certain place in the sky. The only way to explain that energy was that it was a new object. They named it a quasar. The energy from quasars was discovered not by looking, but by listening. Quasars give out radio waves. Radio waves can be picked up with a **radio telescope**.

A *radio telescope*, shown in the photo on the right, is shaped like a soup bowl. In its center is an antenna. The antenna is pointed toward the sky. The radio telescope records sounds made by such objects as quasars. The radio waves travel through space. They are picked up by the antenna. The antenna passes the waves to a receiver. The receiver changes the waves into a pattern. The pattern, drawn on a roll of paper in the recorder, tells astronomers the position of the object. The drawing on the left shows how the telescope operates.

There is another object in space that is even stranger than a quasar. It is known as a **black hole**. Scientists think that when some giant stars collapse, all their star material

Radio telescope: A telescope that picks up and records sounds from space.

Black hole: An area in space from which no light escapes.

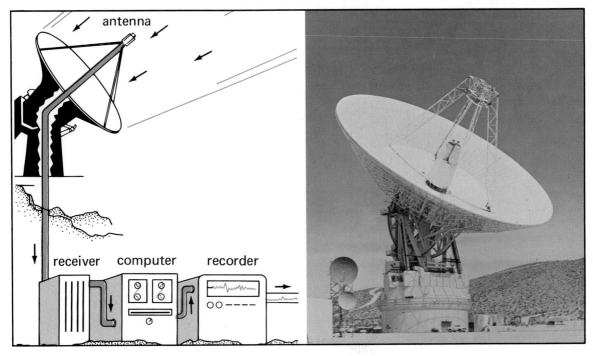

antenna

receiver   computer   recorder

is forced into a space less than 3 kilometers (about 2 miles) across. This area has so much matter that it pulls anything nearby into it. A *black hole* can even pull in light. This means that a black hole cannot be seen. Scientists think black holes exist because there are areas of space where star material seems to disappear. This discovery was made in 1971. The black hole was named Cygnus (**sig**-nus) X-1. A spacecraft discovered X rays coming from the place where matter was disappearing. X rays are thought to be given off when matter is pulled into a black hole.

The idea of a black hole is very exciting. Some scientists think that black holes may be like strange bridges. They may connect one part of space with another. If this is so, then anything that is sucked into a black hole may reappear someplace else. Maybe the "time travel" or "space warps" that you may have seen in science fiction movies are like black holes.

Section Review

Main Ideas: The distance to a star is measured in light-years. Stars differ from each other in size, color, and magnitude. Some stars seem to go through a definite pattern of birth, existence, and death. There are some objects, such as quasars and black holes, that we do not know very much about.

Questions: Answer in complete sentences.

1. Why are light-years and not kilometers used to measure the distance to a star?
2. How do stars differ in size and color?
3. What is a radio telescope?
4. Describe the characteristics of quasars and black holes.
5. Explain the steps that some stars go through as they are born, exist, and die.

Have you ever done follow-the-dot puzzles? If you have, then you will like learning about the patterns that people see in the night sky. For years people have imagined that the twinkling dots in the sky were the outlines of real objects. When you finish this section, you should be able to:

☐ **A.** Identify five groups of star patterns.
☐ **B.** Explain the cause for the apparent movement
of stars.

Ancient people thought that the skies were a magical place. They thought that the stars formed part of the outlines of kings and queens. They saw magical beasts and even giant objects.

People saw what they were familiar with. Hunters saw animals. Other people saw famous heroes from stories. Beliefs about the star patterns were passed down from one group of people to the next. Groups of stars that form patterns in the sky are called **constellations** (kahn-steh-**lay**-shunz). There are 88 *constellations*. The patterns

Constellations: Groups of stars that form patterns in the sky.

appear to look like animals, people, or objects. It takes a little imagination to see some of them.

Look at the three drawings of the sky shown below. Look at the star patterns. The first pattern shows the constellation **Orion** (oh-ry-un). People think *Orion* looks like a hunter. The three stars across the center are supposed to be his belt. The small stars below his belt are his sword. The two stars above Orion's belt are his shoulders. The two stars at the bottom are the hunter's legs. The star at Orion's left shoulder is a red star. It is named Betelgeuse (**bet**-ul-jooz). The star at his right leg is a blue star. It is named Rigel (**ry**-jel). Which star is hotter, Betelgeuse or Rigel?

Another constellation is **Cassiopeia** (kas-ee-oh-**pay**-ah). People think the pattern forms the crown of the queen *Cassiopeia*. Other people see her chair. Look at the drawing of the queen. Do you see her crown?

The third drawing shows **Cygnus** (**sig**-nus). People think *Cygnus* looks like a swan. Do you? There is a very bright star in Cygnus called **Deneb** (**den**-eb). *Deneb* is a white star. Is it hotter or cooler than Rigel?

Orion: A constellation that looks like a hunter.

Cassiopeia: A constellation.

Cygnus: A constellation that looks like a swan.

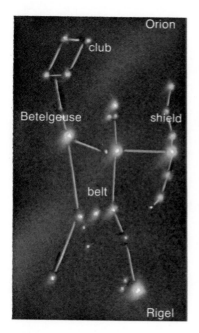

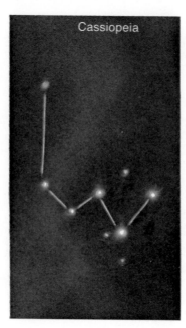

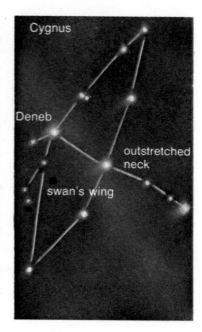

338

The constellations are not seen in the exact same place in the sky all night. They seem to move across the sky. The constellations seem to move because earth is rotating on its axis.

The constellations seen from earth in the winter are different from those seen in summer. This occurs because the earth travels around the sun. However, there are two constellations that can be seen all year in the Northern Hemisphere. You have probably seen them. They are the **Big Dipper** and **Little Dipper**. No matter where earth is, the North Pole is pointed toward these two constellations.

The *Big Dipper* and *Little Dipper* look like spoons or ladles. Look at the drawing above. The two stars at the end of the dipper of the Big Dipper are called *pointer stars*. An arrow drawn from these two stars will point to the last star of the handle of the Little Dipper. That star in the Little Dipper is called **Polaris** (poh-**lar**-is). *Polaris* is the North Star. Polaris is a star that does not seem to move. It is always above earth's North Pole. People use the North Star to tell their direction.

Big Dipper, Little Dipper: Constellations that are seen all year in the Northern Hemisphere.

Polaris: The North Star. A star always above earth's North Pole.

ACTIVITY

Making a constellation projector

A. Obtain these materials: black construction paper, clear tape, flashlight, safety pin, scissor, shoe box, tracing paper.

B. Cut out a square at one end of the shoe box. At the other end, cut out a circle so that the head of the flashlight fits into the hole.

C. Cut pieces of black paper and tracing paper that are slightly larger than the square opening.

D. On each sheet of tracing paper, trace one of the three groups of dots shown below.

E. Place each sheet of tracing paper over a piece of black paper.

F. Make a hole through each dot with an open safety pin so that the hole is made through the black paper, too.

G. Face that end of the box about 25 cm from a wall.

H. Darken the room. Turn on the flashlight.

1. What do you see on the wall?
2. What constellation is projected with the first star pattern?
3. What constellation is projected with the second?
4. What constellation is projected with the third?

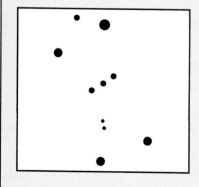
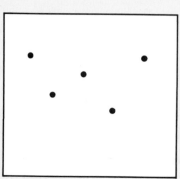
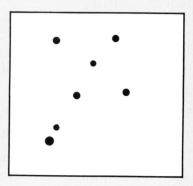

Section Review

Main Ideas: There are 88 constellations. People think the constellations look like people, animals, or objects. Orion, Cassiopeia, Cygnus, the Big Dipper, and the Little Dipper are constellations.

Questions: Answer in complete sentences.

1. What do we call stars that form patterns in the sky?
2. Why do constellations seem to move across the sky?
3. What is the main idea shown in the first drawing of this section?
4. Why do we see different constellations at different times of the year?
5. Name and describe the objects, people, or animals shown in the star patterns on the right.

People in Science

Susan Jocelyn Burnell

This young Irish scientist has made an important discovery in astronomy. While a student at Cambridge University in England, she studied the radio waves coming to earth from outer space. She used a giant antenna that received radio waves and sent the waves to a computer. The computer changed the waves into printed charts. Susan Burnell studied the charts for changes in the radio waves. One day she noticed some very suspicious wiggly lines on the charts. Radio waves were coming from deep space. Soon she noticed more of these waves. What Susan Burnell discovered were objects that scientists now call **neutron** (**nyoo-trahn**) stars. *Neutron* stars have the same weight as the sun but are only about the size of a city. They have a very strong magnetic field and spin quite rapidly.

17-3.

The Universe

Have you seen any science fiction movies lately? You may have seen pictures of gigantic space platforms. On them people live and work. Plants are able to grow. The people wear normal clothing because there is oxygen there. Wouldn't it be fun to ride on one? You are on one! It is called earth and it is whizzing through space. When you finish this section, you should be able to:

☐ **A.** Describe the group of over 100 billion stars that includes our solar system.
☐ **B.** Classify three types of *galaxies* by their shapes.
☐ **C.** Explain three theories about how everything in space was formed.

Galaxy: A group of billions of stars.

As you travel on the space platform earth, you can see many stars and some planets. You are looking at part of a **galaxy** (gal-ux-ee).

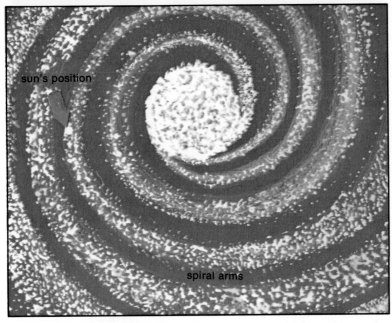

A *galaxy* is a group of billions of stars. The earth is in the **Milky Way** Galaxy. The *Milky Way* contains about 100 billion stars, including our sun. Look at the drawings above. From the side, the Milky Way is shaped like a huge disc with a bulge at its center. From above, it appears to have arms that spiral around the center. That is why the Milky Way is called a spiral galaxy. The distance from one edge of the Milky Way to the other is about 100,000 light-years. Our solar system is about 30,000 light-years from the center of the Milky Way. Look at the drawings again. The arrows point to the position of the sun in the solar system.

You are moving around the center of the Milky Way at 1,000,000 kilometers per hour (620,000 miles per hour). At that speed it would take you about one second to travel from Los Angeles to San Diego.

Milky Way: Our galaxy.

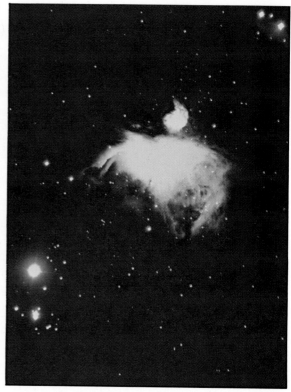

Andromeda Galaxy: A spiral galaxy close to our galaxy.

Nebulae: Clouds of dust and gas.

The Milky Way is not the only galaxy. By using radio telescopes, scientists have discovered millions of galaxies. Sixteen of these galaxies are within 3 million light-years of ours. One of the closest is called the **Andromeda** (an-**drah**-mih-duh) **Galaxy**. From earth this galaxy is seen in the same area of the sky as a constellation also named Andromeda. However, the galaxy is millions of light-years farther away from earth than the constellation. The *Andromeda Galaxy* is also a spiral galaxy. How is a spiral galaxy shaped?

The Milky Way contains dust and gases. Sometimes the dust and gases form clouds. The clouds are called **nebulae** (**neb**-yoo-lay). Look at the two pictures above. The first picture is of the Orion *nebula*. The second is the Horsehead nebula. Do you see a horse's head?

There are other types of galaxies that are not spiral.

Some galaxies have the shape of a circle that has been stretched out. They are called **elliptical** (ee-**lip**-tih-kul) **galaxies.** *Elliptical galaxies* have little dust and gas. Within them are trillions of stars. Another type is called an irregular galaxy. They got this name because they have no definite shape. Within irregular galaxies are clouds of gas, dust, and stars.

Galaxies have different shapes. Now scientists think galaxies group together, forming even larger structures that are cigar-shaped or flattened like pancakes.

All of the galaxies and the space they exist in are called the **universe** (**yoo**-nih-vers). How was the *universe* formed? Scientists have many theories. A theory is a possible explanation for what is observed. Scientists do experiments to test their theories. A good theory explains all of their observations.

Elliptical galaxy: A galaxy that has the shape of a stretched-out circle.

Universe: All the galaxies and the space they exist in.

ACTIVITY

Making a model of the Milky Way

A. Obtain these materials: sheet of graph paper, pencil, ruler.

B. Use the following information to prepare a scale drawing of the Milky Way Galaxy. It is 100,000 light-years across. The center of the galaxy is 30,000 light-years from our solar system. Its thickness near earth is 3,000 light-years. Its thickness at the center is 10,000 light-years.

C. Label your scale drawing to show the following information. The galaxy is rotating. The speed of our solar system around the galaxy is 240 kilometers per second. It will take 230 million years for our solar system to make one revolution around the Milky Way Galaxy.

Here is one theory. Over 10 billion years ago, everything in the universe was packed together. Suddenly there was a giant explosion. Everything went flying outward. The galaxies, stars, and planets were formed.

Another theory states that galaxies are always moving out of the universe. New galaxies are always forming to take their places.

A third theory states that the universe explodes, comes together, and explodes again. This is believed to happen about every 80 billion years. There are still other theories about how the universe was formed.

Section Review

Main Ideas: The Milky Way and the Andromeda galaxies are spiral galaxies. Galaxies may also be irregular or elliptical. There are many theories about how the universe was formed.

Questions: Answer in complete sentences.

1. What name is given to the group of 100 billion stars that includes our solar system?
2. Describe the three types of galaxies.
3. Describe three theories about how the universe was formed.
4. What is the main idea shown in the drawings that show the location of the sun in the Milky Way?
5. A nebula contains many galaxies. Is this statement true or false? Explain your answer.

CHAPTER REVIEW

Science Words: Match the terms in column A with the definitions in column B.

Column A

1. Quasar
2. Constellation
3. Polaris
4. Galaxy
5. Light-year
6. Elliptical
7. Nebula
8. Andromeda Galaxy
9. Magnitude
10. Black hole

Column B

A. The brightness of a star as seen from the earth
B. A place from which no light escapes
C. An object the size of a star that gives off as much energy as hundreds of millions of stars
D. The closest galaxy to ours
E. A cloud of dust and gas
F. A galaxy that is the shape of a stretched-out circle
G. A group of billions of stars
H. A pattern of stars in the sky
I. A star that is always above the North Pole
J. The distance light travels in a year

Questions: Answer in complete sentences.

1. Compare three types of galaxies.
2. Describe the galaxy that our solar system is in.
3. Explain what is meant by the term *light-year*. Why don't astronomers use kilometers instead of light-years?
4. A person looking at stars through a telescope notices that some of them appear to have different colors. Give an explanation for these colors.
5. If a person said that our sun is made of recycled material (material that is used again), what might he or she mean?
6. Does a radio telescope use light? Explain.

Building and using an astrolabe

A. Obtain these materials: small weight such as a washer or nut, piece of cardboard (25 cm square), tape, protractor, pencil.

B. Place a degree mark at the lower left-hand corner of the cardboard. Place a 90° mark at the upper right-hand corner. Using the string as a guide, draw a curved line from the lower left-hand corner to the upper right-hand corner. Make additional marks at 10° intervals from 0° to 90° using the protractor.

C. Tie the weight to the string. Tape the free end to the upper left corner. You have made an **astrolabe** (**as**-troh-layb). This is used to locate objects in the sky. You sight objects along the top edge of the cardboard. When you use the *astrolabe* to sight an object at the horizon, the string should cross the 0° mark.

D. Prepare a chart to record the number of degrees that objects are above the horizon. Sight the following: tops of trees, chimneys, moon, brightest star. CAUTION: DO NOT SIGHT THE SUN. YOU COULD DAMAGE YOUR EYES. Record your data.

   1. What is the astrolabe reading for an object straight ahead?

   2. What is the astrolabe reading for an object directly above you?

   3. What is the astrolabe reading for an object halfway between the horizon and the position directly above you?

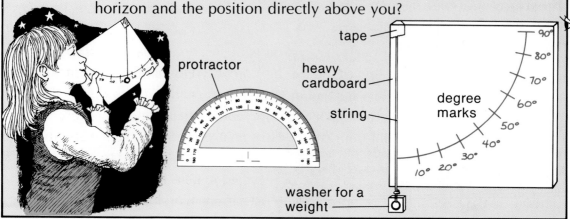

tape

protractor

heavy cardboard

string

degree marks

90°
80°
70°
60°
50°
40°
30°
20°
10°

washer for a weight

CAREERS

Astronaut ▶

An **astronaut** has an exciting job. Most *astronauts* are good jet pilots who take special training. They ride on special airplanes to experience the weightlessness of space. They learn how to use radar, computers, and even space-age clothing and food containers. Astronauts have to be in topnotch physical condition. Their job requires them to work very hard for a long time.

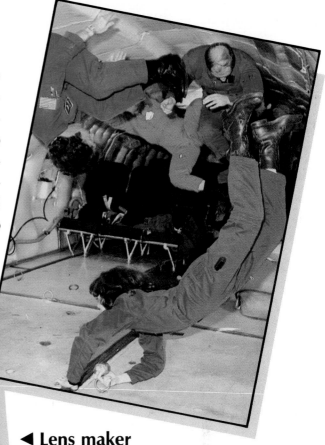

◀ Lens maker

A **lens maker** grinds clear pieces of glass into various shapes. Many telescopes contain lenses that have been carefully ground. The *lens maker* has to have a good eye for detail. The glass that is used cannot have any marks or scratches. Lens makers also have to be very patient and able to handle delicate objects. Lens makers usually learn their trade by working with an experienced lens maker for many years.

GLOSSARY/INDEX

In this Glossary/Index, the definitions
are printed in italics.

Absorb (ab-**sorb**): *to take in*, 101

Abyssal plain (uh-**bis**-ul): *flat part of ocean floor*, 11, 14, 18, 19

Acoustics (uh-**koo**-sticks): *the study of sound and how it affects people*, 100, 108

Agar (**ah**-gar): *a tasteless, odorless material made from seaweed*, 44

Algae (**al**-jee): *plantlike protists that have chlorophyll and grow in water*, 235, 236

Alligators, 279–280

Ameba (ah-**mee**-buh): *a one-celled animal-like protist with no regular shape*, 232

Amphibians (am-**fib**-ee-unz): *cold-blooded vertebrates that must live in or near water*, 275–277; blood system of, 277; compared to reptiles, 278; heart of, 276–277; structures of, 277; water essential to, 276

Andromeda (an-**drah**-mih-duh) **Galaxy:** *a spiral galaxy close to our galaxy*, 344, 346

Angiosperms (an-jee-uh-**spermz**): *seed-bearing plants that form their seeds inside a flower*, 251

Animals, cells of, 226, 229; classification of, 290; cold-blooded, 274, 275, 278, 281; land, 278; need plants, 242; ocean, 50–51; sunlight essential to, 307; warm-blooded, 281, 284, 287, 288; with backbones, 272–288; with four-chambered heart, 280; without backbones, 254–270

Antennas (an-**ten**-uz): *jointed structures on the heads of many arthropods that are used for feeling, smelling, and hearing*, 265, 341

Aqualung (ak-wuh-lung): *an air tank worn on a diver's back*, 58, 62

Armature (**ahr**-muh-cher): *the coil of wire in a generator*, 194

Arthropods (**ahr**-thruh-pahdz): *invertebrates with jointed legs and an outer skeleton*, 264–270; five groups of, 265–270

Asteroids (**as**-ter-oydz): *rocky objects that orbit the sun*, 324

Astronaut (**as**-stro-not): *an American who travels in space*, 299, 301, 349

Astronomer (as-**stron**-oh-mer): *a scientist who studies objects in space*, 317, 321

Auditory nerve (**awe**-dih-tore-ree): *the nerve that carries sound messages to the brain*, 127

Autumnal equinox (awe-**tum**-nal ee-**kwi**-noks): *the first day of fall in the Northern Hemisphere*, 297

Axis: *an imaginary line around which the earth spins*, 296, 297, 298

Backbone: *a column of bones that extends up the center of the back*, 143

Bacteria (bak-**teer**-ee-uh): *the smallest one-celled organisms that are clearly alive*, 234

Ball-and-socket joint: *a kind of joint where the bones can move in many directions*, 146–147

Bathyscaphe (**bath**-ih-scaf): *an underwater ship*, 59, 62

Bats, 98, 99, 100, 285, 288

Battery, 169, 170, 171, 191

Bell, Alexander Graham, telephone invented by, 104, 107

Biceps (**by**-seps): *the muscle on the top side of the upper arm*, 151, 153, 155, 156

Big Dipper: *a constellation that is seen all year in the Northern Hemisphere*, 339, 341

Biologist, marine, 62, 65

Birds, 1, 6, 281, 283

Black hole: *an area in space from which no light escapes*, 335–336

Blood, carries carbon dioxide, 273; carries food to cells, 115, 140, 157, 276; carries oxygen to cells, 157, 228, 276; carries wastes away, 115, 140, 157, 273; flows through muscles, 155–156

Body system (**sis**-tum): *groups of organs that work together*, 116, 117

Bones, 139–149; and minerals, 140; and voluntary muscles, 151, 153, 154; muscles attached to, 157; *See also* Skeletal system

Boosters: *powerful rockets that help spacecraft reach orbit*, 327

Boyle, Robert, sound experiments of, 89

Brain, and hearing, 127; and immovable joint, 148, 149; and sight, 129, 132; and taste, 120, 122; and touch, 137; as part of nervous system, 116, 117; protected by cranium, 142; sends messages to muscles, 153

Breaker: *a wave in which the crest has tumbled forward,* 33, 36

Carbon dioxide (kar-bon die-ox-side): *a gas found in the air,* 241, 242; carried by blood, 273, 274; on Mars, 315; on Venus, 313

Cardiac muscle (kar-dee-ak): *a type of muscle that the heart is made of,* 156

Cartilage (kar-tuh-lij): *a soft substance that is found where some bones meet,* 145–146, 149; *a firm but bendable material that forms the skeleton,* 274

Cassiopeia (kas-ee-oh-pay-ah): *a constellation,* 338, 341

Cell(s) (selz): *tiny living parts of the body,* 115; *tiny living parts of which all organisms are made,* 226–229; and spores, 248; and viruses, 230–231; food carried to, 115; of animals, 242, 256; of bones, 140; of muscles, 156–157, 158; of plants, 232; of plants compared to animals, 229; of sponges, 255; of vertebrates, 273; oxygen carried to, 115, 226, 227, 229; red blood, 228, 273; reproduction of, 115, 227; types of, 115–117

Cell membrane (mem-brayn): *outside covering of a cell,* 115, 226, 229

Cell wall: *a stiff protective layer around plant cells,* 229

Centipede (sen-tuh-peed): *an arthropod with many body segments and one pair of legs on most segments,* 269–270

Central processing unit (CPU): *the "brain" of a computer,* 213, 216

Characteristic (kar-ik-ter-is-tik): *something that helps set one thing apart from another,* 223, 225

Charge(s) (char-jez): *the electrical property of matter,* 165–168; positive and negative, 165–168, 170

Chip: *a small electric circuit,* 211–212, 216

Chlorophyll (klor-uh-fil): *green material in plants' cells that helps them make their own food,* 228–229, 232, 235, 236, 237, 240–242, 246

Circuit (ser-kut): *the path through which current electricity flows,* 170; closed, 170; design of, 219; four parts of, 170; kinds of, 170, 173, 177; open, 170; parallel, 177–181; series, 173–176

Circuit breaker: *a safety device for circuits that opens a switch to break a circuit,* 179, 181

Classification (klas-ih-fih-kay-shun): *a way of sorting things into groups according to ways they are alike and ways they are different,* 222–225; of animals, 290; of bacteria, 234; of birds, 283; of plants, 290; of reptiles, 283

Closed circuit, 170

Cold-blooded animals: *vertebrates whose body temperature stays the same as the temperature of the surroundings,* 274, 275, 278, 281

Comets: *objects that are made of ice and rock particles and orbit the sun,* 324

Computer: *a device that stores and handles information,* 212–216, 341; used in space travel, 313, 315, 327; uses of, 214–216

Computer program: *a series of directions for a computer to follow,* 214

Conclusion: *a final statement based on observations,* 3

Conductors (kun-duk-terz): *materials that allow current to flow through them easily,* 169–172, 180

Conservation (kahn-ser-vay-shun): *careful use of a natural resource,* 207–208, 210, 291

Constellations (kahn-steh-lay-shunz): *groups of stars that form patterns in the sky,* 337–341

Continental shelf (kahn-tih-nen-tul): *part of the ocean bottom near land,* 11, 14, 18, 19

Continental slope: *part of the ocean bottom where the continental shelf plunges downward sharply,* 11, 14

Copepods (koh-peh-podz): *tiny shrimplike animals,* 49, 54

Copernicus, Nicolaus (ko-purr-nih-kus): *a Polish scientist who in 1543 wrote that the earth moved around the sun,* 312

Core: *the central part of the sun,* 305–306

Corona (kuh-roh-nuh): *the faint, white light seen around the sun during a solar eclipse,* 307, 308

Cranium (kray-nee-um): *group of skull bones that surround the brain,* 142

Craters (kray-terz): *bowl-shaped holes,* 300, 304, 315, 322

Crest: *the highest point of a wave,* 32, 33, 36

Current(s): *water that moves in a certain direction,* 26–30, 65; caused by sun, 29, 30; caused by temperature, 64; caused by wind, 27–28; deep, 29–30

Current electricity: *the flow of negative charges, or electrons,* 170

Cycads (sy-kadz): *the earliest plants that reproduced by seeds,* 249–250

Cygnus (**sig**-nus): *a constellation that looks like a swan*, 338, 341

Cytoplasm (**sight**-uh-plazm): *the liquid inside the cell where the cell's activities take place*, 227

Decibel (**des**-ih-bel): *unit of measurement of sound intensity*, 95–96

Desalination (dee-sal-ih-**nay**-shun): *the process of removing salt from ocean water*, 47–48

Diaphragm (**dy**-uh-fram): *part of a camera that controls how much light enters*, 132

Diatoms (**dy**-uh-tahmz): *tiny ocean plants*, 44

Dinosaurs, 223, 249, 278, 280

Disease, caused by bacteria, 234; caused by viruses, 231; spread by insects, 269

Disk: *magnetic tape that stores information in a computer*, 213

Dislocation (dis-loh-**kay**-shun): *a bone forced out of its usual position in a joint*, 148

Dolphins, 85, 286, 287

Dry cell, 169, 170, 171, 191

Dwarfs: *small stars*, 332

Ear canal: *a narrow tube inside the ear that carries sound vibrations into the head*, 126

Eardrum: *the part of the ear at the end of the ear canal*, 127

Earth, 295; compared to the moon, 301; moon revolves around, 303; oxygen of, 315; rotation of, 295–296

Earthquakes, 32, 36

Echo (**eh**-ko): *a sound reflected from an object*, 98–101

Echo sounder: *an instrument that sends out sounds that hit the ocean bottom*, 59, 62

Edison, Thomas, invented the first phonograph, 104, 107

Eggs, of birds, 281; of insects, 267–268; of reptiles versus amphibians, 278; of the platypus, 285

Electrical appliance: *a device that uses electricity*, 169

Electricity (ih-lek-**tris**-ih-tee): *a form of energy*, 164–182; and chips, 211–212, 216; and generators, 194–196; and sound energy, 102–108; conductors of, 169–172; current, 169–172; in relation to magnetism, 188–196; measurement of, 198–202; produced by fuels, 205–206; produced by nuclear reaction, 206, 208–209; produced by solar cells, 209–210; produced by water, 203–206;

static, 164–168, 169; used in computers, 212–216

Electromagnet (ih-lek-troh-**mag**-net): *a magnet made with current electricity*, 190–192, 206

Electron(s) (ih-lek-trahn): *the smallest negative charge*, 168, 170, 172; and dry cells, 175; and terminals, 175–176; move through circuit, 177–178

Ellipses: *the shapes of the orbits of planets*, 312

Elliptical galaxy (ee-**lip**-tih-kul): *a galaxy that has the shape of a stretched out circle*, 345, 346

Endoskeleton (en-doh-skel-uh-tun): *a hard support structure inside the body of some vertebrates*, 273, 274

Energy (**eh**-ner-jee): *the ability to do work*, 69–70, 72, 165; electricity changed into, 199–202; forms of, 199–200; from fuel, 205–206; from sunlight, 209, 210, 228, 241, 306, 307; heat, 199–200, 205–206; light, 79–82; needed by muscle cells, 157; of a star, 334; of motion, 200; sound, 79–82

Euglena (yoo-**glee**-nuh): *a one-celled organism that is like both an animal and a plant*, 232

Exoskeleton (ek-so-skel-uh-tun): *the hard outer covering of arthropods*, 264–265, 268, 273

Extinct (ek-**stinct**): *does not exist anymore*, 55, 56, 65

Faraday, Michael: *19th century scientist who discovered the way to produce electricity from magnetism*, 193–194

Farsightedness: *difficulty in seeing close-by objects*, 131

Ferns: *plants with roots, stems, and leaves, and that reproduce by spores*, 248–249

Fish, 273–275, 277; fins of, 275; structures of, 277; with skeletons, 274

Flatworm: *a worm with one body opening and a long, flattened body*, 256, 257

Food, carried to cells by blood, 115, 157; from ocean, 44–45; important to bones, 140; made by plants, 243, 248

Food chain: *a pattern of who-eats-whom*, 50–51, 54–55, 56, 65

Force: *a push or a pull*, 165; magnetic, 185–187

Fossil fuels (**fah**-sil **fyoo**-ellz): *fuels formed from remains of plants and animals*, 46, 48

Fossils, 18, 60

Frequency: *the number of vibrations made in one second*, 92–93, 96

Fuel (fyoo-el): *anything that can be burned to produce heat*, 205, 207; used in rockets, 326, 328

Fungi (fun-jy): *plantlike protists that cannot make their own food*, 236–237

Fuse: *a safety device for circuits with a piece of wire that melts to break the circuit*, 179, 181

Galaxy (gal-ux-ee): *a group of billions of stars*, 342–346; spiral, 343, 344, 346

Galileo: *Italian astronomer who wrote book using Copernicus' ideas*, 312, 318

Galvanometer (gal-vuh-**nahm**-uh-ter): *an instrument that can measure a weak electric current*, 193, 195

Gas(es), a form of matter, 207; above the sun's surface, 306; as medium for sound, 88, 90; made from a liquid, 16; of stars, 332

Generator (jen-uh-ray-ter): *a machine in which current electricity is produced with magnetism*, 194–196, 203–206

Genetics (juh-**neh**-tiks): *study of how characteristics are passed along from one generation to the next*, 252

Giants: *stars that swell and become large*, 332

Gills: *structures in some water-dwelling animals that pick up oxygen from the water*, 274, 275, 276

Gymnosperms (**jim**-nuh-spermz): *seed-bearing plants that form seeds on cones exposed directly to the air*, 250

Hearing, 123–127. *See also* Sound.

Heart, four-chambered compared to three-chambered, 280; heard by stethoscope, 88; made of muscles, 116, 154, 156; of amphibians, 276–277, 279–280; of fish, 273–274; of reptiles, 278

Heat, and ocean currents, 29, 30; and pollution of rivers, 209; energy, 199–200

Helium (**heel**-ee-um), 305–306, 334

Herb: *a plant without a woody stem*, 245

Hinge joint: *a kind of joint where the bones can move back and forth or up and down*, 146

Hollow-bodied animal: *a simple invertebrate with one body opening that is surrounded by tentacles*, 256, 258

Hydroelectric plant (hy-droh-ih-**lek**-trik): *a power plant at which falling water is the energy source*, 205

Hydrogen (hy-druh-gen), 305–306, 334

Hypothesis: *a scientific guess*, 3

Input: *the information that goes into a computer*, 213, 216

Insects, 267–269, 270, 273, 276; eaten by centipedes, 270; eaten by lizards, 280

Insulators (in-suh-lay-terz): *materials that do not allow current to flow through them*, 171, 172

Intensity: *the loudness or softness of a sound*, 91–92, 94, 95, 96

Invertebrates (in-ver-tuh-brayts): *animals without backbones*, 254–270; compared to vertebrates, 273; spiny-skinned, 262–263

Investigate: *to study carefully*, 2

Involuntary muscles (in-**vahl**-un-teh-ree): *muscles, such as the heart, that cannot be controlled*, 154

Io: *one of Jupiter's moons*, 318

Iris (eye-rus): *the colored part of the eye*, 129, 132

Jawbone: *a bone that is part of the head*, 143

Joint: *the place where two bones meet*, 146; immovable, 148, 149; kinds of, 146–148, 149

Jupiter (joo-pih-ter): *the fifth planet from the sun in the solar system*, 317, 318, 321, 324

Kelp: *the largest kind of seaweed*, 235

Kilowatt-hour: *a unit used to measure electricity use*, 201, 202

Leaf: *the plant structure that usually makes food*, 243, 246; eaten by caterpillars, 268; of ferns, 248

Lens (lenz): *the part of the eye that changes light into a pattern*, 129–130, 132

Ligaments (lig-uh-ments): *strong bands of material that hold bones in place at joints*, 147, 149

Light, traveling through the eye, 129–130, 131, 132

Light energy, from the sun, 209–210, 228, 295, 297, 298; speed of, 81, 90; travels, 79–82

Light-year: *the distance light travels in one year*, 331

Lines of force: *lines around a magnet that show where the magnetic force is found,* 185–187, 189

Liquid(s), as sound media, 90; changed into a gas, 16

Little Dipper: *a constellation that is seen all year in the Northern Hemisphere,* 339, 341

Lunar eclipse (loo-ner ee-klips): *occurs when the earth passes between the moon and the sun,* 304

Lungs, of amphibians, 275; of reptiles, 279

Magnets: *objects that pick up or attract iron, nickel, and cobalt,* 184; and speakers, 106; and electricity, 188–196, 205; poles, 184, 194

Magnetic field: *the space around a magnet in which there is a magnetic force,* 185, 189

Magnetic force, 185–187, 189

Magnitude (mag-nih-tood): *the brightness of a star as seen from earth,* 332

Mammals: *vertebrates that have hair and feed milk from their bodies to their young,* 284; groups of, 288; in the sea, 286; meat-eating, 285, 286; most intelligent, 287; plant-eating, 286, 287; pouched, 285, 288

Maria (muh-ree-uh): *smooth places on the moon's surface,* 300–301, 304

Marine biologist, 62, 65

Marrow (mar-roh): *a soft substance in the hollow of some bones,* 144

Mars (marz): *a planet in the solar system,* 312, 315–316, 324

Mechanical energy (muh-kan-ih-kul): *the energy of motion,* 200

Media: *more than one medium,* 87–90

Medium: *matter through which sound can travel,* 87–90

Membrane (mem-braine): *the thin skinlike covering of a cell,* 115, 226, 229; and viruses, 231

Mercury (mer-kyer-ee): *the planet in the solar system closest to the sun,* 312–313

Metamorphosis (met-uh-mor-fuh-sis): *a series of major changes in the structure of an animal as it develops from its early stages to become an adult,* 268, 276

Meteor (mee-tee-or): *a burning meteoroid,* 322, 324

Meteorite: *a meteoroid that lands on a surface,* 322, 324

Meteoroids (mee-tee-er-oydz): *chunks of iron, nickel, and other materials that move through space,* 322, 324

Microscope, 223, 226, 229

Mid-ocean ridge: *mountain chain on the ocean floor,* 11, 14

Milky Way: *our galaxy,* 343, 344, 345, 346

Millipede (mil-uh-peed): *an arthropod with many body segments and two pairs of legs on most segments,* 270

Minerals, in ocean water, 15–19; make up bones, 140; used by plants, 243

Mollusk (mahl-usk): *an invertebrate with a soft body, usually protected by a shell,* 259; three kinds of, 259–261, 263

Molten (mol-ten): *melted by heat,* 21, 23, 24

Moon(s), 299–304; and tides, 38, 40, 41; changing appearance of, 301; compared to the earth, 301; hit by meteorites, 322; light from, 301; motion of, 300; of Neptune, 320; of Saturn, 319; of Uranus, 320; of Jupiter, 318; phases of, 301, 302, 303; volcanoes on, 300

Morse, Samuel: *first person to send a message using the telegraph,* 103

Mosses: *small plants without real roots, stems, or leaves,* 247–248

Muscle cells, exercise important to, 157; requiring energy, 157, 158; three types of, 156–157, 158

Muscles, 150–158; attached to exoskeleton, 264; functions of, 150; types of, 151, 153, 154, 155–158

Muscular system: *all the muscles of the body,* 150

Musical instruments, 73, 75–78

Natural gas: *a fossil fuel in gas form,* 46

Natural resource: *something useful found in nature,* 207, 210

Neap (neep) **tides:** *low tides that are not very low; high tides that are not very high,* 40–41

Nearsightedness: *difficulty in seeing far-away objects,* 130

Nebulae (neb-yoo-lay): *clouds of dust and gas,* 344

Negative terminal: *part of the dry cell that has extra electrons,* 176

Neptune (nep-toon): *a planet in the solar system,* 317, 320–321

Nerve cell(s): *cell that carries information,* 115, 134; and hearing, 127; and sight, 129

Nervous (nerv-us) **system:** *the system that controls all other systems in the body,* 116, 117; of land-living animals, 277; sense of taste as part of, 120, 122

Nose, 116–117, 118
Nuclear reaction (nyoo-klee-er ree-ak-shun): *a reaction that occurs when tiny particles of matter are split apart*, 206; waste product of, 208–209, 210
Nucleus (nyoo-klee-us): *the part of the cell that controls its activities*, 115, 156, 227, 230

Observe: *to watch closely*, 2
Ocean, and fossil fuels, 46; farming, 45; forms of life in, 49–51; movements of, 26–41; pollution of, 52–56; resources in, 43–48; salt removed from, 47–48; three areas of, 49; water of, 15–19. *See also* Current(s), Tides, Waves.
Ocean bottom, 10–14; changes in, 14
Ocean floor: *part of the ocean bottom that lies at the bottom of the continental slope*, 11, 14; changes in, 20–24; exploration of, 57–62; layers of sediments on, 60–61, 62
Olfactory nerve (ol-fak-tore-ee): *nerve that carries smell messages to the brain*, 117, 120
Optic nerve (op-tik): *the nerve that carries sight messages to the brain*, 129
Orbit: *the path of one object in space around another*, 312, 316; of outer planets, 317, 320–321
Orbiter: *the part of the shuttle that orbits and returns to the earth*, 327–328
Organ: *group of tissues that works together*, 116, 117
Organism: *a living thing*, 225; eaten by sponges, 255; grown from cells, 248; one-celled, 232
Orion (oh-ry-un): *a constellation that looks like a hunter*, 338, 341, 344
Outer ear: *the part of the ear that gathers sound vibrations*, 126, 127
Output: *the information that comes out of a computer*, 213, 215, 216
Oxygen, absent in space, 326; carried to cells by blood, 115, 157, 228, 276; needed by animals, 242; needed by cells, 226, 227, 229, 273; on earth, 315; picked up by gills, 274, 275; released by plants, 241, 242; supplied by four-chambered heart, 280

Parallel circuit: *a circuit with more than one path through which charges can flow*, 177–181; compared to series circuit, 178
Paramecium (par-uh-mee-see-um): *an animal-like protist shaped like a slipper*, 232

Pelvis (pel-vis): *the hipbones and backbone*, 144
Percussion instrument (per-kush-shun): *an instrument that produces a musical sound when hit*, 77–78
Pesticides (pes-tih-sidz): *chemicals sprayed on crops*, 53–56
Petroleum (peh-troh-lee-um): *a fossil fuel in liquid form*, 46
Phases (fay-zes): *the shapes the moon appears to be as seen from the earth*, 301
Phonograph, 104–105, 106, 107, 108
Photosphere (foh-toh-sfeer): *the surface of the sun*, 306
Photosynthesis (foh-toh-sin-thuh-sis): *the process by which plants use light energy to make food*, 240, 246
Pitch: *the highness or lowness of a sound*, 92–93, 94, 95, 96
Pivot joint: *a kind of joint where the bones can move around and back*, 147
Planets: *the main bodies in space that revolve around the sun*, 299; four closest to the sun, 312–316; in the solar system, 310–328; outer, 317–321
Plankton (plank-tun): *tiny plants and animals on the ocean surface*, 49, 54
Plants, cells of, 226, 228–229, 232; classification of, 239–242, 290; needed by animals, 242; ocean, 49–51; release oxygen, 241, 242; structures of, 243–246; sunlight essential to, 307; types of, 240, 247–252; use chlorophyll, 240–242
Pluto (ploo-toh): *a planet in the solar system*, 317, 320–321
Polaris (poh-lar-is): *the North Star, always above earth's North Pole*, 331, 339
Poles: *the ends of a magnet*, 184, 186, 187, 194
Pollution (poh-loo-shun): *the adding of harmful materials to the environment*, 52, 208–210; noise, 100–101; of ocean, 52–56; prevention of, 53
Population: *a group of the same kind of plants or animals living in the same place*, 1
Positive terminal: *part of the dry cell that has a shortage of electrons*, 176
Primates: *the most intelligent mammals*, 287, 288
Protists: *a group of living things that are not animals or plants, but have some characteristics of each*, 232, 233, 234; eaten by mollusks, 260; plantlike, 235–237
Ptolemy (tul-uh-mee): *ancient Greek astronomer*, 311–312
Pupil (pyoo-pul): *the opening in the center of your iris*, 129, 132

Quasar (kway-zar): *an object about the size of a star that gives off huge amounts of energy*, 334–335, 336

Radio telescope: *a telescope that picks up and records sounds from space*, 335, 344

Receiver (ri-see-ver): *the part of the telephone through which you hear*, 104, 106

Receptors (ree-sep-torz): *the nerve cells in the skin*, 134–137

Record: *to write down information*, 2

Reflected (ree-flek-ted): *bounced off of something*, 97–99

Repel (rih-pel): *to move away from*, 166, 187

Reproduction: *the process by which living things make more of their own kind*, 248, 249

Reptiles (rep-tylz): *cold-blooded vertebrates that have thick skins made of scales or plates*, 278, 284; classification of, 283; compared to amphibians, 278; three main groups of, 279–280

Retina (reh-tih-nuh): *the back part of the eye where images are focused*, 130, 132

Revolution: *the movement of one object around another*, 296, 298; of the moon, 303

Ribs: *twelve pairs of bones that surround and protect the heart and lungs*, 144

Rocket: *an engine that burns fuel and moves forward by pushing exhaust backward*, 326–328

Rocks, changed by waves, 35, 36; from the moon, 300; mosses on, 247; on the ocean bottom, 18

Rodents: *mammals with chisel-like teeth*, 286

Root(s): *the plant structure that takes in water and keeps the plant in the ground*, 243–246, 247; of ferns, 248–249

Rotation: *the spinning of an object*, 295–296

Roundworm: *a worm with a round body pointed at both ends*, 257

Salt, in ocean water, 15–17, 19, 29, 30; removed from ocean, 47–48

Satellite (sat-uh-lite): *an object in space that revolves around a planet*, 300, 304; placed in orbit by rockets, 326, 328; transmit sound waves, 107

Saturn (sa-tern): *the sixth planet from the sun in the solar system*, 317, 319, 320, 321

Sea anemone (uh-nem-uh-nee): *an ocean animal*, 50, 256

Sediments (sed-uh-ments): *sand, clay, and other materials that settle in water*, 17–19; and fossil fuels, 46; layers of, on ocean floor, 60–61, 62

Seeds: *the structure by which most plants reproduce*, 249, 250, 251, 269

Segmented worm: *a worm with a body that is divided into many similar parts*, 257–258, 259, 264

Sense organs: *parts of the body that are sensitive to smell, taste, hearing, sight, and touch*, 114–119

Series circuit: *a circuit with only one path through which charges can flow*, 173–176; compared to parallel circuit, 178

Sewage (soo-ij): *waste materials carried by sewers and drains*, 52–53, 54

Sharks, 49, 272, 274, 277

Silicon (sil-ih-kahn): *a common material found in the earth*, 209, 211, 216

Skeletal muscle: *a type of muscle containing long, cylinder-shaped cells*, 156–157

Skeletal system: *the bones of the body*, 140–144; four functions of, 140; names of bones in, 141–144; produces blood cells, 144

Smell, 116–117, 118; affected by taste, 120, 122; as a safety device, 117, 122

Smooth muscle: *a type of muscle containing long, thin, and pointed cells*, 156

Sodium chloride (so-dee-um klor-ide): *a salt*, 1

Soil, and water, 245; earthworms good for, 258; enriched by peat moss, 248; formed by mosses, 247; held in place by grass, 244

Solar cell: *a piece of silicon that can produce energy from sunlight*, 209–210

Solar eclipse (soh-ler ee-klips): *occurs when the moon passes between the earth and the sun*, 303, 304, 306–307

Solar flares: *bright areas in the sun's atmosphere from which hot gases shoot out*, 306, 308

Solar system: *the nine planets, their moons, and the sun*, 310–328

Solids, as good media for sound, 87, 88, 90

Sonic boom (sah-nik boom): *loud sound produced when a jet is moving faster than sound*, 81

Sound, 68–110; as energy, 69, 70, 71, 72; as noise pollution, 100–101; as vibrations, 75, 92–93, 99, 124, 126–127; causes of, 68–72; changed into electrical energy, 102–108; instruments for, 73–78; messages through, 102–108; range of, 99; speed of, 81, 90; traveling to the brain, 126–127; travels

through, 79–82, 85–90; variations of, 91–96
Sound wave: *a vibration that moves through matter,* 84–108; reflection of, 97–99
Southern Hemisphere, 297
Space, around a magnet, 185–187; around a flowing current, 189
Space probe: *a rocket launched into space to send information back to earth,* 313, 315
Space shuttle: *a reusable spacecraft that can orbit the earth and return like an airplane,* 325, 327–328
Species: *all of the same kind of living thing,* 1, 54, 65; affected by pollution, 54–56
Spiders, 266, 270
Spinal cord: *a large nerve that carries messages to the brain,* 137, 143
Spirogyra (spy-roh-**jy**-rah): *a freshwater alga one cell wide and many cells long,* 235
Sponge: *a simple invertebrate that has one body opening and small holes all over its body,* 255, 256, 258
Spores: *special cells made by some living things that develop into new organisms like the organisms that made them,* 248, 249
Spring tides: *very high and very low tides,* 40–41
Stars: *objects in space made of hot gases,* 305, 330–346; colors of, 332, 336; distance from earth, 331, 336; energy of, 334; size of, 332; shooting, 322; temperature of, 332, 333
Static electricity: *a type of electricity produced when objects gain or lose negative charges,* 164–168, 169
Stem(s): *the plant structure that carries food and water through the plant and that also gives support,* 243–246, 247; of cycads, 249; of ferns, 248–249; underground, 245
Stethoscope (**steth**-uh-skope): *an instrument used to hear heartbeats,* 88
Stringed instrument: *an instrument with one or more strings,* 73–74
Structure (**struk**-cher): *part of a living thing, such as a wing, leg, or leaf,* 223, 225
Submarine canyon (sub-muh-**reen kan**-yun): *a groove cut in the continental shelf and slope,* 18
Sulfur oxides (**sul**-fer **ahk**-sides): *materials released when coal or oil is burned,* 208
Summer solstice: *the first day of summer in the Northern Hemisphere,* 297
Sun, 305–308; and tides, 40, 41; creates currents, 29, 30; energy produced by, 209–210, 228, 295, 297, 298, 334; essential to life on earth, 307; reflected on moon, 301; used in photosynthesis, 240–241, 242

Sunspots: *dark spots on the sun,* 306, 308
Supergiants: *very large stars,* 332
Supersonic (soo-per-**sah**-nik): *faster than the speed of sound,* 82

Taproot: *the main root of a root system,* 244–245, 246
Taste, 119–120; affected by smell, 120, 122; four basic kinds, 119–120
Taste buds: *groups of cells on the tongue that are sensitive to taste,* 119, 120, 122
Taste nerves: *nerves that carry taste messages to the brain,* 120, 122
Telegraph (**tel**-uh-graf): *a device for sending messages using a code,* 103
Telephone, 104, 106, 107, 108
Telescope: *an instrument that makes distant objects appear closer and larger,* 317–318, 321
Tendons (**ten**-dunz): *tough cords that connect muscles to bones,* 153, 157
Terminals: *parts of a dry cell to which wires are connected,* 175–176
Tides: *the rise and fall of ocean water,* 37–41; caused by the moon, 38
Tissue (**tish**-oo): *group of cells that works together,* 116, 117
Touch, 133–137; as a safety device, 137
Trade winds: *winds that blow from east to west toward the equator,* 28
Transmission lines: *power lines that carry electricity from its source to where it is used,* 206
Transmitter (trans-**mit**-ter): *the part of the telephone you speak into,* 104, 106
Trees, apple, 251; cells of, 228, 229; evergreen, 250; mosses on, 247; oak, 225; pine, 225, 250; stems of, 245
Trenches: *deep ocean valleys,* 22
Triceps (**try**-seps): *the muscle on the bottom side of the upper arm,* 151, 153, 155, 156
Trough (trof): *the lowest point of a wave,* 32, 33
Tsunami (tsoo-**nah**-mee): *giant wave caused by movements at the ocean floor,* 36
Tuning fork (**too**-ning): *a device used to tune musical instruments,* 71
Turbines (**ter**-bynz): *waterwheels that are used at electrical power plants,* 203–206

Ultrasonic (ul-truh-**sah**-nik): *sound frequency that is higher than 20,000 vibrations per second,* 98–99

Universe (yoo-nih-vers): *all the galaxies and the space they exist in,* 345–346

Uranus (yoo-ray-nus): *a planet in the solar system,* 317, 320, 321

Vacuum: *space that does not contain matter,* 89

Venus (vee-nus): *a planet in the solar system,* 312–313, 321

Vernal equinox: *the first day of spring in the Northern Hemisphere,* 297

Vertebrae (ver-tuh-bray): *the small bones that make up the backbone,* 143

Vertebrates (ver-tuh-brayts): *animals with backbones,* 255, 272–288; compared to invertebrates, 273

Vibrate (vi-brayt): *to move back and forth quickly,* 70–71, 72, 124, 126–127

Vibrations, and music, 75; and sound energy, 85–90, 92–93, 99, 104, 105, 106, 110

Viruses (vy-rus-uz): *particles much simpler than cells that can only reproduce within living cells,* 230–231, 234

Volcanoes, 24, 310; and ocean floor, 61; on Jupiter's moon, 318; on earth's moon, 300; on Venus, 313

Voluntary muscles (vahl-un-teh-ree): *muscles that can be controlled,* 151, 154, 155

Voyager 2: *spacecraft sent to Saturn for photographs,* 317, 319, 321

Warm-blooded animals: *vertebrates whose body temperature does not change,* 281, 284, 287, 288

Water, and desert plants, 246; essential to amphibians, 276; essential to plants, 241, 243, 247; from the ocean, 15–19, 47–48; used to produce electricity, 203–206

Watt: *a unit that measures how much electricity is needed to run an electrical appliance,* 21

Wave(s), 31–36; parts of, 32

Westerlies (west-ter-leez): *winds that blow from west to east away from the equator,* 28

Whales, 49, 55–56, 223, 286, 287

White dwarf: *a star about the size of the earth that has begun to shrink,* 334

Whooping cranes, 2–5

Wind(s), and ocean currents, 27–28, 30; causes waves, 32, 36; trade, 28; westerlies, 28

Wind instrument: *an instrument made of a hollow tube through which air can flow,* 75–76

Winter solstice: *the first day of winter in the Northern Hemisphere,* 297

Worms, groups of, 256–258; segmented, 257–258, 259, 264

PHOTO CREDITS

235 *bottom left*—Runk/Schoenberger/Grant Heilman, *bottom right*—Bob Evans/Peter Arnold; p. 236 *top*—Steve Solom/Bruce Coleman, *bottom left*—Jacques Jangoux/Peter Arnold, *bottom right*—John Shaw/Bruce Coleman; p. 237 *top*—Runk/Schoenberger/Grant Heilman; p. 239—Grant Heilman; p. 240—Manfred Kage/Peter Arnold; p. 242—Animals Animals; p. 245—Grant Heilman; p. 246—M.P. Kahl/Bruce Coleman; p. 247—Dr. E.R. Degginger; p. 248 *top*—Carolina Biological Supply Co., *bottom right*—Phil Degginger, *bottom left*—Raymond A. Mendez/Earth Scenes; p. 250 *top*—Harold R. Hungerford, *bottom*—Dr. E.R. Degginger; p. 251 *top*—M.E. Warren/Photo Researchers Inc.; p. 252—Geraldine Wurzburg; p. 254—Anne L. Doubilet; p. 255—Carl Roessler/Animals, Animals; p. 256 *left*—A. Kerstitch, *right*—Grant Heilman; p. 257 *top*—William E. Ferguson, *bottom*—Dr. E.R. Degginger; p. 259—Dr. E.R. Degginger; p. 261—David Doubilet; p. 262 *right*—Fred Bavendan/Peter Arnold, Inc., *left*—Dr. E.R. Degginger; p. 263—Dr. E.R. Degginger; p. 264 *right*—Dr. E.R. Degginger, *bottom left*—Walter Chandoah, *top left*—D.R. Speckler/Animals, Animals; p. 265—Dr. E.R. Degginger; p. 266 *right*—R. Carr/Bruce Coleman, Inc., *left*—Harry N. Darrow/Bruce Coleman, Inc.; p. 267 *bottom right*—Peter Ward/Bruce Coleman, Inc., *top right*—Breck P. Kent/Animals, Animals, *top left*—William E. Ferguson; *bottom left*—Harold Hungerford; p. 269—William E. Ferguson; p. 270—Jack Dermid/Bruce Coleman, Inc.; p. 272—David Doubilet; p. 274—Carl Roessler/Animals, Animals; p. 275 *top*—Bill Wood/Bruce Coleman, Inc., *bottom*—Tom McHugh/Photo Researchers, Inc.; p. 275, 276—Z. Leszczynski/Animals, Animals; p. 278—Tom McHugh/Photo Researchers, Inc.; p. 279 *left*—Walter Chandoah, *right*—Mark Boulton/Photo Researchers, Inc.; p. 280 *top*—Dr. E.R. Degginer, *center*—Z. Leszczynski/Animals, Animals, *bottom*—Tom McHugh/Photo Researchers, Inc.; p. 281 *top* —Clem Haagner/Bruce Coleman, Inc., *bottom*—Roger Tory Peterson/Photo Researchers, Inc.; p. 284— Taronga Zoo, Sydney, Tom McHugh/Photo Researchers, Inc.; p. 285 *top*—Carolina Biological Supply Company, *center*—Tom McHugh/Photo Researchers, Inc., *bottom*—Dr. E.R. Degginger; p. 286 *top*— Leonard Lee Rue III/Animals, Animals, *left*—Kenneth W. Fink/Bruce Coleman, Inc.; p. 287 *top*—Walter Chandoah, *right*—Susan Kuk Lin/Photo Researchers, Inc.; p. 291 *right*—Jeff Foott/Bruce Coleman, Inc., *left*—Mike Lockhart/U.S. Fish & Wildlife Service.

Unit VI: pp. 292, 293—NASA; p. 295 *top*—Gregory Edwardo/International Stock Photo, *bottom*—Mark Bolster/International Stock Photo; pp. 299, 300—NASA; p. 303—Los Alamos Scientific Laboratory; p. 304—Ronn Maratea/International Stock Photo; p. 305—James Sugar/Black Star; p. 306—NASA; p. 307— Robert Phillips/EXXON Enterprises; p. 310—NASA; p. 311—The Bettmann Archive; p. 313—NASA; p. 315—NASA; p. 316—G.V. Levin/Biospherics, Inc.; p. 317—NASA; p. 318 *top*—The Granger Collection, *bottom right*—NASA, *bottom left*—NASA; pp. 319, 320—NASA; p. 322—UPI; pp. 324, 325, 326, 330, 335—NASA; p. 341—Jonathan Blair/Woodfin Camp; p. 344 *left*—Photography by Orien A. Ernest, Copyright © 1978 by Astro Media Corp., *right*—Copyright by The California Institute of Technology and Carnegie Institution of Washington. Reproduced by permission from the Hale Observatories; p. 349 *left*— Perkin-Elmer, *right*—NASA.

ART CREDITS

Gary Allen pp. 12, 14, 28, 38, 40, 52, 59

Helen Cogancherry pp. 1, 6, 7, 98, 99, 103, 121, 125, 167, 194, 218

Network Graphics, Inc. pp. 227, 229, 231, 245

William Hunter-Hicklin p. 337

Marion Krupp pp. 115, 126, 130, 137, 148, 153

Matthew Snow pp. 228, 241, 243, 244, 245, 268, 276

Joel Snyder pp. 224, 240, 249, 260, 268, 269, 273, 278, 282, 290

John Kier pp. 295, 296, 297, 301, 303, 306, 312, 320, 327, 334, 336, 338, 341, 342, 346

Pat Stewart pp. 13, 34, 47, 54, 64, 76, 87, 92, 97, 106, 107, 110, 194, 281

Marc Thorner pp. 320

Vantage Art, Inc. pp. 3, 4, 13, 39, 56, 60, 61, 75, 118, 130, 132, 165, 177, 178, 282, 308, 314, 326, 333, 337, 348

Matthew Weiderecht/Network Graphics pp. 296, 312